The Complete Dolly Parton Illustrated Discography

Daniel Selby

The Complete Dolly Parton Illustrated Discography
©2021 Daniel Selby / BearManor Media. All Rights Reserved.
All photographs / illustrations are copyright of their respective owners, and are reproduced here in the spirit of publicity. While we have made every effort to acknowledge photograph credits we apologize for any and all omissions, and will make every effort to make any appropriate changes in future editions of this book if necessary.

No part of this book may be reproduced in any form or by any electronic or mechanical means, including information storage and retrieval systems, without written permission from the publisher or author, except in the case of a reviewer, who may quote brief passages embodied in critical articles or in a review.

Note: Many foreign 45 releases were issued with the same catalog # and picture sleeves for different countries, especially neighboring. Also some were re–issued with a different design / number at a later time. Not all are presented here. Nor are all Greatest Hits, Best Of or similar compilation albums documented as almost 240 have been released by various labels and countries through the years on Dolly. Album release dates, recording dates and other information researched through Billboard and Cashbox magazines / websites, press releases and RCA Records archives. I have not listed all chart statistics for every release. In addition release dates will tend to be US dates and foreign dates may differ, unless it is a foreign release of course. I have strived to be as accurate as possible, but occasionally mistakes make it through. If found, please send corrections (with sources) to me through: bookwriter@gmail.com. All I can do is try to make it right and produce a good, enjoyable book. Even Dolly has said nothing is ever perfect! This has been a labor of love.
Thank you!

Published in the USA and abroad by:

www.bearmanor–digital.myshopify.com/

Cover Layout & Interior Design:
From Design to Done Graphics / Daniel Selby

ISBN: 978-1-62933-700-5

Special Thanks

    First and foremost a ***Special Thanks*** to: Dolly Parton for continually writing and producing some of the finest music that truly has withstood the test of time. For always having a giving, good heart and for giving back to others from the ***very*** beginning of your career. For always being a team player and for teaching me what happiness truly is through music. I can't imagine a world without Dolly Parton, her music and the love that she shares with everyone. It may be cliché but I can honestly say about Dolly Parton: "**I Will Always Love You.**"

    To Allan for once again supporting me and this writing project and for helping with technical issues as they arose... and they did! Also for all the love the last 34 years.

    Thank you to worldradiohistory.com/ for all the back copies of Billboard, Cashbox and other industry magazines that helped *tremendously* with research of chart placement, sales, release dates, studios used, reviews and interview quotes.

    Also thanks to Wikipedia for several articles on Dolly, some album release information and chart placement. I have enjoyed adding to Dolly's Wiki material myself over the years!

Dedication

I dedicate this book to my late, younger sister Debra. It was because of her that I started listening, *really* listening to Dolly Parton. Debra would save up her money and buy Dolly Parton albums in her youth, starting in 1977 with "Here You Come Again." Debra had seen the album in the store in Livermore, California where we lived, knew little of Dolly other than she looked "Very pretty" on the album cover. Debra loved the track "Me and Little Andy." I gave her a few of Dolly's albums as birthday and Christmas gifts as well over the years. One being Debra's favorite, 1980's "Dolly, Dolly, Dolly" released on April 14, 1980 which I gave to her for Christmas 1980. Debra had always hoped to meet Dolly. She went to many Dolly concerts and waited outside stage doors or gates at a fairground when possible. She was never able to meet and give Dolly a hug and thank her for the music as she had always wanted to do, but ever hopeful she never stopped trying until she could no longer go to concerts. Debra died at age 47 on July 10, 2017 after an aggressive fight with an equally aggressive cancer and in her final days she continued to play Dolly's albums on CD. The cancer had spread to her spine and robbed her of the ability to walk. CD's could be changed in bed, whereas LP's would be more of a challenge. But I know if she has her way Debra is still listening to Dolly Parton in heaven while walking her own Golden Streets of Glory.

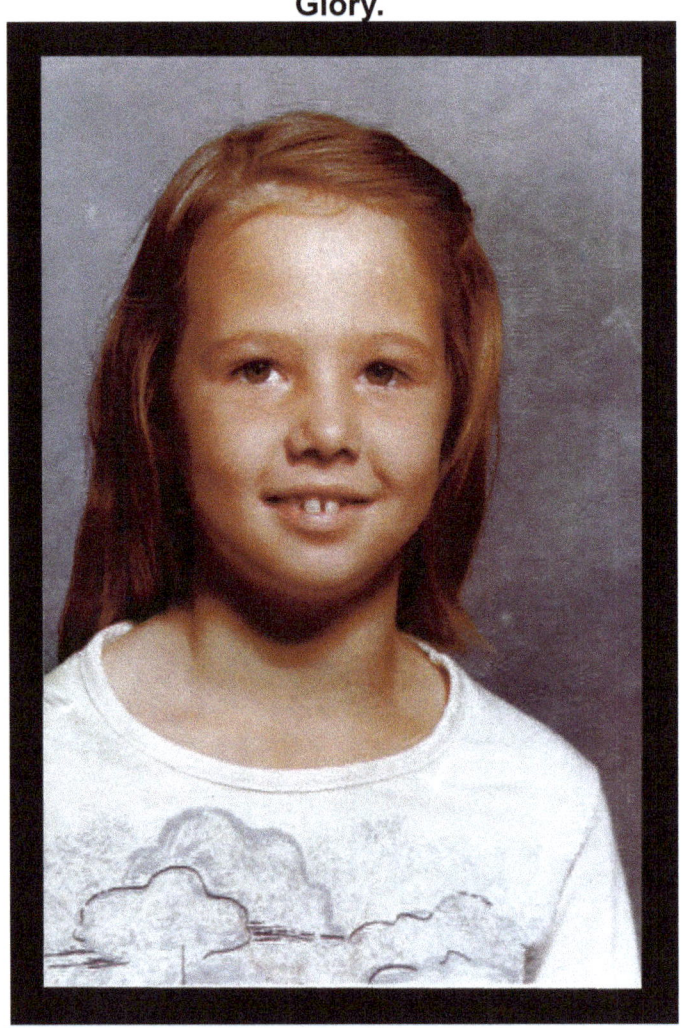

Debra in 1977 at age 8

Some Early History On Dolly Parton

      Dolly Rebecca Parton was born January 19,1946, in a one–room cabin on the banks of the Little Pigeon River in Pittman Center, Tennessee. She was the fourth of twelve children born to Avie Lee Caroline (née Owens; 1923–2003) and Robert Lee Parton Sr. (1921–2000). Sadly brothers Floyd and Randy have passed away in the last few years. Dolly's infant brother, Larry Parton, died 4 days after birth in 1955.

      Dolly inherited her middle name from her mother's great–great–grandmother Rebecca (Dunn) Whitted. Dolly's father, known as "Lee", worked in the mountains of East Tennessee, first as a sharecropper and then later tending his own small tobacco farm and acreage. He had, on occasion, also worked construction jobs to supplement the farm's small income. Despite her father's illiteracy, Dolly has often commented that he was one of the smartest people she ever knew in regards to business and making a profit.

      Dolly's mother, Avie Lee, cared for their large family. Her 11 pregnancies (the tenth being twins) in 20 years made her a mother of 12 by the time she was 35. Often in poor health, she still managed to keep a loving home and entertain her children with Smoky Mountain folklore and ancient ballads. The songs were initially sung by immigrants moving from the British Isles to southern Appalachia over a century earlier. Avie Lee's father, Jake Owens, was a Pentecostal preacher, and Dolly and her siblings all attended church regularly. Dolly has long credited her father for her business savvy, and her mother's family for her musical abilities. When Dolly was very young, the family moved from the Pittman Center area to a farm up on nearby Locust Ridge. Many of her treasured memories of youth happened there. The farm acreage and surrounding woodland inspired her to write the song "My Tennessee Mountain Home" in 1972. Years after her parents sold the property, Dolly bought it back in the later 1980s and her brother Bobby Lee helped with restoration and new construction. The Homestead has been used in a few of Dolly's productions, either on LP jackets or TV shows. For approximately 6 to 7 years, Dolly and her family lived in the rustic, one–room cabin before moving to a better one.

      Dolly has described her family as being "dirt poor." Her father paid the doctor who helped deliver her, Dr. Robert F. Thomas, with a bag of cornmeal. She outlined her family's poverty in some of her early songs; "Coat of Many Colors" and "In the Good Old Days (When Times Were Bad)" among them. There is even a song about the family doctor— "Dr. Robert F. Thomas" that appears on Dolly's "My Tennessee Mountain Home" LP from 1973.

      This was a predominately Pentecostal area located north of the Greenbrier Valley of the Great Smoky Mountains. Music played a very important role in Dolly's early life. She was brought up in the Church of God in Cleveland, Tennessee, in a congregation her grandfather, Jake Robert Owens, pastored. Her earliest public performances were in the church, beginning at age 6. At 7, she started playing a homemade guitar. When she was eight, her uncle Bill bought her her first real guitar. Dolly began performing as a child, first singing on local radio and television programs in the East Tennessee area. Then by 10, she was appearing on *The Cas Walker Show* on both WIVK Radio and WBIR–TV in Knoxville, Tennessee. At 11, in 1957, she recorded the single "Puppy Love" b/w "Girl Left Alone" for *Goldband Records* out of Lake Charles, LA, release # 1086. The single was released in late April of 1959, but failed to chart. The material from that first recording session has been licensed on various compilations though the years. The single has also been pressed several times by Goldband after Dolly became famous with the note that it was Dolly's first recording and is a collectors item. It should be noted that Dolly's song "Puppy Love" was not the same song recorded by Donny Osmond in 1972 which was written by Paul Anka who had the first hit with it in 1959. Dolly's version was written by her and her uncle and often song writing partner, Bill Owens.

      It was also in 1959 when she was 13 that Dolly first appeared on the Grand Ole Opry in Nashville. While at the Opry she first met Johnny Cash, who encouraged her to follow her dreams regarding her career. Dolly's first Grand Ole Opry performance was alongside her Uncle Bill Owens on July 25, 1959 and they received three encores.

      Next, on the *Circle B Records* label (release #CB–102), Dolly recorded a duet "So Little I

Wanted, So Little I Got" with uncle Bill Owens in 1962. The flip side was "Forbidden Love." This record failed to make the charts. In 1962 Dolly and her Uncle Bill Owens were signed to Tree Publishing and Dolly scored a recording contract with Mercury Records due to Nashville veteran Buddy Killen. There Dolly recorded "It's Sure Gonna Hurt," written by her and uncle Bill Owens, backed with "The Love You Gave Me." It made little dent in the charts.

In Nashville in 1963, and for Somerset Records out of Burbank, California Dolly recorded one side of an LP. The album was titled "Hits Made Famous by Country Queens." Dolly's side was titled; "Dolly Parton Sings Hits Made Famous By Kitty Wells," more on that album in the section titled; Other Recorded Works.

After graduating from Sevier County High School in 1964, Dolly moved to Nashville the next day. Her initial success came as a songwriter, having signed with Combine Publishing shortly after her arrival; with her frequent songwriting partner, her uncle Bill Owens, she wrote several charting songs, including two top–10 hits: Bill Phillips's "Put It Off Until Tomorrow" (1966) and Skeeter Davis's "Fuel to the Flame" (1967). Her songs were recorded by many artists during this time period, including Kitty Wells and Hank Williams Jr.

Dolly would go on to record a couple of singles in the mid 1960's for various labels that would not chart. She was then signed to Monument Records where she released a number of singles as well as her first album. First up was the single "What Do You Think About Lovin'" b/w "I Wasted my Tears" in 1964 (MN45–869) which did not chart followed in 1965 by "Happy Birthday, Baby" b/w "Old Enough To Know Better (Too Young To Resist)" (MN45–897) which was produced by Ray Stevens and this became Dolly's first charting single. It peaked at #108 on the Bubbling Under Hot 100 chart. Later, in 1982, a duet recording of the A side "Happy Birthday, Baby," was included on the album *The Winning Hand* featuring Dolly and Willie Nelson. The recording featured Parton's original 1965 vocals, with new vocals from Nelson overdubbed to create a "duet."

In 1966 Dolly would release a few more singles on Monument Records a few months before she left the label and really starting rolling at RCA Records. The final Monument singles were; "Busy Signal" b/w "I Took Him for Granted" (#MN–45 913) "Don't Drop Out" b/w "Control Yourself" (#MN–45 922), "The Little Things" b/w "I'll Put it Off Until Tomorrow" (#MN45 948), "Dumb Blonde" b/w "The Giving and The Taking" (#MN45 982) which peaked at No. 24 on the Billboard Country Charts in 1967, "Something Fishy" b/w "I've Lived My Life" (#45 1007), "Why, Why, Why" b/w "I Could Wait Forever" (#45 1032). Quite a few of the later singles made up Dolly's first LP; *Hello, I'm Dolly* (SLP–18085) released on Monument on September 8, 1967, just a few days after Dolly's debut as a regular on *The Porter Wagoner Show* on September 5.

Dolly signed with RCA Victor in early October 1967 and had her first session with Porter on October 10th where they recorded, "Just Between You and Me" for a planned first album. The recording was done at RCA Studio A. A few of the sessions also taking place next door at Studio B on occasion as well. The following day on October 11th they recorded "The Last Thing on My Mind" also at Studio A and the response at the session and with RCA brass was so strong the song was rush released only 20 days after recording on October 30th with "Love is Worth Living" (recorded at the same session on October 11th) being the flip side. It was with RCA Records that Dolly really took off. The hits and chart positions kept rising on her new label with each release.

Dolly is one of the most honored country performers of all time, with 25 RIAA certified gold, platinum, and multi–platinum awards as well as 382 nominations and 189 wins for her music and material. She has contributed more to the music industry than any other single person I can think of. She also has charm, beauty and an inner light that glows. There is something meaningful in everything she does. I am not saying she is perfect, but she is pretty damn close! Dolly Parton is real and *totally* relatable. There is more to her than the wigs, make–up, and anything else you can see. I have never come across anyone who did not like Dolly Parton! People seemed to light up when told about this book. I love Dolly's music—country, pop or anything in–between... it transcends categorization and has been covered by a multitude of artists! Good music is good music!

About The Book

This book was born out of my love for music and my love of history. I love doing research and it is easier when you enjoy the subject matter. Like my first music book on the Osmond Family's enormous discography this book was two things– first a labor of love since I love learning new things about those I care for and second a lot of work!

I have added many, many facts about Dolly Parton to Wikipedia and many other webpages over the years so you may have read some of what is in this book already. I simply wanted to bring all I have written together along with information from those who selflessly gave of themselves as well. Many people, knowing my love for Dolly Parton, sent me all kinds of, facts and tid–bits through the years. I kept them all! I also poured over the RCA recording logs loaned to me as well. Dolly's RCA CD Box sets were a wealth of information too concerning recording information!

One thing I have really enjoyed while working on this book has been was what I call "Rediscovering Dolly." That's not to say I had ever forgotten her, nor not played her music... and often. But there were some albums I had not played in a number of years. They were waiting there to be played again and rediscovered. One by one and in chronological order I have played each Dolly album during the writing of this book, playing only vinyl LP's until the albums released were only on CD...before going back to LP again! Give me vinyl over CD's any day!

I would have noticed Dolly eventually, but I would like to thank my late sister Debra for making it happen sooner rather than later.

It should be noted early on in this book, for those interested, that a majority of Dolly's back catalog can be downloaded from sites such as Amazon. This includes her solo work, the work with Porter Wagoner and all of the Trio albums.

I have had a great time listening to all of Dolly's album from first to most recent and watching videos from the decades of her career in the 4 months this book took to put together. Though Dolly has never left my radar since I first discovered her in 1977 though my sister, it is nice rediscovering the music I had not played in a while. I had favorite Dolly Parton albums, and still do, and those where the mainstays, but hearing the other material was like hearing it for the first time all over again!

Enjoy!
~Daniel

Hall of Fame Honors

During her career, Dolly Parton has gained induction into numerous Halls of Fame.
Those honors include:

Nashville Songwriters Hall of Fame (1986)

Small Town of America Hall of Fame (1988)

East Tennessee Hall of Fame (1988)

Country Music Hall of Fame (1999)

Songwriters Hall of Fame (2001)

Junior Achievement of East Tennessee Business Hall of Fame (2003)

The Americana Highway Hall of Fame (2006)

Grammy Hall of Fame – "I Will Always Love You – 1974 Recording" (2007)

Blue Ridge Music Hall of Fame – Songwriter Category (2008)

Gospel Music Hall of Fame (2009)

Music City Walk of Fame (2009)

Country Gospel Music Hall of Fame (2010)

Grammy Hall of Fame – "Jolene – 1974 Recording" (2014)

The National Hall of Fame for Mountain Artisans (2014)

The Happiness Hall of Fame (2016)

East Tennessee Writers Hall of Fame (2019)

A Few Random Dolly Parton Facts:

- Dolly holds the record for the most Top 10 Albums on the *Billboard Top Country Albums Chart* at 43! She has sold more than 100 million records world-wide. Not an easy feat!
- She has earned more than 25 gold, platinum and multi-platinum awards!
- Dolly doesn't think of herself as a star. When, in 2014, Billboard asked if she felt different now than when she first came to Nashville in 1964, she said, "I'm more successful now than I was then, but I still feel like the same girl. I'm just a working girl. I never think of myself as a star because, as somebody once said, 'A star is nothing but a big ball of gas'—and I don't want to be that."
- Dolly has a cookbook out called *Dolly's Dixie Fixin's: Love, Laughter and Lots of Good Food.* It features more than 125 recipes for Southern favorites. There's a catfish recipe, a cream of vegetable soup recipe, and even one for chicken and dumplings! It was released in 2006. It is out of print now and sells on Amazon for between $210 and $274. Another cookbook was released by Dollywood called *Dollywood Presents Tennessee Mountain Home Cooking* and was sold at Dollywood around 1989. This one featured favorite recipes from the Dollywood family.
- Dolly plays at least 10 different instruments.
- Dolly has written more than 5,000 songs.
- The first cloned mammal was named after her. "Dolly" the sheep.
- Dolly can't read music. (Neither could the Beatles)
- Dolly was an uncredited producer of *Buffy, The Vampire Slayer* from 1997–2003.
- Dolly received an Academy Award nomination in 1980 for the song "9 to 5" from the film of the same name and another for 2006's "Travelin' Thru" from the film "Transamerica."
- A stone's throw from Dollywood, Sevierville, Tennessee is where Parton grew up. Between stimulating tourismand her philanthropy, this proud native has given a lot back to her hometown. And Sevierville residents returned that appreciation with a life-sized bronze Dolly that sits barefoot, beaming, and cradling a guitar, just outside the county courthouse. The sculpture, made by local artist Jim Gray, was dedicated on May 3, 1987. Today it is the most popular stop on Sevierville's walking tour.
- Dolly wakes up at 3am to answer mail, make calls and meditate. "I do my little meditations, I do my little spiritual work. I get more work done between 3am and 7am than most people all day, because it's quiet and the energy's all low-key...except mine."
- In February 2021 Dolly asked Tennessee lawmakers to withdraw a bill designed to create a statue of her at the State Capitol. Dolly was touched, but said: "I am honored and humbled by their intention, but I have asked the leaders of the state legislature to remove the bill from any and all consideration," Parton tweeted on Thursday. Continuing she said, "Given all that is going on in the world, I don't think putting me on a pedestal is appropriate at this time. I hope, though, that somewhere down the road, several years from now or perhaps after I'm gone if you still feel I deserve it, then I'm certain I will stand proud in our great State Capitol as a grateful Tennessean."
- Dolly has always been one to give back and even gave one million dollars to help develop the Moderna Covid-19 vaccine, which she has since taken.
- Jeni's Splendid Ice Cream out of Columbus, Ohio announced it would soon, in April 2021, make available a specialty flavor of ice cream in collaboration with Dolly, the sales of which will go directly to Dolly's Imagination Library early childhood literacy program. The flavor is Strawberry Pretzel Pie. Jeni's has over 40 branded 'scoop shops' and retail distributors nationally, look for it!

The Albums →

Hello, I'm Dolly
SLP–18085

Track Listing:
Dumb Blonde / Your Ole Handy Man / I Don't Want to Throw Rice / Put It Off Until Tomorrow / I Wasted My Tears / Something Fishy / Fuel to the Flame / The Giving and the Taking / I'm in No Condition / The Company You Keep / I've Lived My Life / The Little Things

Production Information:
Produced by: Fred Foster
Recorded at: Fred Foster Sound Studio, Nashville, TN
Engineers: Tommy Strong / Mort Thomasson
Cover Photography: Fred Foster
Art Direction: Ken Kim

Singles Released From This Album:
"The Little Things" b/w "I'll Put If Off Until Tomorrow" – June 6, 1966 (Did not chart)
"Dumb Blonde" b/w "The Giving and The Taking" – November 7, 1966 (Peaked at # 24 on the *Billboard* Hot Country Songs chart dated March 18, 1967)
"Something Fishy" b/w "I've Lived My Life" – May 8, 1967 (Peaked at # 12 on the *Billboard* Hot Country Songs chart dated August 5, 1967)

Album Data:
Billboard Chart Debut: November 11, 1967
Highest Chart Position: # 11 on January 12, 1968
Billboard Chart: Hot Country Albums
Number of weeks on Chart: 14

Notes / Trivia:
- Recorded 1964 – 1966
- This album was released on LP on September 18, 1967.
- The original release date was set to be in February 1967, but the release was pushed back for unknown reasons.
- *Billboard* published a review of the album dated October 28, 1967, which said: "Dolly Parton has a little girl voice but it's Lolita in style on the honky–tonking, carousing "Dumb Blonde." She also does extremely well on "I Wasted My Tears," "I Don't Want to Throw Rice," Something Fishy" and "Fuel to the Flame."
- On November 19, 1967 *Cashbox* published a review that said, "Dolly Parton could have a big winner in her possession with this striking album. Singing at the top of her form throughout the entire set, the lark offers "Dumb Blonde," "Put It Off Until Tomorrow," "Fuel to the Flame," "The

Giving and the Taking," and eight others. Give this one a careful listen. It should pull in a healthy amount of chart action."
- Liner notes by producer Fred Foster.
- Three of the album's 12 tracks are Dolly's own compositions and seven were co–written with her uncle, Bill Owens. The two remaining tracks, "Dumb Blonde" and "I've Lived My Life," were written by Curly Putman and Lola Jean Dillon.
- This album was re–issued by Monument through CBS Records in 1972 as a two LP set along with 1970's *As Long as I Love* with the title *The World of Dolly* Parton (KZG–31913). *As Long as I Love* was released June 8, 1970 and consisted of two songs previously issued and ten that had been unreleased up to that time. The two LP's had also been issued together as: *Hello, I'm Dolly / As Long as I Love* (BZ–33876) by CBS Records in 1971.

Dumb Blonde Single

Just Because I'm A Woman
Stereo LSP–3949 / Mono LPM–3949

Track Listing:
You're Gonna Be Sorry / I Wish I Felt This Way At Home / False Eyelashes / I'll Oilwells Love You / The Only Way Out / Little Bit Slow To Catch On / The Bridge / Love And Learn / I'm Running Out Of Love / Just Because I'm A Woman / Baby Sister / Try Being Lonely

Production Information:
Produced by: Bob Ferguson
Recorded at: RCA Victor's "Nashville Sound" Studios, Nashville, TN
Engineer: Al Pachucki

Musicians:
Drums: Jerry Carrigan
Piano: Hargus "Pig" Robbins / David Briggs
Steel Guitar: Lloyd Green
Bass: Junior Huskey
Fiddle: Mack Magaha
Rhythm Guitar: George McCormick / Chip Young
Electric Guitar: Wayne Moss
Electric Banjo: Charles Trent
Vocal Accompaniment: Anita Carter / Dolores Edgin

Singles Released From This Album:
"Just Because I'm A Woman" b/w "I Wish I Felt This Way At Home" – May 27, 1968 (Peaked at # 17 on the Hot Country Singles chart dated September 14, 1968. It also peaked at # 8 in Canada on the *RPM* County Singles chart)

Album Data:
Billboard Chart Debut: May 4, 1968.
Highest Chart Position: # 22 on June 14, 1968.
Billboard Chart: Hot Country Albums.
Number of weeks on Chart: 9

Notes / Trivia:
- This album was released on LP on April 15, 1968.
- This was Dolly's first LP on her new label: RCA Records.
- Liner notes by Porter Wagoner.
- The title song, in which a woman admonishes her boyfriend for passing judgment on her previous sexual encounters even though he is guilty of the same behavior, was regarded as

something of a daring statement to make at the time. It was written by Dolly in response to her husband's questioning (and subsequent reaction) if she'd ever been with a man before him.
- "The Bridge" is distinctive because of its subject matter and rather sudden ending. It tells the story of a woman who meets a man on a bridge and falls in love with him, then becomes pregnant with his child. He leaves her which leads the woman back to the bridge where they met and she apparently commits suicide. The last verse states, "My feet are moving slowly, closer to the edge, here is where it started, and here is where I'll end it..." before simply ending, midway through the verse.
- Dolly re–recorded the title track for the 2003 tribute album *Just Because I'm a Woman: Songs of Dolly Parton*.

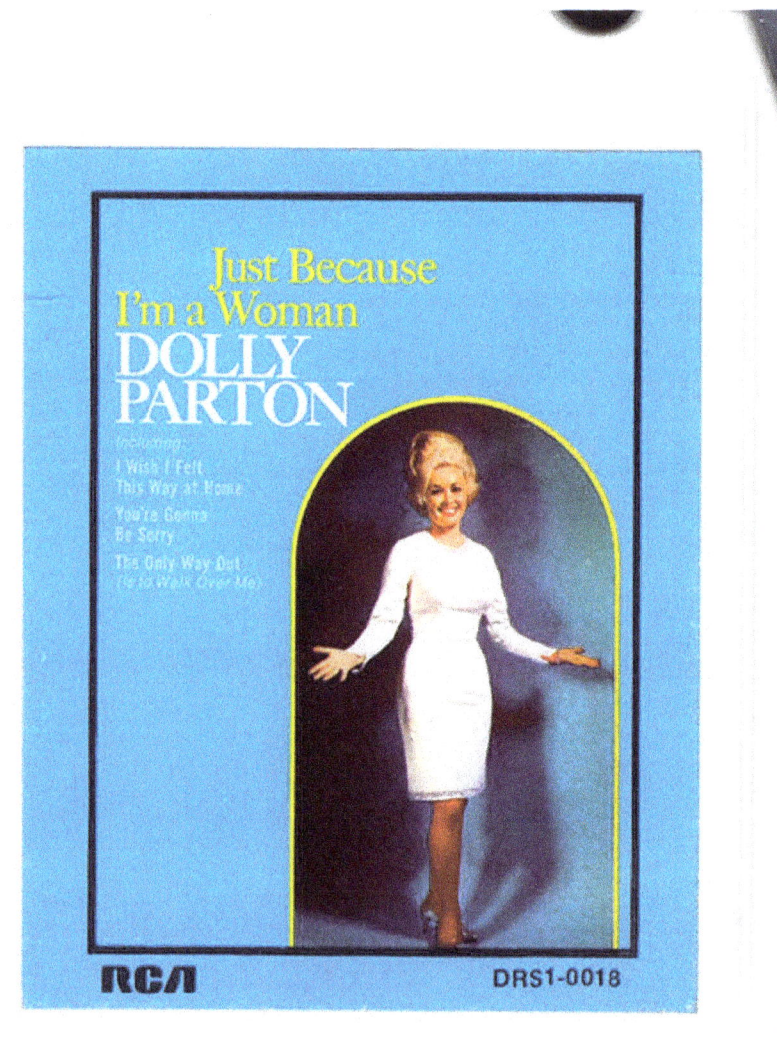

A 1970's 8–Track cartridge re–issue of the album.

In The Good Old Days (When Times Were Bad)
LSP–4099

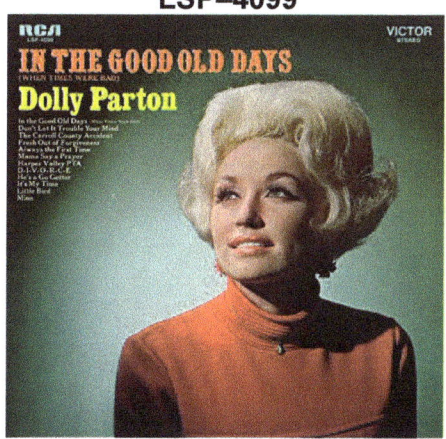

Track Listing:
Don't Let It Trouble Your Mind / He's A Go Getter / In The Good Old Days (When Times Were Bad) / It's My Time / Harper Valley PTA / Little Bird / Mine / The Carroll County Accident / Fresh Out Of Forgiveness / Mama Say a Prayer / Always the First Time / D–I–V–O–R–C–E

Production Information:
Produced by: Bob Ferguson
Recorded at: RCA Victor's "Nashville Sound" Studios, Nashville, TN
Engineer: Al Pachucki

Musicians:
Drums: Kenneth Buttrey / Jerry Carrigan
Bass: Junior Huskey
Piano: Hargus Robbins
Steel Guitar: Lloyd Green
Fiddle: Mack Magaha
Guitars: Jerry Reed / Jerry Stembridge / Wayne Moss
Electric Banjo: Buck Trent
Rhythm Guitar: George McCormick
Vocal Accompaniment: June Page / Dolores Edgin / Joseph Babcock

Singles Released From This Album:
"In The Good Old Days (When Times Were Bad)" b/w "Try Being Lonely" – October 14, 1968 (Peaked at # 25 on the Hot Country Singles chart dated December 21, 1968).

Album Data:
Billboard Chart Debut: Match 1, 1969.
Highest Chart Position: # 15 on March 28, 1969.
Billboard Chart: Hot Country Albums.
Number of Weeks on Chart: 11

Notes / Trivia:
- This album was released on LP and 8–Track on February 3, 1969 .
- The tongue–in–cheek track "He's a Go Getter" plays on an unpredicted joke, "When his wife gets off from work, he'll go get 'er."
- In the title song, Dolly looks back on her impoverished upbringing, concluding that while she values the lessons it taught her, she would not want to go back.

- Liner notes by Dolly Parton
- In the February 15, 1969 issue of *Billboard* the review reads, "Without doubt this will be a big hit LP for Dolly Parton...just as it will be considered a great package of entertainment by her friends. The key to the LP is her empathy on "In the Good Old Day (When Times Were Bad)", but also she tugs the heartstrings on "D–I–V–O–R–C–E" and gets through to the emotion on "The Carroll County Accident."
- Also on February 15, 1969 *Cashbox* published a review of the album, "Gaining in strength as one of the more popular country female artists, Dolly Parton follows up her chart single of "In the Good Old Days (When Times Were Bad)" with a strong LP that should solidify her position with the disk buyers. In addition to her own hit single, the LP features such monster titles as "D–I–V–O–R–C–E" and "Harper Valley PTA", among others."
- Dolly re–recorded the title song for her 1973 album *My Tennessee Mountain Home.* Dolly also re–recorded "The Carroll County Accident" with Buck Trent (who plays banjo on this LP) for his 2018 album *Spartanburg Blues.*
- The album was reissued on cassette tape in the US and Germany in 1987 and CD in Portugal in 1997 without any bonus material. It was later released as a digital download on July 26, 2019.

US 1980's Cassette Tape Re–Issue

My Blue Ridge Mountain Boy
LSP-4188

Track Listing:
In The Ghetto / Games People Play / 'Til Death Do Us Part / Big Wind / Evening Shade / I'm Fed Up With You / My Blue Ridge Mountain Boy / Daddy / We Had All The Good Things Going / The Monkey's Tale / Gypsy, Joe And Me / Home For Pete's Sake

Production Information:
Produced by: Bob Ferguson
Recorded at: RCA Victor's "Nashville Sound" Studios, Nashville, TN
Engineers: Al Pachucki
Assistant Engineers: Roy Shockley and Milt Henderson

Musicians:
Drums: Jerry Carrigan / James Isbell
Bass: Junior Huskey
Piano: Hargus Robbins
Steel Guitar: Lloyd Green / Pete Drake
Fiddle: Mack Magaha
Guitars: Fred Carter Jr / Jerry Stembridge / Wayne Moss
Electric Banjo: Buck Trent
Rhythm Guitar: George McCormick
Vocal Accompaniment: June Page / Dolores Edgin / Joseph Babcock

Singles Released From This Album:
"Daddy" b/w "He's a Go Getter" – March 10, 1969 (peaked at # 40 on the Hot Country Singles chart dated May 31, 1969)
"In The Ghetto" b/w "The Bridge" – June 23, 1969 (peaked at # 50 on the Hot Country Singles chart dated September 6, 1969)
"My Blue Ridge Mountain Boy" b/w "'Til Death Do Us Part" – September 8, 1969 (peaked at # 45 on the Hot Country Singles chart dated November 15, 1969)

Album Data:
Billboard Chart Debut: October 11, 1969
Highest Chart Position: # 6 on December 26, 1969
Billboard Chart: Hot Country Albums
Number of Weeks on Chart: 28

Notes / Trivia:

- This album was released on LP and 8–Track on September 8, 1969.
- The track "Daddy" was recorded on September 9, 1968 at sessions for Dolly's previous album *In the Good Old Days (When Times Were Bad)*.
- Dolly re–recorded the title song for her 1982 album *Heartbreak Express*.
- A song recorded during the May 1969 album sessions but not used was "Everything Is Beautiful (In Its Own Way)".
- Dolly confirmed that the man on the album cover is her reclusive husband, Carl Dean.
- A review of the album in the September 20, 1969 issue of *Billboard* said, "Undoubtedly, this is the best composite album that Miss Dolly Parton has created. Her country version of "In the Ghetto" is now on the country singles chart and should provide plenty of LP sales impetus. While her "Daddy," "Gypsy, Joe and Me," and "Home for Pete's Sake" are tearjerkers in the traditional vein. "Games People Play" is also a strong contender for honors."
- *Cashbox* also published a review of the album on September 25, 1969, saying, "Dolly Parton effectively changes moods and tempos as she sings her way through this set containing her latest singles in addition to other noteworthy offerings. The set includes, besides title track, "In the Ghetto," "Games People Play," "Big Wind," "Daddy" and "We Had All the Good Things Going." Rapid chart action can be expected on this one.

Ad for the 1969 album *My Blue Ridge Mountain Boy*.

The Fairest of Them All
LSP–4288

Track Listing:
Daddy Come and Get Me / Chas / When Possession Gets Too Strong / Before You Make Up Your Mind / I'm Doing This for Your Sake / But You Loved Me Then / Just the Way I Am / More Than Their Share / Mammie / Down from Dover / Robert

Production Notes:
Produced by: Bob Ferguson
Recorded at: RCA Victor's "Nashville Sound" Studios, Nashville, TN
Engineers: Engineers: Al Pachucki
Assistant Engineers: Roy Shockley and Milt Henderson
Cover Photography: Bill Goodman
Album Liner Notes: Judy H. Ogle

Musicians:
Piano: Hargus "Pig" Robbins
Drums: Jerry Carrigan
Steel Guitar: Lloyd Green
Bass: Junior Huskey
Fiddle: Mack Magaha
Rhythm Guitar: George McCormick
Guitar: Wayne Moss / Jerry Stembridge
Electric Banjo: Buck Trent
Background vocals: Joseph Babcock / Dolores Edgin / June Page

Singles Released From This Album:
"Daddy Come And Get Me" b/w "Chas" – December 8, 1969 (peaked at # 40 on the Hot Country Singles chart dated March 7, 1970)

Album Data:
Billboard Chart Debut: March 14, 1970.
Highest Chart Position: # 13 on May 8, 1970.
Billboard Chart: Hot Country Albums.
Number of Weeks on Chart: 17

Notes / Trivia:
- This album was released on LP and 8–Track on February 2, 1970.
- Recording sessions for the album began on September 4, 1969, at RCA Studios in Nashville, Tennessee. Two additional sessions followed on October 30 and 31. "I'm Doing This for Your

Sake" was recorded during the September 10, 1968 session for 1969's *In the Good Old Days (When Times Were Bad)*. "Mammie" and "But You Loved Me Then" were recorded during sessions for 1969's *My Blue Ridge Mountain Boy*, on May 13 and 21, 1969, respectively.
- "Down from Dover" was covered by Nancy Sinatra and Lee Hazelwood in 1972.
- Parton re–recorded "Down from Dover" in 2001 for her album *Little Sparrow*, with one added verse.
- Dolly has joked that the album cover is one of the funniest she has ever appeared on. She was attempting to look like a fairy–tale character.
- *Billboard's* review of the album on February 14, 1970 which said, "A very strong album in more ways than one. "Daddy Come and Get Me" is in the traditional jilted love vein, then "Down from Dover" follows. The "Dover" tune is very beautiful and well produced, but the theme is perhaps a little too strong for airplay, even in this day of enlightenment. "Just the Way I Am" is beautiful and not so strong. Dolly Parton is sensational, as usual."
- *Cashbox* published a review a week before on, February 7, 1970, which said, "Many of Dolly Parton's male fans will agree that she is "The Fairest of Them All", and all her fans will agree that vocally, she's one of country music's brightest young stars. Teeing off this set with her current single, Dolly goes on to sing a host of strong tunes, most of which are her own compositions. Should be a nice chart spot on tap for this package. Watch it closely for action."

Dolly in 1969 at RCA Studio B

The Golden Streets of Glory
LSP–4398

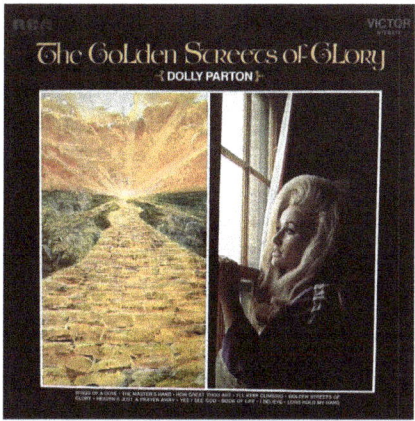

Track Listing:
I Believe / Yes I See God / The Master's Hand / Heaven's Just a Prayer Away / Golden Streets of Glory / How Great Thou Art / I'll Keep Climbing / Book of Life / Wings of a Dove / Lord Hold My Hand

Production Information:
Produced by: Bob Ferguson
Recorded at: RCA Victor's "Nashville Sound" Studios, Studio A, Nashville, TN
Engineers: Engineers: Al Pachucki
Assistant Engineer: Roy Shockley
Cover Photography: Les Leverett

Singles Released From This Album:
"Golden Streets of Glory" / "Comin' For To Carry Me Home" (peaked at # 23 on the Hot Country Singles chart dated May 21, 1971)

Album Data:
Highest Chart Position: # 22 on April 9, 1971
Billboard Chart: Hot Country Albums
Number of weeks on chart: 8

Notes / Trivia:
- This album was released on LP and 8–Track on February 15, 1971.
- Recording sessions for the album took place at RCA Studios in Nashville, Tennessee, on May 11, 12 and 13, 1970.
- "Would You Know Him (If You Saw Him)" recorded May 11, 1970, was recorded during the album sessions but remained unreleased until the 2010 compilation album *Dolly Parton– Letter To Heaven: Songs Of Faith And Inspiration*. The compilation included this complete album along with songs from the albums: Porter Wagoner and Dolly Parton – Once More / Dolly Parton – Dolly / Dolly Parton – Joshua / Dolly Parton – Love Is Like A Butterfly / Dolly Parton – The Seeker / We Used To
- Side 2 of the album's single *Comin' For to Carry Me Home* was recorded January 25, 1971, but was not included on the album.
- This album was also issued in 1997 on CD as *Dolly Parton I Believe*.
- The album was nominated for Best Sacred Performance at the 14th Annual Grammy Awards on March 14, 1972.
- "How Great Thou Art" was recorded during the album sessions on May 12, 1970 but released on the album "The Best of Dolly Parton" on November 9, 1970.

- The *Billboard* review published February 27, 1971 said, "Sacred music is an essential part of the country field, and with this album Dolly Parton shows her knowledge of this material. Her vocals are full of sincerity and include such standards as "How Great Thou Art," "Wings of a Dove," and "I Believe."
- *Cashbox* reviewed the album in the issue dated February 13, and said, "There has always been a tremendous similarity between country music and gospel music, and with this album, Dolly Parton closes the gap. Already one of the top female vocalists in her field, this new LP will practically immortalize her. It is honest, sincere, direct, and religious–all in one. "I Believe," "Yes, I See God," "Heaven's Just a Prayer Away," "Book of Life," "Lord, Hold My Hand" and "Wings of a Dove" are only a sampling of the selections that will make this new Dolly Parton album one of the all time best sellers."
- Liner notes and the song "Book of Life" were written by Dolly's grandfather Rev. Jake Owens.
- The album was made available for digital download world wide on August 19, 2016.

Here Dolly is shown with the real live inspiration of "Daddy Was An Old Time Preacher Man", a real old time preacher for most of his life, Dolly's Grandfather. Here he is shown at the recording session of Dolly's sacred album "Golden Streets Of Glory". He wrote one of the songs, "Book Of Life", also the liner notes.

Joshua
LSP–4507

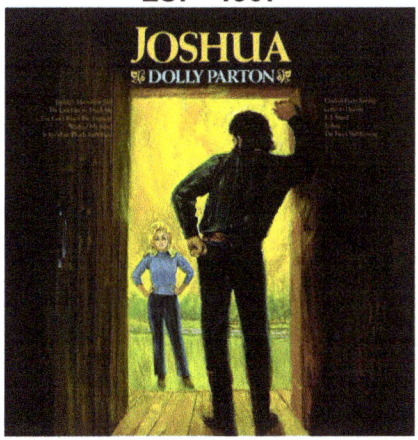

Track Listing:
Joshua / The Last One to Touch Me / Walls of My Mind / It Ain't Fair That It Ain't Right / J.J. Sneed / You Can't Reach Me Anymore / Daddy's Moonshine Still / Chicken Every Sunday / The Fire's Still Burning / Letter to Heaven

Production Information:
Produced by: Bob Ferguson
Recorded at: RCA Victor's "Nashville Sound" Studios, Nashville, TN
Engineers: Engineers: Al Pachucki
Assistant Engineer: Roy Shockley
Cover Art: Bill Myers

Singles Released From This Album:
"Joshua" / "I'm Doing This for Your Sake" – November 9, 1970 (peaked at # 1 on the Hot Country Singles chart in February 1971)

Album Data:
Highest Chart Position: # 16 on May 21, 1971
Billboard Chart: Hot Country Albums
Number of weeks on chart: 12

Notes / Trivia:
- This album was released on April 12, 1971 on LP, 8–Track and Cassette.
- Recording sessions for the album began at RCA Studios in Nashville, Tennessee, on April 20, 1970. Three additional sessions followed that fall on October 21, 1970; January 26 and February 11, 1971.
- "Walls of My Mind," "You Can't Reach Me Anymore," and "The Fire's Still Burning" were recorded during the October 31, 1969 session for Dolly's album *The Fairest of Them All*.
- The title song was Dolly's first # 1 solo single.
- Dolly received her first Grammy nomination in the Best Country Female Vocal category for the title song.
- The B side of the single release from this album was taken from the album *The Fairest of Them All* but was recorded during the sessions for the album *In The Good Old Days (When Times Were Bad)* on September 10, 1968.
- The Billboard review published in the April 24, 1971 issue said, "Dolly Parton took "Joshua" right to the top of the country singles chart, and she should now take him right to the top of the LP chart as well, with this exceptional album followup. Most of the tunes are originals, and

there are many standouts, among them "You Can't Reach Me Anymore," "The Last One to Touch Me," and "Chicken Every Sunday.""
- In the April 10, 1971 issue of *Cashbox* the review said, "Dolly Parton's "Joshua" has to be one of the all–time best country records ever recorded. Now the title tune of her latest album, it enables those who missed it the first time around to hear it along with nine other fine selections. Always a best seller, this LP containing "The Last One to Touch Me," "Walls of My Mind," "Chicken Every Sunday," "Letter to Heaven" and "J.J. Sneed" which are outstanding tracks, is sure to top the charts shortly."
- The album was made available for digital download world–wide on December 4, 2015.

First pressing of Joshua Single

Coat of Many Colors
LSP–4603

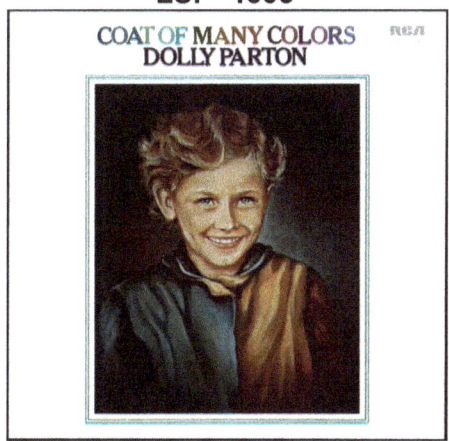

Track Listing:
Coat of Many Colors / Traveling Man / My Blue Tears / If I Lose My Mind / The Mystery of the Mystery / She Never Met A Man (She Didn't Like) / Early Morning Breeze / The Way I See You / Here I Am / A Better Place to Live

Production Information:
Produced by: Bob Ferguson
Recorded at: RCA Victor's "Nashville Sound" Studios, Nashville, TN
Engineers: Al Pachucki
Assistant Engineer: Roy Shockley
Cover Painting: Les Leverett
Liner Notes: Dolly Parton

Musicians:
Piano: David Briggs / Hargus "Pig" Robbins
Drums: Jerry Carrigan
Steel Guitar: Pete Drake
Bass: Bobby Dyson
Fiddle: Johnny Gimble / Mack Magaha / Buddy Spicher
Guitar: Dave Kirby / George McCormick / Billy Sanford / Jerry Shook
Electric Banjo: Buck Trent
Vocal Accompaniment: The Nashville Edition

Singles Released From This Album:
"My Blue Tears" b/w "The Mystery of the Mystery" – June 14, 1971 (peaked at # 17 on the Hot Country Singles chart September 3, 1971)
"Coat of Many Colors" b/w "Here I Am" – September 27, 1971 (peaked at # 4 on the Hot Country Singles chart)

Album Data:
Highest Chart Position: # 7 on January 21, 1972
Billboard Chart: Hot Country Albums
Number of weeks on chart: 23

Notes / Trivia:
- This album was released on LP, 8–Track and Cassette on October 4, 1971.
- "She Never Met a Man (She Didn't Like)" and "A Better Place to Live" were recorded during the

October 30, 1969 session for Dolly's album *The Fairest of Them All* and "Early Morning Breeze" was recorded during the January 26, 1971 session for Dolly's album *Joshua*.
- The album was nominated for Album of The Year at the 1972 CMA Awards on October 16, 1972.
- Songs recorded during the album's sessions but not released until 2007 include: "My Heart Started Breaking," recorded on January 25, 1971. "Just as Good as Gone," recorded on April 27, 1971. "The Tender Touch of Love," recorded on April 16, 1971. There was also an acoustic demo of "My Blue Tears" recorded on January 25, 1971.
- Marie Osmond cut a demo of "Coat of Many Colors" in 1973 prior to signing with MGM Records.
- Goldie Hawn recorded a version of *My Blue Tears* on her 1972 solo album "Goldie" for Reprise Records (MS–2061 / March 1972). Goldie's version was arranged by Dolly Parton and Porter Wagoner. Recording took place at Jack Clement Studios in Nashville in December 1971 and engineered by veteran Charlie Tallent. Dolly and Porter were in attendance and photos on the back jacket show Goldie, Dolly and Porter at the recording session.
- The album made *Time* magazine's list of the 100 Greatest Albums of All Time and on *Rolling Stone*'s 2020 list of the 500 Greatest Albums of All Time it landed at # 257. Dolly has cited the title track on numerous occasions as her personal favorite of all the songs she has written.
- Over the years, Dolly would re–record a number of songs from the album. "Traveling Man" was re–recorded in 1973 for Parton's *Bubbling Over* album. "My Blue Tears" was re–recorded in 1978 with Emmylou Harris and Linda Ronstadt for a Trio album project. The recording would eventually surface on Ronstadt's 1982 album *Get Closer*. Dolly also cut the song for a third time, including it on her 2001 album, *Little Sparrow*. Parton re–recorded "Early Morning Breeze" for 1974's *Jolene* and again for inclusion as a bonus track on the Walmart edition of her 2014 album, *Blue Smoke*. The 2007 bonus track "My Heart Started Breaking" was later re–recorded and included on Dolly's 1975 album, *Dolly*. Dolly re–recorded "Here I Am" as a duet with Sia for the 2018 soundtrack album, Dumplin'.
- The October 16, 1971 review published in *Billboard* said, "The top stylist's new single, the touching ballad "Coat of Many Colors," kicks off what should prove to be her biggest selling album to date. Most of the material is her own, with a few strong numbers penned by Porter Wagoner. The recent hit single, "My Blue Tears," is spotlighted along with other standouts such as "She Never Met a Man" and "The Way I See You."
- *Cashbox* published a review a week earlier on October 9, 1971 which said, "It's hard to believe it's possible, but Dolly's releases still get better and better each time you listen and each time a new one hits the market. This one's another bulls–eye with her new single as the title track and her previous hit "My Blue Tears" for drawing power, an extraordinary self–penned tune (even for Dolly) in "She Never Met a Man (She Didn't Like)" for programming appeal and a trio of Porter Wagoner tunes to put the icing on the country cake. Bound for top chart honors."

In 1978 a Dolly Parton doll hit the market. The doll also had other clothing options like this Coat of Many Colors. This outfit also included a wonderful sound sheet (pictured separately in the gallery) that had Dolly's mother, Avie Lee Parton, telling the story of the coat!

Touch Your Woman
LSP–4686

Track Listing:
Will He Be Waiting / The Greatest Days of All / Touch Your Woman / A Lot of You Left in Me / Second Best / A Little at a Time / Love Is Only As Strong (As Your Weakest Moment) / Love Isn't Free / Mission Chapel Memories / Loneliness Found Me

Production Information:
Produced by: Bob Ferguson
Recorded at: RCA Victor's "Nashville Sound" Studios, Nashville, TN
Engineers: Al Pachucki and Tom Pick
Assistant Engineers: Roy Shockley and Mike Shockley
Cover Photography: Les Leverett

Singles Released From This Album:
"Touch Your Woman" b/w "Mission Chapel Memories" – February 14, 1972 (peaked at # 6 Hot Country Singles chart)

Album Data:
Highest Chart Position: # 19 on April 21, 1972
Billboard Chart: Hot Country Albums
Number of weeks on chart: 10

Notes / Trivia:
- This album was released on LP and 8–Track on March 6, 1972.
- Recording session for the album began at RCA Studios in Nashville, Tennessee, on December 14, 1971. Two additional sessions followed on January 1 and 12, 1972.
- "Love Isn't Free" was recorded during the October 30, 1969 session for Dolly's album *The Fairest of Them All*.
- The title song was nominated for a Grammy in the category of *Best Country Vocal Performance, Female*. The show was broadcast March 3, 1973 on CBS–TV.
- The album was made available for digital download world–wide on October 10, 2014.
- *Billboard* published a review in the March 18, 1972 issue that said, "Miss Parton is currently enjoying a highly successful career and this LP will take her higher up the ladder as both a fine stylist and a superb songwriter. Produced by Bob Ferguson, this terrific package is a showcase for the beautiful voice and writing talent of the lovely country girl. "Second Best," "Will He Be Waiting," "A Little at a Time," and the title tune all penned by Miss Parton are highlights."
- *Cashbox* published a review a week earlier on March 11, 1972 which said, "Dolly Parton has a

unique voice, partly because of its tone and partly because of the emotion she places behind her singing. On this LP of ten new cuts, she reaches new heights of emotion in both her singing and songwriting. Sticking to pure country music roots as far as song structure goes, Dolly however, shows a very progressive attitude when it comes to writing lyrics in tunes such as "The Greatest Days of All," "Second Best," "Will He Be Waiting" and "Mission Chapel Memories" the latter which was co–written with Porter Wagoner."

Touch Your Woman
Promo mono single / Green label / Plug side

Sings My Favorite Songwriter, Porter Wagoner
LSP–4752

Track Listing:
Lonely Comin' Down / Do You Hear the Robins Sing / What Ain't to Be, Just Might Happen / The Bird That Never Flew / Comes and Goes / Washday Blues / When I Sing for Him / He Left Me Love / Oh, He's Everywhere / Still on Your Mind

Production Information:
Produced by: Bob Ferguson
Recorded at: RCA Victor's "Nashville Sound" Studios, Nashville, TN
Engineers: Al Pachucki and Tom Pick
Assistant Engineer: Roy Shockley
Cover Photography: Les Leverett

Musicians:
Electric Bass / Bass Guitar: Bobby Dyson
Rhythm Guitar / Banjo: Bobby Thompson
Electric Guitar: Dave Kirby
Steel Guitar: Pete Drake
Flat Top Guitar: Jerry Stembridge / Chip Young
Rhythm Guitar: Billy Sanford
Electric Banjo: Buck Trent
Fiddle: Mack Magaha / Johnny Gimble
Drums / Piano: Jerry Carrigan
Piano / Organ: Hargus Robbins
Vocal Accompaniment: The Nashville Edition

Singles Released From This Album:
"Washday Blues" b/w "Just As Good As Gone" – July 10, 1972 (peaked at # on the Hot Country Singles chart on)
"When I Sing for Him" b/w "Lord Hold My Hand" – September 4, 1972 (peaked at # Hot Country Singles chart on)

Album Data:
Highest Chart Position: # 33 on December 22, 1972
Billboard Chart: Hot Country Albums
Number of weeks on chart: 7

Notes / Trivia:
- This album was released on LP and 8–Track Tape on October 2, 1972.

- All songs written by Porter Wagoner.
- The October 14, 1972 review in *Billboard* said, "Dolly Parton is coming on as the leading female country singer in the business. Here, she does "Lonely Comin' Down," "Do You Hear the Robins Sing" and "Still on Your Mind." "When I Sing for Him" is an excellently done gospel tune. Another stirring LP from Dolly!"
- *Cashbox* gave a glowing review of the album in their October 7, 1972 issue : "Dolly Parton—which is more beautiful, her voice or her looks? Whatever the answer, the combination of the two is simply devastating! Dolly radiates her inner soul through both her looks and her voice, and has shown time and time again that purity of feeling wins out over flashy singing tricks—her talent stands the test of time. In her liner notes, Dolly emphatically states that Porter Wagoner is her favorite songwriter, and for that reason she has recorded an album of his songs exclusively. The team of Dolly's performance and Porter's writing is another "perfect combination." A superlative album."

An early 1970's tour poster

My Tennessee Mountain Home
APL-1-0033

Track Listing:
The Letter / I Remember / Old Black Kettle / Daddy's Working Boots / Dr. Robert F. Thomas / In The Good Old Days (When Times Were Bad) / My Tennessee mountain Home / The Wrong Direction Home / Back Home / The Better Part of Life / Down on Music Row

Production Information:
Produced by: Bob Ferguson
Recorded at: RCA Victor's "Nashville Sound" Studios, Nashville, TN
Engineer: Tom Pick
Assistant Engineer: Roy Shockley
Cover Photography: Louis Owens
Back Cover Photography: Bill Preston

Musicians:
Guitar: Jimmy Colvard
Rhythm Guitar: Jerry Stembridge / Dave Kirby / Bobby Thompson
Dobro / Petal Steel Guitar: Pete Drake
Bass: Bobby Dyson
Drums: Jerry Carrigan
Electric Banjo: Buck Trent
Fiddle: Mack Magaha / Johnny Gimble
Piano: Hargus "Pig" Robbins / Ron Oates
Harmonica: Charlie McCoy / James Riddle
Harp: Mary Hoephinger
Vocal Accompaniment: The Nashville Edition

Singles Released From This Album:
"My Tennessee Mountain Home" b/w "The Better Part of Life" – December 4, 1972 (peaked at #15 on the Hot Country Singles chart)

Album Data:
Highest Chart Position: # 19 on June 1, 1973
Billboard Chart: Hot Country Albums
Number of weeks on chart: 10

Notes / Trivia:
- This album was released on LP, 8 Track and Cassette on April 2, 1973.
- The cover is a gate–fold on the first issue release. The interior, in addition to recording credits contains photos of Dolly as a child as well as photo of her parents and other relatives. About the cover Dolly writes: "This is **MY TENNESSEE MOUNTAIN HOME**— the house I lived in from the time I was five years old until I was ten years old. I remember these years most of all."
- Songs recorded for this album but not released at the time included: "Eugene, Oregon" and Dolly's original recording of "What Will Baby Be?"
- Dolly would later re–record "What Will Baby Be?" for her 1992 album *Slow Dancing with the Moon*.
- The song "Sacred Memories" which was one of the first recorded for the album on September 1, 1972 was not released until 1974 on Dolly's album *Love Is Like A Butterfly*.
- Dolly performed the title song on her 1994 live album *Heartsongs*.
- Overdub sessions took place for this album on December 12, 1972 at RCA Studio A, Nashville, TN

The back cover photo

Bubbling Over
APL-1-0286

Track Listing:
Bubbling Over / Traveling Man / Alabama Sundown / Afraid to Live and Afraid of Dying / Love with Me / My Kind of Man / Sometimes and Old Memory Get in My Eye / Pleasant as May / The Beginning / Love, You're So Beautiful Tonight

Production Information:
Produced by: Bob Ferguson
Recorded at: RCA Victor's "Nashville Sound" Studios, Nashville, TN
Engineers: Al Pachucki and Tom Pick
Assistant Engineer: Roy Shockley
Cover Photography: Les Leverett

Singles Released From This Album:
"Traveling Man" b/w "I Remember" – June 1973 (peaked at # 20 on the Billboard Country Singles Chart. The single pealed at No. 12 in Canada on the RPM Country Singles chart.)

Album Data:
Highest Chart Position: # 14 on February 1, 1974
Billboard Chart: Hot Country Albums
Number of weeks on chart: 20

Notes / Trivia:
- This album was released on LP, 8–Track and Cassette on September 10, 1973.
- This album was also issued in the Quad format on LP, 8–Track and Open reel tape.
- The album's single, "Traveling Man", is a re–recording of a song previously included on Dolly's 1971 album *Coat of Many Colors*. Side B of the single– "I Remember," was taken from her previous album.
- "The Beginning" would later be recorded as a duet with Porter Wagoner and included on their 1975 album *Say Forever You'll Be Mine.*
- *Billboard* published a review on September 22, 1973, that said, "Dolly must write a dozen or so hits a week, and since Porter Wagoner resumed his writing career, he's almost keeping pace. The two of them supply the bulk of the material for this, another in the huge collection of Dolly's album outputs, and it – as the others before it – tops the last one out. It ranges from the happy uptempo to the tearful ballad, and no one fills this range better than Dolly. "Love with Me," "Pleasant as May" and "Love, You're So Beautiful Tonight" are the best cuts on the album."
- *Cashbox* reviewed the album in their October 6, 1973 issue saying, "An eagerly awaited album, Dolly Parton's new release will elicit immediate effervescence upon the initial listening,

but then again isn't that what bubbling over is all about! "Traveling Man," Dolly's last chart single is included on the album. An easy listening blend of country music at its finest this new album will prove an inevitable success for the inimitable Miss Parton. Some of the more outstanding tracks are "Bubbling Over," "Sometimes an Old Memory Gets in My Eye" and "Love with Me."

The Quadraphonic 8–Track release of the *Bubbling Over* album.

Jolene
APL–1–0473

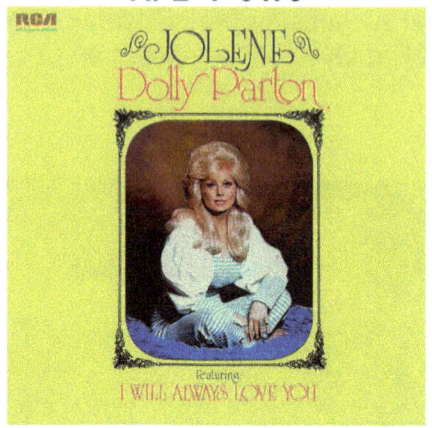

Track Listing:
Jolene / When Somebody Wants to Leave / River of Happiness / Early Morning Breeze / Highlight of My Life / I Will Always Love You / Randy / Living on Memories of You / Lonely Comin' Down / It Must Be You

Production Information:
Produced by: Bob Ferguson
Recorded at: RCA Victor's "Nashville Sound" Studios, Nashville, TN
Engineers: Tom Pick
Assistant Engineer: Roy Shockley

Musicians:
Dolly Parton: Vocals / Guitar
Guitar: Jimmy Colvard / Dave Kirby / Bobby Thompson / Chip Young
Petal Steel Guitar: Pete Drake / Stu Basore
Bass: Bobby Dyson
Drums: Jerry Carrigan / Larrie Londin / Kenny Malone
Banjo: Buck Trent
Fiddle: Mack Magaha / Johnny Gimble
Piano: Hargus "Pig" Robbins / David Briggs
Harmonica: Onie Wheeler
Vocal Accompaniment: The Nashville Edition
Cover Photography: Hope Powell
Art Direction: Herb Burnette

Singles Released From This Album:
"Jolene" b/w "Love, You're So Beautiful Tonight" – October 15, 1973 (peaked at # 1 on the Billboard Country Singles chart dated February 1, 1974.)
"I Will Always Love You" b/w "Lonely Comin' Down" – March 11, 1974 (peaked at # 1 on the Billboard Country Singles Chart on June 7, 1974.)

Album Data:
Highest Chart Position: # 6 on April 19, 1974
Billboard Chart: Hot Country Albums
Number of weeks on chart: 23

Notes / Trivia:
- This album was released on LP, 8 Track and Cassette on February 4, 1974.
- The song "Jolene" was covered by Olivia Newton–John in 1976 on her MCA album *Come On Over*.
- The album was released during the time period Dolly was embarking on a solo career, after having spent seven years as part of The Porter Wagoner Show on television and his touring road show. The album's song "I Will Always Love You," was reportedly written to express the sorrow Dolly felt over the professional breakup.
- This album, along with a couple of the other older albums, were re–issued to tie in with Dolly's 2007 UK Tour. This re–issue included 4 unreleased songs from the albums sessions. They include: "Another Woman's Man" recorded May 22, 1973 / "Cracker Jack" recorded June 12, 1973 / "Barbara on Your Mind" recorded June 12, 1973 / "Last Night's Lovin'" recorded June 12, 1973.
- "Early Morning Breeze" is a re–recording of a song which previously appeared on Dolly's album *Coat of Many Colors* and was recorded January 26, 1971.
- "Lonely Coming Down" had first appeared on Dolly's Porter Wagoner tribute album *Sings My Favorite Songwriter, Porter Wagoner* from 1972 and was recorded May 3, 1972.
- This album was re–issued on vinyl LP at least twice in recent years. First by Music on Vinyl on July 10, 2015 and again in LP by Sony in 2019.
- Dolly's original 1974 recording of the song "I Will Always Love You" appeared in Martin Scorsese's film *Alice Doesn't Live Here Anymore*, and the 1996 film *It's My Party*. The song also won Parton Female Vocalist of the Year at the 1975 CMA Awards. Dolly re–recorded the song in 1982 for "The Best Little Whorehouse in Texas" film. Released as the first single from the soundtrack Dolly took the song to the # 1 spot on the Country Singles Chart for the 2nd time!

1976 Germany 45 release of *Jolene* backed with *Coat of Many Colors*

Love Is Like A Butterfly
APL-1-0712

Track Listing:
Love Is like A Butterfly / If I Cross Your Mind / My Eyes Can See Only You / Take Me Back / Blackie, Kentucky / Gettin' Happy / You're the One That Taught Me How to Swing / Highway Headin' South / Once Upon A Memory / Sacred Memories

Production Information:
Produced by: Bob Ferguson
Recorded at: RCA Victor's "Nashville Sound" Studios, Nashville, TN
Engineers: Tom Pick
Assistant Engineer: Roy Shockley
Vocal Accompaniment: The Lea Jane Singers
Cover Photography: Hope Powell
Art Direction: Herb Burnette – Pinwheel Studios

Singles Released From This Album:
"Love Is Like A Butterfly" b/w "Sacred Memories" – August 5, 1974 (peaked at # 1 on the Hot Country Singles chart on November 8, 1974)

Album Data:
Highest Chart Position: # 7 on November 8, 1974
Billboard Chart: Hot Country Albums
Number of weeks on chart: 23

Notes / Trivia:
- This album was released on LP, 8 Track and Cassette on September 16, 1974.
- Parton used the song as the opening theme for her 1976–77 TV variety show *Dolly!*
- A version of the title track, sung by Clare Torry, was used as the theme to BBC–TV comedy series *Butterflies.*
- The track "Sacred Memories" was originally recorded September 1, 1972 during session work for the album *My Tennessee Mountain Home.* It was included as a bonus track on the 2007 CD reissue of *My Tennessee Mountain Home* by Legacy / Sony.

A 1974 trade ad for the album *Love Is Like A Butterfly*

The Bargain Store
APL-1-0950

Track Listing:
The Bargain Store / Kentucky Gambler / When I'm Gone / The Only Hand You'll Ever Hold / On my Mind Again / I Want To Be What You Need / Love to Remember / You'll Always Be Special to Me / He Would Know / I'll Never Forget

Production Information:
Produced by: Porter Wagoner & Bob Ferguson
Recorded at: RCA Victor's "Nashville Sound" Studios, Nashville, TN
Engineers: Tom Pick
Assistant Engineer: Roy Shockley
Vocal Accompaniment: The Lea Jane Singers
Cover Photography: Hope Powell
Art Direction: Herb Burnette – Pinwheel Studios

Singles Released From This Album:
"The Bargain Store" b/w "I'll Never Forget" – January 13, 1975 (peaked at # 1 on the Billboard Country Singles chart in April 1975.)

Album Data:
Highest Chart Position: # 9 on April 25, 1975
Billboard Chart: Hot Country Albums
Number of weeks on chart: 23

Notes / Trivia:
- This album was released on LP, 8 Track and Cassette on February 17, 1975.
- The single off the album was Dolly's fifth # 1 in a row. Surprisingly, several country radio stations in the south banned the single from their play list at the time. They felt the line, "The bargain store is open come inside, you can easily afford the price" was inappropriate for listeners making this the only song Dolly has ever had that was banned from radio. Still, the single rocketed up the charts to # 1.

Dolly
APL-1-1221

Track Listing:
The Seeker / My Heart Started Breaking / Hold Me / I'll Remember You As Mine / Because I Love You / We Used To / The Love I Used To Call Mine / Bobby's Arms / Only The Memory Remains / Most Of All Why

Production Information:
Produced and Arranged by: Porter Wagoner
Recorded at: RCA Victor's "Nashville Sound" Studios, Nashville, TN
Engineer: Tom Pick
Assistant Engineer: Roy Shockley
Vocal Accompaniment: The Lea Jane Singers and The Nashville Edition
Orchestration: Bill McElhiney
Cover Photography: Dennis Carney
Art Direction: Herb Burnette – Pinwheel Studios

Singles Released From This Album:
"The Seeker" b/w "Love With Feeling" – May 19, 1975 (peaked at # 2 on the US Country Singles chart on August 8, 1975 and in Canada peaked at #1 on the *RPM* Country Singles chart)
"We Used To" b/w "My Heart Started Breaking" – September 8, 1975 (peaked at # 9 on the US Country Singles Chart)

Album Data:
Highest Chart Position: # 14 on November 21, 1975
Billboard Chart: Hot Country Albums
Number of weeks on chart: 19

Notes / Trivia:
- This album was released on LP, 8 Track and Cassette on September 15, 1975
- Though simply titled "Dolly" this album is sometime referred to as *Dolly The Seeker – We Used To* due to the cover graphics. The label simply reads "Dolly."
- *The Seeker* and *We Used To* were recorded at the same session on December 9, 1974.
- A review by *Billboard* dated September 27, 1975 said: "A collection of Dolly's favorite love songs plus her two latest singles. She wrote all of the tunes and is one of the better writers around. All beautiful songs, beautifully done. Best cuts: "Most Of All Why," "Because I Love You" and "Only The Memory Remains." Dealers: Display country, pop and MOR."
- *Cashbox* published a review on October 4, 1975 that said, "Produced and arranged by Porter Wagoner, this LP is a collection of love songs written by Dolly, most of them sad songs —

songs of remembering lost love. Most are ballads with only a few uptempo cuts."

The UK cassette tape of the album

The Japanese LP version of the album

All I Can Do
APL–1–1665

Track Listing:
All I Can Do / The Fire That Keeps You Warm / When The Sun Goes Down Tomorrow / I'm a Drifter / Falling Out of Love with Me / Shattered Image / Boulder to Birmingham / Preacher Tom / Life's Like Poetry / Hey, Lucky Lady

Production Information:
Produced by: Dolly Parton & Porter Wagoner
Recorded at: RCA Victor's "Nashville Sound" Studios, Nashville, TN
Engineer: Tom Pick
Assistant Engineer: Roy Shockley
Vocal Accompaniment: The Lea Jane Singers
Arrangements by: Porter Wagoner
Cover Photography: Hope Powell
Art Direction: Herb Burnette – Pinwheel Studios

Singles Released From This Album:
"Hey, Lucky Lady" b/w "Most of All Why" – February 9, 1976 (peaked at # 19 in the US on the Hot Country Singles chart and # 11 in Canada on the RPM chart)
"All I Can Do" b/w "The Fire That Keep You Warm" – July 5, 1976 (peaked at # 3 in the US on the Hot Country Singles chart and # 1 in Canada on the *RPM* chart)
"Shattered Image" b/w "I'm a Drifter" – November 19, 1976 (UK only release)

Album Data:
Highest Chart Position: # 3 on November 19, 1976
Billboard Chart: Hot Country Albums
Number of weeks on chart: 25

Notes / Trivia:
- This album was released on LP, 8 Track and Cassette on August 16, 1976.
- The album was nominated for Best Country Vocal Performance, Female at the 19th Annual Grammy Awards.
- Dolly would re–record "Shattered Image" for her 2002 album *Halos & Horns.*
- "Falling Out of Love with Me" was covered by country–rock band *Pinmonkey* in 2002 with Dolly providing vocals on the recording.
- "The Fire That Keeps You Warm" was previously recorded by Dolly Parton and Porter Wagoner on May 23, 1974 as a duet for their 1974 album *Porter & Dolly*. The song was written by Dolly.
- A song recorded for, but not released on the *All I Can Do* album, was a song Dolly wrote called "To Daddy." Dolly's own version of the song later appeared on her 1995 compilation *The*

Essential Dolly Parton One
- *Hey Lucky Lady* was recorded December 9, 1974.
- *Billboard* published a review in its August 28, 1976 issue that said, "Exceptional LP by the enigmatic lady who has reached the pinnacle of country music success and is now making her impact, deservingly, on the pop music market. Few artists write better songs than Parton, and no one can sing them better. A powerful performer, Parton provides an album for country and pop chart consideration. Her version of Emmylou Harris' "Boulder to Birmingham" is a striking, heartfelt song, sung without pretension and with a surplus of feeling. Effective blend of slow ballads and uptempo numbers, contains a pair of her hit singles and a couple more that should make good singles. Incisive liner notes by Don Cusic add depth to an already noteworthy LP."
- *Cashbox* also published a review on August 28, 1976 that read, "Making a positive move into the progressive sound, Dolly makes her current single the theme of the total offering. Other self-penned selections are "The Fire That Keeps You Warm," "When the Sun Goes Down Tomorrow," "I'm a Drifter," "Falling Out of Love with Me," "Shattered Image," "Preacher Tom" and "Hey, Lucky Lady." Also included are "Life's Like Poetry" (Merle Haggard) and "Boulder to Birmingham" (Emmylou Harris/Bill Danoff). A Dolly Parton/Porter Wagoner production."

The picture sleeve of "All I Can Do" release from Germany.

New Harvest … First Gathering
APL-1-2188

Track Listing:
Light Of a Clear Blue Morning / Applejack / My Girl (My Love) / Holdin' On to You / You Are / How Does It Feel / Where Beauty Live in Memory / (You're Love Has Lifted Me) Higher and Higher / Getting In My Way / There

Production Information:
Produced and Arranged by: Dolly Parton
Co-Produced by: Gregg Perry
Tracks 1, 3,4, 5, 6 and 9 strings and vocals recorded at: Sound Shop Studios
Engineer: Rich Adler
Tracks 2, 7, 8, 10 recorded at Creative Workshop Studios, Nashville, TN
Engineer: Brent Maher
Tack piano overdubbed at: Lee Hazen's Studio, Nashville, TN
Mixed at: Sound labs, Los Angeles, CA
Mixed by: Armin Steiner
Assistant Mix Engineer: Rich Adler
LP Mastered at: The Mastering Lab.
Cover Photography: Nick Sangiamo and David Gahr
Inner Spread LP Artwork: Richard Sparks
Art Direction: Acy Lehman

Singles Released From This Album:
"Light of A Clear Blue Morning" b/w "There" – March 21, 1977 (peaked at # 11 in the US on the Hot Country Singles chart and # 1 in Canada on the RPM chart)
"You Are" b/w "Jealous Heart" (European only release)
"Applejack" b/w "You Are" (European only release)
"Higher and Higher" b/w "Applejack" (European only release)

Album Data:
Highest Chart Position: # 1 on May 13, 1977.
Billboard Chart: Hot Country Albums
Number of weeks on chart: 29

Notes / Trivia:
- This album was released on LP, 8 Track and Cassette on February 14, 1977.
- Dolly would rerecord the title song for her 1992 film *Straight Talk*; for this recording, she changed the lyrics of verse two. A third recording of the song appeared on an album of spirituals Dolly released in 2003 titled *For God and Country*. Glen Campbell covered the song on his 1991 album *Unconditional Love*
- "(Your Love Has Lifted Me) Higher and Higher" was nominated for Best Country Vocal Performance, Female at the 20th Annual Grammy Awards in 1978.
- The album won Best Country Album at the AMA's in 1978.

1977 promotional ad from Billboard Magazine

Here You Come Again
APL–1–2544

Track Listing:
Here You Come Again / Baby Come Out Tonight / It's All Wrong, But It's All Right / Me And Little Andy / Lovin' You / Cowgirl and The Dandy / Two Doors Down / God's Coloring Book / As Soon As I Touched Him / Sweet Music Man

Production Information:
Produced by: Gary Klein
Executive Producer: Charles Koppleman
Recorded at: Sound Labs and Capitol Recording Studios Los Angeles, CA – June, July & August 1977.
Engineers: Armin Steiner
Assistant Engineer: Linda Tyler (at Sound Lbs) and Don Henderson (at Capitol)
Cover Photography and art direction: Ed Caraeff
Lettering by: Michael Manoogian

Singles Released From This Album:
"Here You Come Again" b/w "Me and Little Andy" – September 26, 1977 (peaked at #1 in the US on the Hot Country Singles chart and Canada on the *RPM* chart.) (US Gold status on February 1, 1978)
"Two Doors Down" b/w "It's All Wrong, But It's All Right" – February 27, 1978 (peaked at # 19 on the Hot 100 Chart and # 12 on Adult Contemporary in the US. In Canada it peaked at # 26 on RPM Top Singles and #7 in Adult Contemporary)
"It's All Wrong, But It's All Right" b/w "Two Doors Down" – February 27, 1978 (peaked at # 1 in the US on the Hot Country Singles chart and Canada on the *RPM* chart. The release was part of a double–A–sided single, the other mentioned above and in the trivia below.)
"Me And Little Andy" b/w ""Cowgirl and the Dandy" – April 1980 (European only release)

Album Data:
Highest Chart Position: # 1 on December 23, 1977.
Billboard Chart: Hot Country Albums
Number of weeks on chart: 57

Notes / Trivia:
- This album was released on LP, 8 Track and Cassette on October 3, 1977.
- This album was Dolly's first album to be certified platinum by the Recording Industry Association of America, for selling a million copies. Gold status of the album had been reached on December 21, 1977 and platinum on April 28, 1978.

- Though *Here You Come Again* was originally written in 1975 and rejected by Brenda Lee, B.J. Thomas was the first artist to record the title song for his self–titled 1977 album, but never released the song as a single. Lesley Gore recorded a cover of the song in her 1982 album "The Canvas Can Do Miracles" and Maureen McGovern recorded a slower, sensual bluesy version for her 1988 album, *State of the Heart*.
- Dolly first recorded her composition "God's Coloring Book" on April 16, 1971 during sessions for the album *Coat of Many Colors* but that original recording was not released until the "Dolly" 4 disc set in 2009.
- On January 13, 1978 Dolly re–recorded a more loose, pop–oriented version of "Two Doors Down" with a slight disco sound so as not to compete with another singer who had recorded the Dolly penned song. RCA released this new version as a double–A–sided single, with the flip side, "It's All Wrong, but It's All Right" which was intended for country airplay, and "Two Doors Down" intended for the pop airplay. "Two Doors Down" topped the U.S. country charts, and was a top–20 pop hit for Parton, and went on to be one of her most popular hits.
- "Two Doors Down" won Dolly a Songwriter Achievement Award in 1979.
- Dolly performed the slower version of "Two Doors Down" on Cher's 1978 TV Special; *Cher...Special* which aired on April 3, 1978. Dolly was nominated for an Emmy in the category of "Best Supporting Actress in a Variety or Musical Special" for her appearance.
- "It's All Wrong, But It's All Right" was featured in the 1979 drama film *Norma Rae*, in which actress Sally Field won the Academy Award for Best Actress for her portrayal as Norma Rae Webster.
- The title cut was nominated in 1979 for a Grammy Award and won for for "Best Female Country Vocal Performance."

The picture sleeve of the single release from Germany
This single contained a different B side than released in the US.

Heartbreaker
AFL–1–2797

Track Listing:
I Really Got The Feeling / It's Too Late To Love Me Now / We're Through Forever (Til Tomorrow) / Sure Thing / With You Gone / Baby, I'm Burning / Nickels and Dimes / The Man / Heartbreaker / I Wanna Fall In Love

Production Information:
Produced by: Gary Klein and Dolly Parton
Executive Producer: Charles Koppelman
Recorded at: Sound Labs and Capitol Recording Studios, Los Angeles, California
Engineers: Armin Steiner
Assistant Engineers: Linda Tyler (at Sound Labs) and Don Henderson (at Capitol)
Cover Photography and Art Direction: Ed Caraeff Studio

Singles Released From This Album:
"Heartbreaker" b/w "Sure Thing" – July 24, 1978 (peaked at # 1 in the US on the Hot Country Singles chart and Canada on the *RPM* chart)
"It's Too Late To Love Me Now" b/w "With You Gone" (South African only release)
"Baby, I'm Burnin'" b/w "I Really Got The Feelin'" – November 6, 1978 (peaked at # 25 in the US on the Hot Country Singles chart and # 1 in Canada on the *RPM* chart)
"I Really Got The Feeling" b/w "Baby, I'm Burnin'" (Peaked at # 1 in the US on the Hot Country Songs Chart)

Album Data:
Highest Chart Position: # 1 on September 8, 1978.
Charts: Billboard Chart Hot Country Albums / Canadian Country Charts
Number of weeks on chart: 45

Notes / Trivia:
- This album was released on LP, 8 Track and Cassette on July 17, 1978.
- The Dolly penned song "Nickels and Dimes" was recorded by International singer Nana Mouskouri on her album "Roses Love Sunshine" released in 1979.
- The single "Baby, I'm Burnin'" b/w "I Really Got The Feeling" was released as a double A sided single with "Baby, I'm Burnin'" geared toward the pop chart and the flip side the country chart.
- A 12" disco re–mix single was released of "Baby, I'm Burnin'" clocking in at 4:31 with the flip side being a disco remix of "I Wanna Fall In Love" coming in at 5:18.

- Dolly used "Baby, I'm Burnin'" as the theme to her 1987–1988 variety show, *Dolly!*
- The album was certified Gold for 500,000+ copies sold on August 16, 1978.

A 1978 Trade Ad for the album *Heartbreaker*

Great Balls of Fire
AHL–1–3361

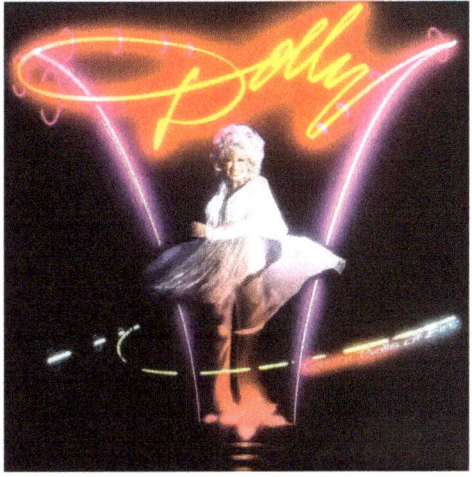

Track Listing:
Star of the Show / Down / You're The Only One / Help! / Do You Think That Time Stands Still / Sweet Summer Lovin' / Great Balls of Fire / Almost in Love / It's Not My Affair Anymore / Sandy's Song

Production Information:
Produced by: Dean Parks and Gregg Perry
Executive Producers: Dolly Parton and Charles Koppelman
Recorded at: Sound Labs Inc, A&M Recording Studios and Salty Dog, Los Angeles, California
Engineers: Eric Prestidge
Assistant Engineers: Linda Tyler (at Sound Labs, Inc)
Mixed at Spectrum Studios
Vinyl mastering by: Bernie Grundman at A&M Recording Studios.
Cover Photography and Art Direction: Ed Caraeff Studio

Musicians:
Piano: Gregg Perry
Bass: Abraham Laboriel
Synthesizer: Gregg Perry / Dean Parks
keyboards: Michael Omartian / David Foster / Bill Payne
Drums–Percussion: Jim Keltner
Steel Guitar: Joe McGuffee
Guitars, alto flute: Dean Parks
Banjo: Herb Pedersen
Horns: Earle Dumler / Chuck Findley / David Grisman / Gary Herbig / Jim Horn / Quitman Dennis
Harp: Dorothy Remsen
Conga: Lenny Castro
Tambourine: Stephanie Spruill
Background Vocals: Anita Ball / Richard Dennison / Roy Galloway / Carol Carmichael Parks / Herb Pedersen / Ricky Skaggs / Stephanie Spruill / Julia Waters / Maxine Waters

Singles Released From This Album:
"You're The Only One" b/w "Down" – May 14, 1979 (peaked at # 1 in the US on the Hot Country Singles chart and Canada on the *RPM* chart)
"Sweet Summer Lovn'" b/w "Great Balls of Fire" – August 6, 1979 (peaked at # 7 in the US and # 1 on the Yugoslavian Singles chart)
"Star of the Show" b/w "Down" (released in Europe only)

Album Data:
Highest Chart Position: # 4 on July 27, 1979
Billboard Chart: Hot Country Albums
Number of weeks on chart: 26

Notes / Trivia:
- This album was released on LP, 8 Track and Cassette on May 28, 1979.
- The album was certified Gold for 500,000+ copies sold on November 13, 1979.
- The album was rated a Top Album Pick in the June 9, 1979 issue of Billboard.
- The most country sounding track on the LP is the cover of the Beatles' "Help!," has a neo-bluegrass arrangement which is helped along by background vocals by Ricky Skaggs and Herb Pedersen.
- "Sandy's Song" is said to be a thank you Dolly wrote for her manager, Sandy Gallin.
- On June 9, 1979 *Billboard* published a review that said: "Parton has now firmly established herself in the pop field and reinforces her universal appeal with a collection of songs that showcase her versatility. Aiding Parton's sweet vocal are a conglomeration of stellar players which gives the material the needed punch. Among the musicians are Jim Keltner, Dean Parks, David Foster, Michael Omartian, Bill Payne, David Grisman and others. String and horn arrangements add sweetening to the material. Parton mixes the album among original and cover material including the Beatles' "Help." Best cuts: "You're The Only One," "Help," "Star Of The Show," "Do You Think That Time Stands Still." Dealers: Another attractive package is a sales stimulant."

Japanese 45 picture insert for "You're The Only One." b/w "Down"

Dolly, Dolly, Dolly
AHL1-3546

Track Listing:
Starting Over Again / Same Old Fool / Old Flames Can't Hold A Candle to You / You're The Only One I Ever Needed / Say Goodnight / Fool For Your Love / Even A Fool Would Let Go / Sweet Agony / I Knew You When / Packin' It Up

Production Information:
Produced by: Gary Klein
Executive Producer: Charles Koppelman
Recorded at: Sound Labs, Inc and Capitol Recording Studios
Engineers: John Arrias
Assistant Engineers: Don Henderson (at Capitol Recording Studios) and Sheridan Eldridge (at Sound Labs)
Cover Photography: Ron Slenzak
Art Direction: Henry Vizcarra and Tim Bryant
Design: Henry Vizcarra

Musicians:
Drums: Eddie Anderson
Piano: Gregg Perry
Keyboards: Ron Oates / Red Young
Guitars: Jeff Baxter / Steve Cropper / Jay Gradon / Albert Lee / Joe McGuffee / Michael Severs / Fred Tackett
Bass: Leland Sklar
Bass Guitar: Abraham Laboriel / Nathan East
Percussion: Lenny Castro
Horns: George Bohanon / Chuck Findley / Gary Grant / Gary Herbig / Jim Horn / Tom Saviano / Tom Scott / Dick Hyde
Background Vocals: Anita Ball / Alexandra Brown / Richard Dennison / Roy Galloway / William "Bill" Greene / Gene Morford / Jim Salestrom / Stephanie Spruill
Harmonica: Terry McMillian
String & vocal arranger: Nick DeCaro
Background vocals & vocal contractor: Denise DeCaro
Music contractor: Frank DeCaro

Singles Released From This Album:
"Starting Over Again" b/w "Sweet Agony" – February 25, 1980 (peaked at # 1 in the US on May 24, 1980 on the Hot Country Singles chart and # 2 In Canada on the *RPM* chart)
"Old Flames Can't Hold a Candle To You" b/w "I Knew You When" – June 23, 1980. (peaked at # 1 in August 1980 on the Hot Country Singles chart)

Album Data:
Highest Chart Position: # 7on May 30, 1980.
Billboard Chart: Hot Country Albums
Number of weeks on chart: 30

Notes / Trivia:
- This album was released on LP, 8–Track and Cassette on April 14, 1980
- Cheryl Ladd recorded a version of "You're The Only One I Ever Needed" on her second LP for Capitol Records "Dance Forever" in 1979.
- Reba McEntire recorded a version of "Starting Over Again" in 1995 on her album of the same name. Reba's version was a top 20 hit peaking at # 19.

Old Flames Can't Hold A Candle To You promo single

9 to 5 and odd Jobs
AHL-1-3852

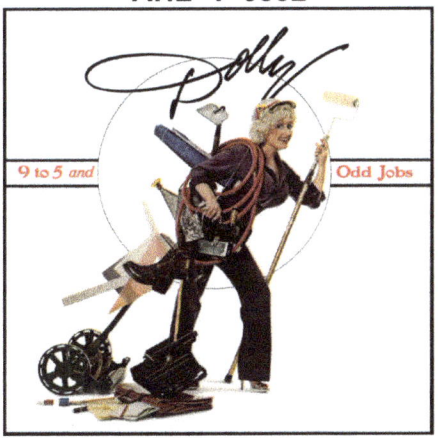

Track Listing:
9 to 5 / Hush–A– Bye Hard Times / The House Of The Rising Sun / Deportee (Plane Wreck At Los Gatos) / Sing for the Common Man / Working Girl / Detroit City / But You Know I Love You / Dark As A Dungeon / Poor Folks Town

Production Information:
Produced and arranged by: Mike Post
Associate producer: Gregg Perry
"9 to 5" Produced and arranged by: Gregg Perry
Recorded at: Audio Media Recorders, Nashville, TN, Western Recorders, Hollywood, CA, and Studio 335, Hollywood, CA.
Engineers: Marshall Morgan (at Audio Media), Paul Dobbe and Chuck Britz (at Western Recorders), Larry Carlton (at Studio 335)
Assistant Engineer: Pat McMakin (at Audio Media)
Mixed at: Smoke Tree Ranch Studios, Chatsworth, CA
Mixing engineer: Doug Parry
Second mix engineer: Rick Romano
The song "9 to 5" was recorded at: Sound Labs, Inc, Los Angeles, CA
Engineer: Armin Steiner
"9 to 5" Mixed at Smoke Tree Ranch Studios, Chatsworth, CA
24–Track Mixing engineer: Doug Parry

Cover Photography: Ron Slenzak
Art Direction: Tim Bryant & George Corsillo / Gribbitt
Design: George Corsillo

Singles Released From This Album:
"9 to 5" b/w "Sing for The Common Man" – November 3, 1980 (peaked at #1 in the US on the Hot Country Singles chart and Canada on the *RPM* chart)
"But You Know I Love You" b/w "Poor Folks' Town" – March 16, 1981 (peaked at # 1 in the US on the Hot Country Singles chart and # 2 in Canada on the *RPM* chart)
"House of the Rising Sun" b/w "Working Girl" – August 3, 1981 (peaked at # 14 in the US on the Hot Country Singles chart)

Album Data:
Highest Chart Position: # 1 on February 13, 1981.
Billboard Chart: Hot Country Albums

Number of weeks on chart: 49

Notes / Trivia:

- This album was released on LP, 8 Track and Cassette on November 17, 1980.
- The album was certified Gold for 500,000+ copies sold on March 6, 1981.
- The single release of the title track went platinum for sales of over 1,000,000 copies sold.
- The title track was written for the 1980 comedy film of the same name starring Jane Fonda, Lily Tomlin and Dolly Parton. The film was released on December 19, 1980.
- The 2009 CD re–issue of the album contains three bonus tracks, two unreleased: "Everyday People," (previously unreleased) "9 to 5 (Love to Infinity Radio Mix 2008)" and "9 to 5 (Karaoke Mix 2009)" (previously unreleased).

But You Know I Love You Picture sleeve single from Spain.

Heartbreak Express
AHL-1-4289

Track Listing:
Heartbreak Express / Single Women / My Blue Ridge Mountain Boy / As Much As Always / Do I Ever Cross Your Mind / Release Me / Barbara On Your Mind / Act Like A Fool / Prime Of Our Love / Hollywood Potters

Production Information:
Produced and arranged by: Dolly Parton and Gregg Perry
Recorded and mixed at: Smoke Tree Ranch Studios, Chatsworth, CA
Engineers: Doug Parry
Assistant Engineer: Rick Romano
Cover Photography: Herb Ritts
Art Direction: Phyllis Chotin & Michelle Hart / Media Arts
Design Concept: Dolly Parton
Hairstyle: Colleen Owens

Singles Released From This Album:
"Single Women" b/w "Barbara on Your Mind" – February 1, 1982 (peaked at # 8 in the US on the Hot Country Singles chart and # 1 in Canada on the *RPM* chart.)
"Heartbreak Express" b/w "Act Like A Fool" – May 3, 1982 (peaked at # 7 in the US on the Hot Country Singles chart and # 1 in Canada on the *RPM* chart)
"Do I Ever Cross Your Mind" b/w "I Will Always Love You" – July 12, 1982 (A double A sided single "I Will Always Love You," re-recorded for the motion picture "The Best Little Whorehouse in Texas" released in July 1982 and peaked at # 1 on October 16, 1982 on the Hot Country Singles chart.)

Album Data:
Highest Chart Position: # 5 on July 2, 1982
Billboard Chart: Hot Country Albums
Number of Weeks on Chart: 25

Notes / Trivia:
- This album was released on LP, 8 Track and Cassette on March 29, 1982.
- The original recording of "Barbara on Your Mind" first appeared on the 2007 UK re-issue of the 1974 album *Jolene*. The song had been recorded during the *Jolene* album sessions, but not released. The track here is a re-recording with a vastly different musical arrangement.
- "Single Women" is a song, written by *Saturday Night Live* writer Michael O'Donoghue. The song, was originally performed during an *SNL* sketch by Christine Ebersole on the October 10, 1981 broadcast. Dolly's version of the song featured somewhat reworked lyrics, as RCA

requested she eliminate the drug references, fearful that they would cause the song to meet resistance on country radio. The song later inspired a 1984 TV movie titled *Single Bars, Single Women*, starring Shelley Hack, Paul Michael Glaser, Mare Winningham and Tony Danza, which was produced by O'Donoghue. An shortened version of Dolly's recording of the song was used as the movie's theme song.

- "Do I Ever Cross Your Mind" written by Dolly around 1973 was first recorded as a duet with Chet Atkins on September 3, 1976 at RCA Studio B in Nashville for Atkins' album *The Best of Chet Atkins & Friends. Dolly* would record the song for a third time in 1994, this time with Emmylou Harris and Linda Ronstadt. This version would be released on the 1999 album *Trio II*, and would be one of three singles released simultaneously from that album.

Heartbreak Express 8-Track Tape

Burlap & Satin
AHL–1–4691

Track Listing:
OOO–EEE / Send Me The Pillow You Dream On / Jealous Heart / A Gamble Either Way / Appalachian Memories / I Really Don't Want To Know (With Willie Nelson) / Potential New Boyfriend / A Cowboy's Ways / One Of Those Days / Calm On The Water

Production Information:
Produced and Arranged by: Gregg Perry
Executive Producer: Dolly Parton
Recorded at: Sound Shop Studios, Nashville, TN / The Castle (Studio A), Nashville, TN / Record Plant, Los Angeles, CA
Engineers: Ernie Winfrey / Phil Jamtaas
Assistant Engineers: Fran Overall / Jim Scott
Mixed by: Ernie Winfrey at Sound Shop Studios, Nashville, TN
Cover Photography / Art Direction & Design: Ed Caraeff

Singles Released From This Album:
"Potential New Boyfriend" b/w "One of Those Days" – April 11, 1983 (peaked at # 20 on the Hot Country Singles chart on July 1,1983)

Album Data:
Highest Chart Position: # 5 on August 26, 1983
Billboard Chart: Hot Country Albums
Number of weeks on chart: 24

Notes / Trivia:
- This album was released on LP, 8 Track and Cassette on May 2, 1983.
- A 5:46 12" extended play dance remix of "Potential New Boyfriend" was also released. The flip side contained an instrumental version clocking in at 5:50 and a shorter disco vocal version clocking in at 3:48.
- The song "A Cowboy's Ways" was originally written to be sung by Burt Reynolds in the film *The Best Little Whorehouse in Texas*. It was said to be originally titled "The Fields Where Stallions Run." Burt had pre–recorded the song and shot the scene, but the entire segment / song was cut from the film. But when the film is shown on TV this scene is often used and other longer scenes are removed to make room for ads to fit the movie in the two–hour slot. Another song that did not make the cut for the film soundtrack was "A Gamble Either Way."
- The track "Potential New Boyfriend" was Dolly's first ever music video.

- The title track earned Dolly a Grammy nomination for "Best Female Country Vocal Performance."

SOLID GOLD Ad in Billboard magazine for the premiere television performance of *Potential New Boyfriend*

The Great Pretender
AHL-1-4940

Track Listing:
Save The Last Dance For Me / I Walk The Line / Turn, Turn, Turn (To Everything There Is A Season) / Downtown / We Had It All / She Don't Love You (Like I Love You) / We'll Sing In The Sunshine / I Can't Help Myself (Sugar Pie Honey Bunch) / Elusive Butterfly / The Great Pretender

Production Information:
Produced by: Val Garay
Recorded and mixed at: Record One, Los Angeles, CA (October 24 – December 5, 1983)
Engineers: Garay–Bolas
Assistant Engineer: Richard Bosworth / Denny Desnmore
Second Assistant Engineers: Scott Hendricks / Danny Mundhenk / Paul Goldberg / Billy Miranda / David Leonard
Additional Overdubbing at: Right Track Recording, New York City / Bullet Recording, Nashville, TN / Music Mill, Nashville, TN / The Sound Factory, Los Angeles, CA
Mastered at: The Mastering Lab by Doug Sax
Cover Photography: Richard Avedon
Art Direction & Design: Tim Bryant

Singles Released From This Album:
"Save The Last Dance For Me" b/w "Elusive Butterfly" – November 28, 1983 (peaked at # 3 in the US on the Hot Country Singles chart and # 2 in Canada on the *RPM* chart)
"Downtown" b/w "The Great Pretender" – March 12, 1984 (peaked at # 36 in the US on the Hot Country Singles chart and # 20 in Canada on the *PRM* chart)

Album Data:
Highest Chart Position: # 7 on May 11, 1984.
Billboard Chart: Hot Country Albums
Number of weeks on chart: 22

Notes / Trivia:
- This album was released on LP, 8 Track and Cassette on January 23, 1984.
- Also in 1984 Dolly received a star on the Hollywood Walk of Fame. The star is located at 6712 Hollywood Boulevard in Hollywood, California

A 1984 Trade Ad for the album *The Great Pretender*

Real Love
AHL-1-5414

Track Listing:
Think About Love / Tie Our Love (In A Double Knot) / We Got Too Much / It's Such A Heartache / Don't Call It Love / Real Love (Duet with Kenny Rogers) / I Can't Be True / Once In A Very Blue Moon / Come Back To Me / I Hope You're Never Happy

Production Information:
Produced by: David Malloy for David Malloy Productions, Inc.
Recorded and Overdubbed at: Rumbo Recorders, Los Angeles, CA
Engineers: Joe Bogan
Assistant Engineer: Julian Stoll
Additional overdubs recorded at: Sunset Sound, Los Angeles, CA
Overdub engineers: Peggy McCreary / Larry Walsh
Mastered at Capitol Records by: Wall Traugott
Cover Photography: Richard D' Amore
Cover photos hand tinted by: Kalli D' Amore
Art Direction: Tim Bryant

Musicians:
Bass: Bob Glaub
Drums: Paul Leim
Guitars: Dean Parks / Billy Joe Walker, Jr
Keyboards: Steve Goldstein / Randy McCormick
Background vocals: Jennifer Kimball / Richard Marxs / Terry Williams / Gene Morford

Singles Released From This Album:
"Don't Call It Love" b/w "We Got Too Much" – January 7, 1985 (peaked at # 3 in the US and # 5 in Canada on the country chart)
"Real Love" (duet with Kenny Rogers) b/w "I Can't Be True" – April 19, 1985 (peaked at # 1 in the US and Canada)
"Think About Love" b/w "Come Back To Me" – November 11, 1985 (peaked at # 1 in the US and Canada)
"Tie Our Love In A Double Knot" b/w "I Hope You're Never Happy" – April 7, 1986 (peaked at # 17 in the US)

Album Data:
Highest Chart Position: # 9 on May 31, 1985
Billboard Chart: Hot Country Albums
Number of weeks on chart: 40

Notes / Trivia:
- This album was released on LP, Cassette and CD on January 21, 1985
- Rumbo Recorders, located at 20215 Saticoy Street, Canoga Park, CA where a majority of the recording work on this album was done was owned by husband and wife musical team Daryl Dragon and Toni Tennille also known as *The Captain & Tennille.* The studio is no longer in operation and has been gutted. It is rental space for parties now.
- In 1982 both Captain and Tennille and Dusty Springfield had recorded "Don't Call It Love" on their respective albums.
- Dolly had recorded a solo version of the song "Real Love" in November 1984, which was later included on the 1995 album "I Will Always Love You: The Essential Dolly Parton One."
- This was Dolly's final album on RCA Records after 19 years with the label. Though later she would release others on RCA.

**Foreign DVD of *Kenny & Dolly Real Love Concert* from 1985.
This concert showcased both artists separately and together with their hits *Real Love* and *Islands In The Stream* among others.**

Rainbow
C40968

Track Listing:
The River Unbroken / I Know You By Heart (duet with Smokey Robinson) / Dump The Dude / Red Hot Screaming Love / Make Love Work / Everyday Hero / Two Lovers / Could I Have Your Autograph / Savin' It For You / More Than I Can Say

Production Information:
Produced by: Steve "Golde" Goldstein
Executive Producer: Dolly Parton
Recorded at:
Engineers: Richard Bosworth
Assistant Engineer:
Cover Photography: Annie Leibovitz
Art Direction: Tony Lane / Nancy Donald

Singles Released From This Album:
"The River Unbroken" b/w "More Than I Can Say" – November 23, 1987 (peaked at # 63)
"I Know You By Heart" b/w "Could I Have Your Autograph" – February 8, 1988
"Make Love Work" b/w "Two Lovers" – July 25, 1988

Album Data:
Highest Chart Position: # 18 on February 12, 1988
Billboard Chart: Hot Country Albums
Number of weeks on chart: 24

Notes / Trivia:
- This was Dolly's first album on her new label CBS.
- This album was released on LP, Cassette and CD on November 25, 1987.
- The plan when Dolly signed with CBS was for her to alternate between releasing pop and country albums, rather than trying to combine the two styles on each album, but due to *Rainbow*'s poor sales, tepid critical reception and poor singles performance, the plan was abandoned. From then on Dolly more or less focused on recording more country sounding material for the remainder of her association with the label with great success.

White Limozeen
C44384

Track Listing:
Time For Me To Fly / Yellow Roses / Why'd You Come In Here (Lookin' Like That) / Slow Healing Heart / What Is It My Love / White Limozeen / Wait "Til I Get You Home (duet with Mac Davis) / Take Me Back To The Country / The Moon, The Stars And Me / He's Alive

Production Information:
Produced by: Ricky Skaggs
Executive Producer: Dolly Parton
Recorded at: Treasure Isle Recorders, Nashville, TN / Lawrence Welk's Champagne Studio, Nashville, TN
Engineers: Tom Harding / Ed Seay / George Massenburg / Scott Hendricks / Doug Johnson
Assistant Engineer: Brad Jones / Jeff Geidt / Pat Hutchinson / Mike Poole
Mixed at: Eleven–Eleven Sound Studios, Nashville, TN / Treasure Isle Recorders, Nashville, TN
Mastered by: Denny Percell at Georgetown Masters, Nashville, TN
Cover Photography: Robert Blakeman
Art Direction and design: Kosh with Amy Dakos

Singles Released From This Album:
"Why'd You Come In Here (Lookin' Like That)" b/w "Wait "Til I Get You Home" (duet with Mac Davis) – April 24, 1989 (peaked at # 1 in the US and Canada)
"Yellow Roses" b/w "Wait "Til I Get You Home" (duet with Mac Davis) – July 31, 1989 (peaked at # 1)
"He's Alive" b/w "What Is It My Love" – November 6, 1989 (peaked at # 39)
"Time For Me To Fly" b/w "The Stars, The Moon And Me" – January 1990 (peaked at # 39)
"White Limozeen" b/w "The Stars, The Moon And Me" – April 9, 1990 (peaked at # 29)
"Slow Healing Heart" b/w "Take Me Back To The Country" – October 15, 1990

Album Data:
Highest Chart Position: # 3 on December 22, 1989
Billboard Chart: Hot Country Albums
Number of weeks on chart: 100

Notes / Trivia:
- This album was released on LP, Cassette and CD on May 26, 1989.
- REO was the first to record "Time For Me To Fly." It was reported to have taken the writer, Kevin Cronin, of REO, 10 years to write the song.
- Dolly performed the song "Why'd You Come In Here" (as well as the title track to the album) when

she hosted *Saturday Night Live* on April 15, 1989.
- Certified gold on December 6, 1991.
- Dolly started work on this album right after wrapping on the film "Steel Magnolias" on September 15, 1988.

Sheet music to He's Alive

Home For Christmas
C46796

Track Listing:
The First Noel / Santa Claus is Coming to Town / I'll Be Home for Christmas / Rudolph the Red Nosed Reindeer / Go Tell It on the Mountain / The Little Drummer Boy / We Three Kings / Jingle Bells / O Little Town of Bethlehem / Joy to The World

Production Information:
Produced by: Gary Smith
Executive Producer: Dolly Parton
Recorded at: Nightengale Studios, Nashville, TN
Engineer: Gary Paczaosa
Assistant Engineer: Michael Davis / Chrissy Follmar / Brad Jones / John Kunz
Cover Photography: Dennis Carney
Mastered by: Denny Purcell

Musicians:
Keyboards: Michael Davis / Gary Smith
Percussion: Michael Davis / Steve Turner
Fiddle: Jimmy Mattingly
Mandolin: Jimmy Mattingly / Stuart Duncan
Piano: Gary Smith
Hammond B3 Organ: Gary Smith
Drums: Steve Turner
Bass: Paul Uhrig
Acoustic Bass: Paul Uhrig
Acoustic Guitar: Carl Jackson / Kent Wells
Electric Guitar: Kent Wells
Dobro: Robert Williams
Gut String Guitar: Michael Johnson
Steel Guitar: Jack Smith
Hammond Dulcimer: Alisha Jones Wall
Background Vocals: Richard Dennison / Jennifer O'Brien / Howard Smith / Bob Bailey / Theresa J. Comer / Everett Drake / Nuana Dunlap / Gary E. Jenkins / Bobby Jones / Lenoria Ridley / Lawrence D. Thomison / Harry Watkins / Angela Wright / Jason Beddoe / Coby Coffman / Al Coleman / Melissa Coleman / Joy Gardner / Landy Gardner / Vicki Pointer / Rebekah Rayburn / Tanya Sykes / Mark Warren / Carl Jackson / The New Salem Methodist Church Congregation / Trent Ashcraft / Alyson Chance / Hannah Dennison / Vanessa Hollowell / Jake Hoover / Crystal Hunt / Amy Johnson /

Gretchen Johnson / Cole Kiracofe / Ian Kiracofe / Bryan Seaver / Rebecca Seaver / Austin Smith / Brandon Smith / Tiffany Smith / David Turner / Katie Turner / Derek Wells / Dustin Wells

Album Data:
Highest Chart Position: # 74 on December 21, 1990
Billboard Chart: Hot Country Albums
Number of weeks on chart: 2

Notes / Trivia:
- This album was released on LP, CD and Cassette on September 11, 1990
- The album was pressed on vinyl LP only in the Netherlands.
- The album's release was promoted several months later by an ABC–TV special, *Dolly Parton: Christmas at Home* on December 21, 1990. My favorite non-singing part is the chocolate covered cherries story!
- There was a Dolly Parton "Home For Christmas" RADIO SPECIAL PROMO CD 1991 CSK-2159. It had music / interviews / promotional clips. It ran 59:20.
- Album certified Gold on December 27, 1994 for 500,000+ copies sold.

Home For Christmas
The Radio Special
1991 CSK-2159

Eagle When She Flies
C46882

Track Listing:
If You Need Me / Rockin' Years (duet with Ricky Van Shelton) / Country Road / Silver and Gold / Eagle When She Flies / Best Woman Wins (duet with Lorrie Morgan) / What A Heartache / Runaway Feelin' / Dreams Do Come True / Family / Wildest Dreams

Production Information:
Produced by: Steve Buckingham and Gary Smith
Executive Producer: Dolly Parton
Recorded at: Nightengale Studios and The Doghouse, Nashville, TN
Engineer: Gary Paczosa
Assistant Engineers: Joe Bogan / Robert Charles / Chrissy Follmar / Larry Jeffries / Brad Jones / Sean Londin / John David Parker
Strings overdubbed at: Javlina East Studios, Nashville, TN
Mixing Engineer: Gary Paczosa
Mixing Assistant: John Kunz
Cover Photography: Randee St. Nicholas
Art Direction / Design: Bill Johnson
Design Assistant: Jodi Lynn Miller
Makeup: Rachel Dennison
Hair Stylist: David Blair
Clothing Stylist: Tony Chase

Musicians:

The Mighty Fine Band:
Organ: Mike Davis
Fiddle / Mandolin: Jimmy Mattingly
Piano / Keyboards: Gary Smith
Drums: Steve Turner
Bass: Paul Uhrig
Acoustic guitar: Bruce Watkins
Electric guitar: Kent Wells
Background Vocals: Richard Dennison / Jennifer O'Brien / Howard Smith

Additional Musicians:
Percussion: Sam Bacco
Upright Bass; Romantic Roy Huskey
Acoustic Guitar / Mandolin: Mark Casstevens
Acoustic Guitars on *If You Need Me*: Paddy Corcoran / Carl Jackson
Fiddle: Glen Duncan
Steel Guitar / Dobro: Paul Franklin
Guitar / Mandolin: Steve Gibson
Accordion: Joey Miskulin
Fiddle on *What a Heartache:* Mark O'Connor
Hammer Dulcimer: Allisa Jones Wall

Additional vocalists
Lea Jane Berinati / Paddy Corcoran / Joy Gardner / Vince Gill / Vicki Hampton / Emmylou Harris / Carl Jackson / Alison Krauss / Patty Loveless / Lewis Nunley / John Wesley Ryles / Lisa Silver / Harry Stinson / Dennis Wilson / Curtis Young

The Kid Connection: Additional background vocals on "Family"

Singles Released From This Album:
"Rockin' Years" (duet with Ricky Van Shelton) b/w "What A Heartache" – February 4, 1991 (peaked at # 1 in the US and Canada) "Rockin' Years" also appears on Ricky's 1991 album "Backroads." Recorded on November 8, 1990.
"Silver and Gold" b/w "Runaway Feelin'" – May 20, 1991 (peaked at # 15)
"Eagle When She Flies" b/w "Wildest Dreams" – September 16, 1991 (peaked at # 33)
"Country Road" b/w "Best Woman Wins" (duet with Lorrie Morgan) – January 1992 "Best Woman Wins" written by Dolly Parton also appears on Lorrie's 1991 album "Something in Red."

Album Data:
Highest Chart Position: # 1 on May 17, 1991
Billboard Chart: Hot Country Albums
Number of weeks on chart: 73

Notes / Trivia:
- This album was released on LP, Cassette and CD on March 7, 1991
- "What a Heartache" had originally been recorded for the motion picture soundtrack of *Rhinestone* in 1983.
- An version of "Rockin' Years" was recorded in 1988 with Dolly and George Jones but remained unreleased until the 2008 release of George's album *Burn Your Playhouse Down – The Unreleased Duets*.
- Certified gold on July 2, 1991 and platinum on August 4,1992.

Slow Dancing With The Moon
CK53199

Track Listing:
Full Circle / Romeo (with Mary Chapin Carpenter, Pam Tillis, Billy Ray Cyrus, Kathy Mattea, and Tanya Tucker) / (You Got Me Over) A Heartache Tonight" (with Billy Dean) / What Will Baby Be / More Where That Came From / Put a Little Love in Your Heart / Why Can't We? / I'll Make Your Bed / Whenever Forever Comes" (with Collin Raye) / Cross My Heart / Slow Dancing with the Moon / High and Mighty

Production Information:
Produced by: Steve Buckingham and Dolly Parton

Musicians:
Accordion: Joey Miskulin
Acoustic Guitar: Bruce Watkins
Autoharp: Gove Scrivenor
Bass: Paul Uhrig
Pedabro: Paul Franklin
Drums: Steve Turner
Hammered Dulcimer: Alissa Jones–Wall
Fiddle: Jimmy Mattingly
Guitar: Kent Wells / Steve Gibson
Harmonica and Percussion: Terry McMillan
Keyboards: Michael Davis
Mandolin: Jimmy Mattingly / Steve Gibson
Piano: John Barlow Jarvis / Mitch Humphries / Paul Hollowell
Steel Guitar: John Hughey / Paul Franklin / Sonny Garrish
Uilleann Pipes: Paddy Corcoran
Backing Vocals: Alison Krauss / Carl Jackson / Chuck Cannon / Darrin Vincent / Emmylou Harris / Jennifer O'Brien–Enoch / Lari White / Maura O'Connell / Michael English / Rhonda Vincent / Richard Dennison / Ricky Skaggs / Rodney Crowell / Vince Gill

Singles Released From This Album:
"Romeo" b/w "High and Mighty" – January 25, 1993 (peaked at # 27 Hot Country Songs chart)
"More Where That Came From" b/w "I'll Make Your Bed" – April 19, 1993
"Full Circle" b/w "What Will Baby Be" – June 21, 1993

Album Data:
Highest Chart Position: # 4 on March 19, 1993
Billboard Chart: Hot Country Albums

Number of weeks on chart: 35

Notes / Trivia:
- This album was released on CD and Cassette on February 23, 1993.
- Certified gold on April 19, 1993 and certified platinum on October 5, 1993.
- The track "Romeo" was nominated for a Grammy in the "Best Country Vocal Collaboration" category.
- The song "More Where That Came From" appeared in a 2008 Target commercial.
- The song "What Will Baby Be" was originally recorded in 1973 for the album "My Tennessee Mountain Home," but the original version was not released until the *Dolly* box set in 2009.

Romeo picture sleeve (Friends: Mary Chapin Carpenter, Pam Tillis, Billy Ray Cyrus, Kathy Mattea and Tanya Tucker) ZSS–38 74876

Something Special
CK–67140

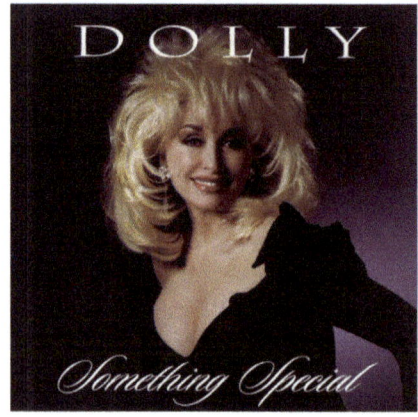

Track Listing:
Wounded Bird / Something Special / Change / I Will Always Love You (with Vince Gill) / Green-Eyed Boy / Speakin' of The Devil / Jolene / No Good Way of Saying Goodbye / The Seeker / Teach Me To Trust

Production Information:
Produced by: Steve Buckingham and Dolly Parton
Recorded at: Nightingale Studio / Sound Emporium Studio / Soundshop Studios / Soundstage Studios / Doghouse Studio / Woodland Sound Studio / Emerald Sound / O'Henry's and Masterfonics in Nashville, TN.
Engineer: Gary Paczosa
Assistant Engineers: Toby Seay / Ed Simonton / Craig White / Marc Frigo / Kevin Ryan / Grant Greene / Richard Landers / Jeff Shannon / John Dickson / Amy Hughs / Robin Dennis / Al Schmidt / Mike Capps / Dave Sinko / Marshall Morgan
Digital Editing: Don Cobb at Georgetown Masters in Nashville, TN.
Mastering Engineer: Denny Purcell at Georgetown Masters in Nashville, TN.
Art Direction: Bill Johnson
Production Assistant: Jennie Carey

Musicians:
Drums: Eddie Bayers / Owen Hale / Steve Turner
Acoustic Guitar: Steve Buckingham
Fiddle: Stuart Duncan / Jimmy Mattingly
Steel Guitar: Paul Franklin
Acoustic Guitar: Steve Gibson / Don Potter / Stuart Smith
Piano: Paul Hollowell / Steve Nathan / Matt Rollings
Bass Guitar: David Hungate / Paul Uhrig
Slide Guitar: Sonny Landreth
Organ: Randy McCormick / Matt Rollings
Percussion / Shaker: Terry McMillan
Acoustic Guitar / Electric Guitar: Brent Mason
Electric Guitar: Brent Rowan / Reggie Young
Conductor / String Arrangements: Dale Oehler

Background Vocals: Bob Bailey / Margie Cates / Suzanne Cox / Richard Dennison / Vicki Hampton / Yvonne Hodges / Carl Jackson / Alison Krauss / Louis Dean Nunley / Chris Rodriguez / Duawne Starling / Pam Tillis

Singles Released From This Album:
"I Will Always Love You" (with Vince Gill) b/w "Speakin' of The Devil" – November 1995 (peaked at # 15 on the Hot Country Singles chart)

Album Data:
Highest Chart Position: # 10 on October 20, 1995
Billboard Chart: Hot Country Albums
Number of weeks on chart: 21

Notes / Trivia:
- This album was released on CD and Cassette on August 22, 1995.
- "I Will Always Love You" with Vince Gill was nominated at the 38th Annual Grammy Awards for Best Country Collaboration with Vocals and was named Vocal Event of the Year at the 30th Annual CMA Awards. This recording marked the third time Dolly had a top 20 hit with the song since its first release in 1974. Dolly had recorded the song in early February 1982 for *The Best Little Whorehouse in Texas* soundtrack. It was released on July 12, 1982, as the first single from the soundtrack. It would eventually peak at number one on the *Billboard* Hot Country Singles chart on , thus Dolly reached the number one position twice with the same song, a rare feat that Chubby Checker had previously achieved when "The Twist" reached number one in 1960 and again in 1962.
- On this album Dolly re–recorded several of her well know hits— in addition to "I Will Always Love You," "Jolene" and "The Seeker" are given new treatments.
- Dolly's association with CBS / Columbia came to an end with the release of this album. Dolly decided to look for a new label at her own leisure. She initially decided on Atlantic Records because she said Doug Morris was the one executive she met with who firmly believed in her and her music. Ultimately Morris lost an executive battle leading to his departure from Atlantic in 1995. Morris was then hired by MCA Records in July 1995 where he formed a joint venture record label with his Rising Tide Records, which became part of Universal Records when Morris was appointed chairman and CEO of MCA Music Entertainment Group in November 1995. Parton said she was in no real hurry to find a new label, but when Morris began working at MCA and approached her to sign she said yes, signing with Universal Records' Nashville branch which had retained the Rising Tide Records name.
- "Speakin' of the Devil" had been used in the 1991 TV film *Wild Texas Wind* co–written by Dolly.

Treasures
RT-53041

Track Listing:
Peace Train (Isitimela Sokuthula) / Today I Started Loving You Again / Just When I Needed You Most Something's Burning / Before The Next Teardrop Falls / After The Goldrush / Walking On Sunshine / Behind Closed Doors / Don't Let Me Cross Over / Satin Sheets / For The Good Times

Production Information:
Produced by: Steve Buckingham
Recorded at: Soundstage (Nashville, Tennessee) / 17 Grand (Nashville) / The Doghouse (Nashville) / The Hit Factory (New York City, New York) / Oceanway (Los Angeles, California)
Engineers: Marshall Morgan / Toby Seay / Al Schmidt / Chris Tergeson
Assistant Engineer: Jeff Demorris / Mel Jones / Ken Ross / Michelle Shelly / Ed Simonton
Cover Photography: David LaChapelle
Additional Photos: Daniel Root / Russ Harrington / Beth Guin / Tony Baker / Tammie Aroyo
Hair and Makeup Stylist: David Blair
Costume Designer: Tony Chase
Clothing Stylist: Frank Chevalier
Album Designer: Jerry Joyner
Art Direction: Virginia Team

Musicians:
Eddie Bayers: Drums (all tracks)
Steve Buckingham: Acoustic Guitar (tracks 1–2, 5), 12–String Electric Guitar (track 4), Baritone guitar (tracks 4 & 7), Mandolin (track 4), Electric Guitar (track 7)
Mark Casstevens: Acoustic Guitar (tracks 3, 5), High String Guitar (track 1)
Dan Dugmore: Lap Steel (track 9)
Paul Franklin: Steel Guitar (track 10)
David Hungate: Bass (tracks 1–10), Upright Bass (track 11)
Pat McInerney: Bodhhrán (track 6)
Farrell Morris: Shaker (track 3), Marimba (track 5), Vibes (tracks 8, 10–11)
Dean Parks: Acoustic Guitar (tracks 1, 3–4, 6–11), Slide Guitar (track 1), Electric Guitar (tracks 4, 6, 7, 10), 12–String Guitar (track 7)
Don Potter: Gut String Guitar (track 5)
Hargus "Pig" Robbins: Piano (tracks 9–10)
Matt Rollings: Keyboard (tracks 1, 3, 7), Wurlitzer (tracks 2, 4–5, 8), B–3 Organ (tracks 2, 4, 7), Piano (tracks 6, 11)
Joe Spivey: Fiddle (tracks 7, 9)
Adam Steffey: Mandolin (track 9)
Reggie Young: Electric Guitar (all tracks)

Background vocals:
Matraca Berg / Steve Buckingham / Richard Dennison / Vicki Hampton / Liana Manis / Darci Monet / Louis Nunley / Jennifer O'Brien / Don Potter / Chris Rodriguez / John Wesley Ryles / Dennis Wilson / Dan Tyminski / Kim Carnes

Choir on track 1:
Bob Bailey, Matraca Berg, Crystal Bernard, Kim Carnes, Andy Landis, Darci Monet, Louis Nunley, Chris Rodriguez, Duawne Starling, Chris Willis

Singles Released From This Album:
"Just When I Needed You Most" b/w "For The Good Times" – September 23, 1996 (peaked at # 62 on November 15, 1996)
"Peace Train" – July 1, 1997 (peaked at # 23 on the *Billboard* Hot Dance Music chart)
"Walking On Sunshine" – August 10, 1999

Album Data:
Highest Chart Position: # 21 on December 20, 1996
Billboard Chart: Hot Country Albums
Number of weeks on chart: 21

Notes / Trivia:
- This album was released on CD and Cassette on September 24, 1996
- The album spawned a dance remix of Dolly's version of the Cat Stevens classic "Peace Train" and was released on several 12" vinyl sets with multiple remixed versions.
- In 1999, a dance remix of Dolly's "Walking on Sunshine" version was released but did not chart.
- A CBS–TV special titled "Treasures" was broadcast on November 30, 1996 to promote the album.
- A music video for *Peace Train* was produced, but was never aired. It was directed by Christopher Ciccone. The unreleased music video was eventually leaked online.

What Dolly said about recording an album of cover song:
"Because it's something I feel like doing…These are great songs. It's a good time to do it because chances are, radio is not going to play any new and original things I'm doing. They didn't play the last two albums. People are excited about the new record here. And I think it's a really good album. I think it's done really well. I just hope my performance is good enough to be played but we'll just have to see."

Treasures TV Special ad

Hungry Again
UMD 80522

Track Listing:
Hungry Again / The Salt in My Tears / Honky Tonk Songs / Blue Valley Songbird / I Wanna Go Back There / When Jesus Comes Calling for Me / Time and Tears / I'll Never Say Goodbye / The Camel's Heart / I Still Lost You / Paradise Road / *Shine On

Production Information:
Produced by: Dolly Parton and Richie Owens
Recorded at: Train Traxx, Nashville, TN and *House of Prayer, Locust Ridge, TN
Engineers: Richie Owens and J. Allen Williams, Jr.
Mix Engineer: Marshall Morgan at The Dog House Studios, Nashville, TN
Assistant Mix Engineer: Toby Seay
Mastered By: Denny Purcell at Georgetown Masters, Nashville, TN
Photography (Front, back, interior): J.R. Rabourn, Jason Pirro, Jim Herrington and Matt Barnes

Musicians:
Bass / Upright Bass: Mark A. Brooks
Banjo: Gary Davis
Acoustic Guitar: Gary Davis / Bob Ocker / Richie Owens
Drums: Bob "Bubba" Grundner
Percussion: Bob "Bubba" Grundner
Piano: Johnny Lauffer
Organ: Johnny Lauffer
Strings: Johnny Lauffer
Accordion: Randy Leago
Fiddle / Mandolin: Gary Mackey
Electric Guitar: Bob Ocker / Richie Owens
Pedal Steel Guitar: Al Perkins
Autoharp / Bouzouki / Dobro / Harmonica / Kona Guitar / Mandolin / Slide Guitar: Richie Owens
Background Vocals: Lois Baker / Jim Boling / Paul Brewster / Darrin Vincent / Rhonda Vincent / Brian Waldschlager / Rachel Dennison / Richard Dennison / Joy Gardner / Teresa Hughes / Louis Dean Nunley / Jennifer O'Brien / Judy Ogle / Ira Parker / House of Prayer Congregation / Honky Tonk Women

Singles Released From This Album:
"Honky Tonk Songs" b/w "Paradise Road" – July 27, 1998 (peaked at # 74 on Billboard's Top Singles Chart)
"The Salt in My Tears" b/w "Hungry Again" – November 9, 1998

Album Data:
Highest Chart Position: # 23 on September 11, 1998
Billboard Chart: Top Country Albums
Number of weeks on chart: 16

Notes / Trivia:
- This album was released on CD and Cassette on August 25, 1998
- When Rising Tide Records closed its Nashville branch in March 1998, Dolly found herself without a label. It was announced in April 1998 that she had signed with Decca Records to release her new album, *Hungry Again*, due to be released in August by subsidiary label MCA. Dolly wrote the album over a three month period in 1997 at her lake cottage outside Nashville and at her Tennessee Mountain Home in Sevierville, which was immortalized in her 1973 hit song. Detailing the writing process for *Billboard*, Dolly said, "I went back home and fasted, not so much in a religious way but as a means of humbling myself and getting into the spirit of things. I ended up with 37 of the best songs I'd written in years, if not the best ever." Dolly said that the songs that made the album resulted in a "more acoustic–type album." She also said that if the album was successful she had enough songs leftover for two or three follow–up albums, which she jokingly said might be titled *Still Hungry*, *Hungry Some More*, or *I'm Full Now*.
- Promotional materials included a Dolly Parton "Hungry Again" promotional plastic lunch box pictured below with inserts including: CD "Hungry Again," Sandwich shaped promotional materials in zip-lock bag, a carrot pen and apple note pad.

Dolly Parton Hungry Again promotional lunchbox

Precious Memories
BE-21749

Track Listing:
Precious Memories / Power in the Blood / In the Sweet Bye-and-Bye / Church in the Wildwood / Keep on the Firing Line / Amazing Grace / Old Time Religion / Softly and Tenderly / Farther Along / What A Friend We Have In Jesus / In The Garden / When The Roll Is Called Up Yonder

Production Information:
Produced by: Richie Owens
Recorded at: Studio 19 / Studio 20
Engineers: Danny Brown / Darrell Puett / Dave Matthews
Overdub Engineer: Jim Pace
Re-Mix Engineer: Dave Matthews
Cover Design: Wade Perry
Arrangements: Dolly Parton

Musicians:
Lead Vocals: Dolly Parton
Bass: Mark Brooks
Mandolin / Fiddle: Sam Bush
Acoustic Guitar / Banjo / Electric Guitar: Gary Davis
Drums: Bob Grundner
Steel Guitar / Dobro Guitar / Kona Lap Guitar: Al Perkins
Fiddle / Mandolin: Gary Mackey
Piano / Strings / Organ: Johnny Lauffer
Background Vocals: The Kinfolks (Louis Owens, Bill Owens, John Henry Owens, Dorothy Jo Owens) / The Kingdom Heirs (Steve French, Arthur Rice, David Sutton, Eric Bennett) / Liana Manis / Rachel Dennison / Steven Hill / Randy Parton

Notes / Trivia:
- This album was released on CD and Cassette on April 17, 1999 and was sold exclusively at Dollywood on Dolly's own Blue Eye label with all proceeds going to the Dollywood Foundation.
- Dolly performed many songs from the album on a TNN special, *Dolly Parton's Precious Memories*, that aired on April 1, 1999, as a part of TNN's 20th Century Hitmakers Week. The special also included performances by Alison Krauss and Union Station and the Cox Family. Parton's siblings Randy Parton and Rachel Dennison also appeared on the show.
- Dolly had sang "Farther Along" in the 1991 TV film Wild Texas Wind which she also co-wrote. It also appeared on the first *Trio* album.

The Grass Is Blue
SUG–CD 3900

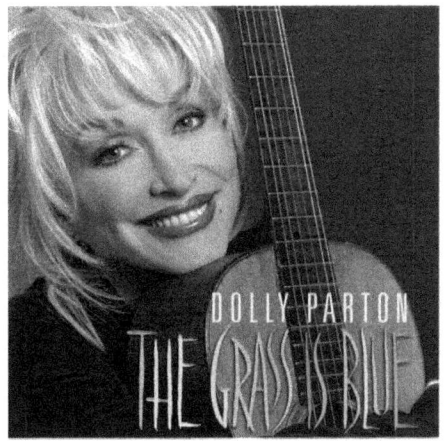

Track Listing:
Travelin' Prayer / Cash on the Barrelhead / A Few Old Memories / I'm Gonna Sleep With One Eye Open / Steady as the Rain / I Still Miss Someone / Endless Stream of Tears / Silver Dagger / Train, Train / I Wonder Where You are Tonight / Will He Be Waiting For Me / The Grass Is Blue / I Am Ready

Production Information:
Produced by: Steve Buckingham
Recorded at: The Sound Kitchen and The Doghouse, Nashville, TN
Engineers: Gary Paczosa
Assistant Engineer: Toby Seay / Marshall Morgan / Sandy Jenkins
Digital Editing: Toby Seay / Marshall Morgan / Chuck Turner
Mastered by: Doug Sax at The Mastering Lab, Los Angeles, CA
Musical director: Jerry Douglas
Production Assistant: Jennie Carey
Cover Photography: Dennis Carney
Recording Studio Photos: Rob Draper / Tim Campbell
Cover: Sue Meyer Design
Hair: Cheryl Riddle

Musicians:
Bass: Barry Bales
Banjo: Jim Mills
Guitar: Bryan Sutton
Rhythm Guitar: Steve Buckingham
Mandolin: Sam Bush
Dobro: Jerry Douglas
Fiddle: Stuart Duncan
Harmony Vocal Group: Dolly Parton / Alison Krauss / Keith Little / Patty Loveless / Claire Lynch / Louis Nunley / Alan O'Bryant / Dan Tyminski / Darrin Vincent / Rhonda Vincent / Barry Bales / Sam Bush / Jerry Douglas / Stuart Duncan

Singles Released From This Album:
"A Few Old Memories" – October 25, 1999
"Silver Dagger" – February 2000

Album Data:
Highest Chart Position: # 24 on November 19, 1999
Billboard Chart: Hot Country Albums

Number of weeks on chart: 35

Notes / Trivia:
- This album was released on CD and Cassette on October 26, 1999
- This album was re–released on vinyl LP on April 18, 2015 in the US & Canada (SUG–LP 3900)
- The album won a Grammy for Best Bluegrass Album and "Travelin' Prayer" was nominated for Best Female Country Vocal Performance.
- Dolly found herself without a record label for the second time in a year when Decca Records closed its Nashville office in early 1999, just months after the release of *Hungry Again*. Throughout the 1990s, she had been losing ground with country radio, though her album sales had remained very strong for much of that time. The idea for the project was brought to Dolly's attention one night in July 1999 when she was having dinner with Steve Buckingham. He mentioned to her that bluegrass fans, when asked which artist they would most like to make a bluegrass album, overwhelmingly cited her. Dolly told *Billboard*, "We were both shocked, but then I thought, since I manage myself now and have my own label and can do what I want, why not do it?" By the end of August 1999, Dolly had recorded the album in Nashville with Buckingham producing and top musicians such as Jerry Douglas, Sam Bush, Stuart Duncan, Alison Krauss, and Rhonda Vincent accompanying. Speaking about the song selection, Dolly said, "I've always loved bluegrass, having grown up in and around mountain music and bluegrass, so I chose some songs I've been singing all my life." She said of the recording process, "It went really fast because these are the world's best bluegrass pickers and singers, who've been doing these songs forever!"

The vinyl LP (above) used a cover photograph taken at the same session as the CD, but a different shot

Little Sparrow
SUG–CD 3927

Track Listing:
Little Sparrow / Shine / I Don't Believe You've Met My Baby / My Blue Tears / Seven Bridges Road / Bluer Pastures / A Tender Lie / I Get A Kick Out Of You / Mountain Angel / Marry Me / Down From Dover / The Beautiful Lie / In The Sweet By and By / Little Sparrow (Reprise)

Production Information:
Produced by: Steve Buckingham
Recorded at: Oceanway Studios (Los Angeles) / The Doghouse (Nashville, TN) and Schnee Studios (Los Angeles, CA)
Engineers: Gary Paczosa
Assistant Engineers: James Bauer / David Bryant / Koji Egawa / Thomas Johnson / Marshall Morgan
Mastered by: Doug Sax at The Mastering Lab, Los Angeles, CA
Cover Photography: Jim Herrington
Art Direction: Kimberly Levitan
Design: Good & Evil Design
Little Sparrow illustration by: Barry Etris

Singles Released From This Album:
"A Tender Lie" – April 2, 2001 (Released to Country Radio)
"Bluer Pastures" – April 2, 2001 (Released to Bluegrass Radio)
"Seven Bridges Road" – April 2, 2001 (Released to Americana Radio)
"Shine" – July 9, 2001

Album Data:
Highest Chart Position: # 12 on February 16, 2001
Billboard Chart: Hot Country Albums
Number of weeks on chart: 37

Notes / Trivia:

- This album was released on CD and Cassette on January 23, 2001
- The album received a Grammy nomination for Best Bluegrass Album and "Shine" won a Grammy for Best Female Country Vocal Performance. The album is dedicated to Dolly's father, Lee Parton, who died in November 2000.
- Dolly had previously recorded two of the tracks featured on the album. "Down from Dover" had originally been recorded on September 4, 1969 and included on her 1970 album, *The Fairest of Them All*. The version on this album contains an extra verse cut from the original. "My Blue Tears" was originally recorded on April 16, 1971 and included on Parton's *Coat of Many Colors*

album. Dolly also recorded the song with Emmylou Harris and Linda Ronstadt in 1978 for an ill–fated Trio project. This recording would eventually surface on Ronstadt's 1982 album, *Get Closer*.

- The 2006 release of the Dolly Parton compilation *The Acoustic Collection: 1999–2002* features a remix of the *Little Sparrow* version augmented with vocals by Kasey Chambers, Norah Jones, and Sinéad O'Connor.
- At the 44th Annual Grammy Awards the album was nominated for Best Bluegrass Album and "Shine" won Best Female Vocal Performance. The "Shine" music video was nominated for Female Video of the Year at the 2002 CMT Music Awards.

A Tender Lie Promo CD

Halos & Horns
SUG-CD 3946

Track Listing:
Halos and Horns / Sugar Hill / Not for Me / Hello God / If / Shattered Image / These Old Bones / What a Heartache / I'm Gone / Raven Dove / Dagger Through the Heart / If Only / John Daniel / Stairway to Heaven

Production Information:
Produced by: Dolly Parton
Recorded at: Southern Sound Studio, Knoxville, TN, February 2002
Engineers: Danny Brown / Scottie Hoaglan / Phil van Peborgh
Remix Engineer: Richard Dennison
Mastered by: Seva David–Louis Ball at Soundcurrent Mastering in Knoxville, Tennessee.
Cover Photography: Annie Leibovitz
Additional photos: Pat Murphy–Racey
Design: Jerry Joyner / Don Bailey / Chris Ferrara
Art Direction: Virginia Team

Musicians:
Dolly Parton: Lead vocals
Steve Turner: Drums, Snare drum / Tambourine / Washboard
Terry Eldridge: Bass guitar / Upright bass
Richard Dennison: Piano
Kent Wells: Acoustic guitar / Baritone guitar / Electric guitar
Brent Truitt / Darrell Webb: Mandolin
Bob Carlin: Claw hammer banjo
Gary "Biscuit" Davis: Banjo / Acoustic guitar
Robert Hale: Acoustic guitar
Randy Kohrs: Dobro / Resonator guitar
Jimmy Mattingly: Fiddle / Mandolin / Viola
Background vocals: Dolly Parton / Eric Bennett / Richard Dennison / Terry Eldridge / Steve French / Robert Hale / Vicki Hampton / Randy Kohrs / Jennifer O'Brien / Arthur Rice / April Stevens / Beth Stevens / Darrell Webb / David Sutton

Singles Released From This Album:
"Dagger Through The Heart" – July 8, 2002
"If" – October 7, 2002 (European release only) (peaked at #73 on UK Singles chart)
"Hello, God" – November 11, 2002 (peaked at # 60 Billboard Hot Country Songs chart)

"I'm Gone" – February 4, 2003

Album Data:
Highest Chart Position: # 4 on July 26, 2002
Billboard Chart: Hot Country Albums
Number of weeks on chart: 38

Notes / Trivia:

- This album was released on CD and Cassette on July 9, 2002.
- Following the release of her 2001 album, *Little Sparrow*, Dolly continued to write. While writing songs at her Tennessee Mountain Home, Dolly said the songs were pouring out of her by the dozens. A representative from Sugar Hill Records confirmed in late January 2002 that Dolly was "writing and arranging" songs for a new album, but recording had not begun so it was unclear when the album might be released. Dollymania had confirmed in February 2002 that Dolly had begun recording the album and that it should be released in summer 2002. Eager to begin recording the songs she had written, Dolly booked a session in Knoxville, initially as a demo session. "I didn't intend to produce a record," Dolly said. "I was just producing these song demos. But it started sounding *so* good that I was getting really excited." Dolly further described the recording process by saying, "I decided I wanted to use everybody from 'up home,' or at least fresh people. There was nothing heavy or hard about it. I just went in with the pickers and we all kicked ideas around. That's how you produce great records anyway—let talented people do what they do. It's fairly 'live,' because I'm not the kind of singer who can start and stop and go back and get the same feeling. I just had a big time doing this."
- The album was nominated for the Grammy Award for Best Country Album in 2003, while "Dagger Through the Heart" and "I'm Gone" were both nominated for Best Female Country Vocal Performance in 2003 and 2004, respectively.
- The album tracks "These Old Bones" and "Sugar Hill" were adapted into episodes of *Dolly Parton's Heartstrings* in 2019.
- There was a songbook of the complete album issued by Warner Music Group. #PFM0219
- The album also includes new versions of two songs Dolly had previously recorded. Dolly had first recorded "Shattered Image" for her 1976 album, *All I Can Do*. "What a Heartache" had originally been recorded in 1983 for the *Rhinestone* soundtrack album. Dolly would record "What a Heartache" for a second time in 1991 for her *Eagle When She Flies* album. When asked why she would choose to re–record songs she has done before, Dolly has said, "I have very strong feelings about them. They've never really had a chance to be all that they can be. I have hundreds of new songs, but there are some that 'want to be done' until I find the right way. When asked why she chose to re–record the album's sixth track, "Shattered Image", Dolly responded, "The reason I decided to re–do it is because of all the shit that comes out in the tabloids. It's like they punish you to death. They tell some God–awful things. Why can't people just leave you alone to live your life as you see fit? So that is why I wanted to drag this song back out, because I was feeling like that."
- The album's fourth track, "Hello, God" was written the day after the September 11 attacks in New York. Speaking about the song, Dolly said, "I realized just how fragile we really are, and how small life is, and how everything can change in the blink of an eye. I hope everything comes across as I meant it. It's like everybody believes that God is their God. But God belongs to everybody."
- The album closes with a cover of the Led Zeppelin hit, "Stairway to Heaven." Speaking about her recording, Dolly said, "I knew I was walking on sacred ground because it is a classic…I was scared to death to send it to Robert Plant and Jimmy Page. They sent word back that it was fine and they loved it. In fact, Robert Plant said he'd always thought of it as a spiritual song, and he was thrilled we'd used a choir on it, because he thought about that, too. If they like it,

that's most important to me. But I do hope the public will accept it too. I even hope they love it."
- A Halos & Horns Radio Special CD (#SUG–CD–3946–I) was sent to select stations. The track list with timings was as follows:

One–Hour With Breaks / Commercial Free
1.) Segment 1 12:14
2.) Segment 1 14:28
3.) Segment 1 10:13
4.) Segment 1 12:42
5.) Segment 1 7:38

Radio Liners
6.) Rusty Miller Promo For Radio Special (W/ Music) 0:41
7.) Dolly Parton Promo For Radio Special (W/ Music) 0:28

Question & Answer
8.) "Dolly, Please Tell Us About Your Earliest Musical Memories And How They Impacted You." 0:41
9.) "One Of Your Signature Songs Is "Coat Of Many Colors", A True Story From Your Childhood. Could You Tell Us The Story Behind The Song?" 1:18
10.) "Tell Us About Moving To Nashville In The Early 60's." 1:16
11.) "You Really Became Known To A National Audience On Porter Wagoner's TV Show. How Did You Meet?" 1:29
12.) "The Early To Mid–70's Was A Period That Saw Your Music Career Really Explode And You Became An International Star. Describe What That Time In Your Life Was Like." 1:08
13.) "How Did You Get Into Acting?" 1:49
14.) "How Did You Feel When You Were Inducted Into The Country Music Hall Of Fame?" 0:56
15.) "Tell Us About Operating Dollywood And What That Experience Has Been Like?" 1:25
16.) "How Did You Stay So Prolific In Your Songwriting?" 0:50
17.) "For Many Years Your Successes Were Crossing Over To Pop From Country. But Your Last Three Albums Have Been A Clear Return To Your Roots Including The New "Halos And Horns" Album. Can You Tell Us About That Change In Style And Direction?" 0:57
18.) "Tell Us About The Making Of "Halos And Horns" And How You Began The Process?" 1:43
19.)   "What Is Your Secret Formula To Success, Longevity And Happiness?" 0:46

Trade Ad for Halos and Horns

For God and Country
SHCD 9756

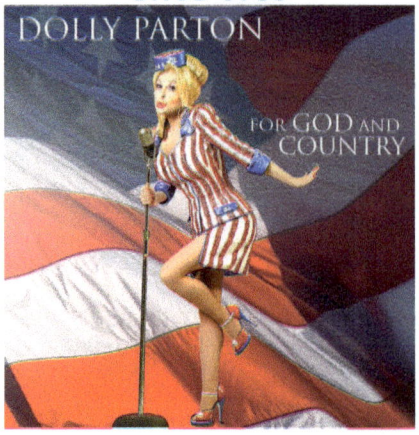

Track Listing:
The Lord Is My Shepard / The Star Spangled Banner / God Bless The USA / Light of a Clear Blue Morning / When Johnny Comes Marching Home / Welcome Home / Gee Ma, I Wanna Go Home / Whispering Hope / There Will Be Peace In The Valley For Me / Red, White and Bluegrass / My Country 'tis of Thee / I'm Gonna Miss You / Go To Hell / Ballad of the Green Beret / Brave Little Soldier / Tie A Yellow Ribbon / Color Me America / The Glory Forever

Production Information:
Produced by: Dolly Parton with Kent Wells and Tony Smith
Recorded at: 2 Monkeys Productions
Engineers: Chuck Ainlay / Dave Sinco / Michael Davis / Patrick Murphy / Russ Long / Tony Smith
Mixed by: Chuck Ainlay (tracks: 4, 5, 7, 12 to 14), / John Guess (tracks: 1 to 3, 6, 8 to 11, 15 to 18)
Assistant Mix Engineer: Jesse Benfield (tracks: 1 to 3, 6, 8 to 11, 15 to 18) / Jesse Benfield (tracks: 4, 5, 7, 12 to 14) / Patrick Murphy (tracks: 1 to 3, 6, 8 to 11, 15 to 18)
Digital Editing: Chuck Ainlay / Erik Hellerman / James Waddell / Jeff Thomas / Jesse Benfield / Michael Davis / Patrick Murphy / Russ Long / Tony Smith
Mixed at: Back Stage Studio and The Tracking Room, Nashville, TN
Mastered by: Benny Quinn at Masterfonics, Nashville, TN
Cover Photography: Dennis Carney
Design (Photo Montages): Don Bailey
Design (Cover Design): Chris Ferrara
Art Direction: Virginia Team for Latocki Team Creative

Musicians:
Acoustic Guitar: Bruce Watkins / Kent Wells / Robert Hale
Banjo: Gary 'Biscuit' Davis
Bass Guitar: Charlie Anderson / Jay Weaver
Dobro: Randy Kohrs
Drums / Percussion: Billy Thomas / Steve Turner
Electric Guitar: Kent Wells
Fiddle: Jimmy Mattingly
Mandolin: Darrell Webb / Jimmy Mattingly
Piano / Organ [Hammond B-3]: Michael Davis / Paul Hollowell
Synth programmed by: Michael Davis / Tony Smith
Backing Vocals: Bob Bailey / Darrell Webb / David Slater / Dolly Parton / Jennifer O'Brien / Kent Wells / Louis Nunley / Lynn Wright / Monty Allen / Richard Dennison / Robert Hale / Sheryl Thomas / Steven Hill / Vicki Hampton / The Fairfield Four additional vocals on "There Will Be Peace in the Valley for Me" / The Harding University Concert Choir – additional vocals on "Whispering Hope"

Singles Released From This Album:
"Welcome Home" – November 2003
"Light of a Clear Blue Morning" – May 2004

Album Data:
Highest Chart Position: # 23 on November 28, 2003
Billboard Chart: Hot Country Albums
Number of weeks on chart: 10

Notes / Trivia:
- This album was released on CD and Cassette on November 11, 2003.
- It is considered Dolly's musical attempt to deal with the aftermath of the September 11, 2001 attacks in New York.
- The music video for the album's first single, "Welcome Home," was shot over the January 10–11, 2004 weekend. It was premiered by CMT on February 4th
- This album has "sub tracks" located between some of the tracks. Track 2.2 is an untitled intro to the album and to Track 3 / Track 5.2 is a story about a WWII veteran / Track 8.2 is an intro to Track 9 / Track 9.2 is an intro to Track 10 / Track 14.2 is an intro to Track 15 / Track 15.2 is an intro to Track 16 and Track 17.2 is a prayer.

The outfit Dolly wore on the album cover and on the album tour.

Those Were The Days
SUG– CD 4007

Track Listing:
Those Were The Days / Blowin' in The Wind / Where Have All The Flowers Gone / Twelfth of Never / Where Do The Children Play / Me And Bobby McGee / Crimson And Clover* / The Cruel War / Turn, Turn, Turn / If I Were A Carpenter / Both Sides Now / Imagine

Production Information:
Produced by: Dolly Parton. *Tommy James and Jimmy Wisner
Recorded at: Two Monkeys Studios, The Tracking Room at Masterfonics, Oceanway, Minutiae Studio in Nashville. Stir Studio in Cardiff, UK. Dollywood's Celebrity Theater in Pigeon Forge, TN. Avatar Studios in New York City. Kensal Town Studio D in London, England. No Can Beat Studios in Hana, Hawaii. Taylor Made Studios in North Caldwell, New Jersey. Sound on Sound Recording in New York City. Chartmaker Studios in Los Angeles, CA.
Engineers: Matt Boynton (Avatar Studios) / Steve Davis (Stir Studio) / Neil DeVor (Chartmaker Studios) / Patrick Murphy (Two Monkeys Studio) / Gary Paczosa (Minutiae Studio) / Sarah Jane Schmeltzer (Dollywood's Celebrity Theater) / Alan Silverman (Sound on Sound Recording) / Glenn M. Taylor (Taylor Made Studios) / J. Carter Tutwiler (No Can Beat Studios)
Assistant Engineer: Brandon Bell (Minutiae Studio) / Courtney Blooding (Chartmaker Studios) / Kyle Dickinson (Two Monkeys Studio) / Adam Dye (The Tracking Room at Masterfonics) / Scott Kidd (Two Monkeys Studio) / Kelly Pribble (Kensal Town Studio D) / Reed Taylor (Sound on Sound Recording) / Aya Takemura (Avatar Studios)
Cover Photography: Dennis Carney
Album Design: Wendy Stamberger

Singles Released From This Album:
"Imagine" – September 27, 2005 (iTunes exclusive release. Then issued to radio on November 7, 2007)
"Both Sides Now" – December 2005 (peaked at # 1 on the *Indie World* Country Singles Chart in March 2006)
"The Twelfth of Never" – January 2006 (peaked at # 3 on the Country Tracks Top 30 chart. (Australian release only)

Album Data:
Highest Chart Position: # 9 on October 28, 2005
Billboard Chart: Hot Country Albums
Number of weeks on chart: 19

Notes / Trivia:
- This album was released on CD on October 11, 2005

- The album's original title was to be "Blue Smoke." This track would remain unreleased until Dolly included it as the title track of her 2014 album.
- The music video for "Imagine" was shot in New York City during the weekend of October 21–23 and features private home videos of John Lennon and Yoko Ono. The video premiered on CMT's website on November 28 and made its television debut three days later on *CMT Top 20 Countdown*.
- Guest vocalists: Judy Collins and Rhonda Vincent special guests on "Both Sides Now" / David Foster special guest on "Imagine" / Mary Hopkin (and the Opry Gang) special guest on "Those Were the Days" / Yusef Islam special guest on "Where Do the Children Play" / Tommy James special guest on "Crimson and Clover" / Norah Jones special guest on "Where Have All the Flowers Gone" / Alison Krauss special guest on "The Cruel War" / Kris Kristofferson special guest on "Me and Bobby McGee" / Roger McGuinn special guest on "Turn, Turn, Turn" / Moscow Circus special guest "Those Were the Days" / Joe Nichols special guest on "If I Were a Carpenter" / Nickel Creek special guest on "Blowin' in the Wind" / Mindy Smith special guest on "The Cruel War" / Dan Tyminski special guest on "The Cruel War" / Keith Urban special guest on "Twelfth of Never" / Porter Wagoner guest vocals on "Those Were the Days" / Lee Ann Womack special guest on "Where Have All the Flowers Gone"
- Dolly told Jon Stewart while on the *Daily Show* to promote the album that she had invited Bob Dylan to sing on "Blowin' in the Wind", but that he declined. She added that she was not sure whether Dylan himself declined or the refusal came from his management.
- "Those Were The Days" was recorded on July 1, 2005 and the Opry Gang consisted of: was recorded on July 1 with Porter Wagoner, Jack Greene, George Hamilton IV, Jan Howard, George Jones, Brenda Lee, Mel McDaniel, Jimmy C. Newman, Jeannie Seely, and Billy Walker.

Those Were The Days Tour Book

Backwoods Barbie
DP925

Track Listing:
Better Get to Livin' / Made of Stone / Drives Me Crazy / Backwoods Barbie / Jesus & Gravity / Only Dreamin' / The Tracks of My Tears / The Lonesomes / Cologne / Shinola / I Will Forever Hate Roses / Somebody's Everything

Production Information:
Produced by: Kent Wells / Dolly Parton
Recorded at: Blackbird Studio A (Nashville) / Kent Wells Production (Nashville) / Sound Kitchen (Franklin) / Emerald Studio A (Nashville)
Engineers: Allan Ditto / Patrick Murphy / Kyle Dickinson
Mixed by: Justin Niebank / Drew Bollman
Editing by: Patrick Murphy / Ben Schmidt / Kyle Dickinson
Mastered by: Alex McCollough at True East Mastering, Nashville, TN
Cover Photography & Art Direction: Kii Arens

Musicians:
Piano: Hargus "Pig" Robbins / Paul Hollowell
Electric Guitar: Tom Bukovac / Rob McNelley / Jerry McPherson / Brent Mason / Derek Wells / Kent Wells
Bass: Mike Brignardello / Steve Mackey
Drums–Percussion: Sam Bacco / Lonnie Wilson
Acoustic Guitar: Kent Wells / Bryan Sutton / Biff Watson
Banjo: David Talbot
Steel Guitar: Terry Crisp / Paul Franklin / Lloyd Green
Fiddle – Mandolin: Aubrey Haynie / Jimmy Mattingly
Fender Rhodes – Hammond B–3 organ – keyboards: Paul Hollowell
Bodhran – Harmonium – Tin whistle: John Mock
Strings: The Nashville String Machine
String arrangements: Kris Wilkinson
Background vocals: Dolly Parton / Christine Winslow / Darrin Vincent / Rhonda Vincent / Marty Slayton / Jennifer O'Brien / Alecia Nugent / Rebecca Isaacs Bowman / Billy Davis / Richard Dennison / Terry Eldridge / Vicki Hampton / Sonya Isaacs / Carl Jackson / Jamie Johnson /

Singles Released From This Album:
"Better Get To Livin'" – August 28, 2007 (peaked at # 48 on Billboard's Hot Country Songs Chart)
"Jesus and Gravity" – February 12, 2008
"Shinola" – July 21, 2008
"Drives Me Crazy" – January 12, 2009

"Backwoods Barbie" – March 9, 2009

Album Data:
Highest Chart Position: # 2 on March 14, 2008
Billboard Chart: Hot Country Albums
Number of weeks on chart: 50

Notes / Trivia:
- This album was released on CD on February 26, 2008.
- The original title of this album was *Country Is as Country Does*.
- Dolly told *The Las Vegas City Life* that she had recorded a song for the album titled "Just a Wee Bit Gay" about a woman and her in–the–closet husband. This track, unfortunately, has not been released as of 2021.
- Best Buy, Target, Walmart, Cracker Barrel and iTunes all offered bonus material on exclusive releases.
- The album has sold 281,000 units in the United States as of December 2020.

The Backwoods Barbie Tour Book

Better Day
528216

Track Listing:
In The Meantime / Just Leaving / Somebody's Missing You / Together You and I / Country Is As Country Does / Holding Everything / The Sacrifice / I Just Might / Better Day / Shine Like The Sun / Get Out and Stay Out / Let Love Grow

Production Information:
Produced by: Kent Wells
Executive Producer: Dolly Parton
Recorded at: The Sound Kitchen / Kent Wells Productions / Blackbird Studios
Engineers: Patrick Murphy / Tony Smith
Assistant Engineer: Ben Schmitt
Digital Editing: Stewart Whitmore
Mixed by: Patrick Murphy at The Sound Kitchen
Mastering: Stephen Marcussen at Marcussen Mastering, Hollywood, CA
Cover Photography: Fran Strine
Photo Assistance: Peter Dokus
Art Direction: Kii Arens
Costume Design: Steve Summers
Hair Stylist: Cheryl Riddle

Musicians:
Piano: Hargus "Pig" Robbins / Paul Hollowell
Hammond B3 Organ / Keyboards: Paul Hollowell
Drums / Percussion: Steve Turner
Bass Guitar: Mike Brignardello / Steve Mackey
Upright Bass: Steve Mackey
Hammond B3 Organ, Synthesizer: Michael Davis
Steel Guitar: Lloyd Green / Steve Hinson
Dobro: Andy Hall / Randy Kohrs
Fiddle / Mandolin: Aubrey Haynie / Jimmy Mattingly
Slide Guitar: Steve Hinson
Electric Guitar: Rob McNelley / Jerry McPherson / Brent Mason / Kent Wells
Harmonica: Richie Owens
Acoustic Guitar: Bryan Sutton / Biff Watson / Kent Wells
Banjo: Dave Talbot
Background Vocals: Jamie Dailey / Christian Davis / Richard Dennison / Vicki Hampton / Emmylou Harris / Becky Isaacs / Sonya Isaacs / Alison Krauss / Jennifer O'Brien / Darrin Vincent / Kent Wells

Singles Released From This Album:
"Together You and I" – May 23, 2011 (peaked at # 67 on UK Singles Chart)
"The Sacrifice" – October 11, 2011

Album Data:
Highest Chart Position: # 11 on July 15, 2011
Billboard Chart: Hot Country Albums
Number of weeks on chart: 13

Notes / Trivia:
- This album was released on CD on June 28, 2011 / and LP on August 16, 2011.
- This album has the 2007 recording of *Country Is as Country Does* which had been recorded for Dolly's previous album *Backwoods Barbie*.
- Dolly originally wrote the song "Together You and I" in the early 1970s and recorded it with Porter Wagoner on their 1974 collaborative RCA album, *Porter 'n' Dolly* (APL–1–0646).
- To promote the album, Dolly embarked on her Better Day World Tour. With 49 shows, the tour visited North America, Europe, and Australia. Dolly's tour begins July 17th in Knoxville, Tenn., and wraps up in the U.S. on August 3rd. The tour will move overseas on August 20th. UK highlights include shows on September 7th and 8th at London's O2 Arena.
- The album was released on August 29, 2011 In the UK, and debuted at # 9 on the UK Album Charts, becoming Parton's highest charting studio album in that country as well as becoming a # 1 album on the UK Country Albums Chart.

The Better Days Tour Book

Blue Smoke
88843 03269 2

Track Listing:
Blue Smoke / Unlikely Angel / Don't Think Twice / You Can't Make Old Friends (duet with Kenny Rogers)* / Homes / Banks of the Ohio / Lay Your Hands On Me / Miss You–Miss Me / If I Had Wings / Lover Du Jour / From Here To The Moon And Back (duet with Willie Nelson) / Try

Production Information:
Arranged and Produced by: Kent Wells / *Produced by Dann Huff
Executive Producer: Dolly Parton
Recorded at: Kent Wells Productions / Starstruck Studios / RTBGV / Blackbird Studios / Doppler Studios / Digital Audio Post / Ben's Studio / Sound Emporium Studios
Engineers: Patrick Murphy / Steve Marcantonio / Todd Tidwell /
Assistant Engineer: Kyle Dickinson / Taylor Tharpe / Shawn Daugherty / Seth Morton / Mike Lancaster / Russell Terrell
Mastering: Stephen Marcussen at Marcussen Mastering, Hollywood, CA
Cover Photography:
Art Direction:

Musicians:
Piano: Jim "Moose" Brown / Richard Dennison / Paul Hollowell / Charlie Judge
Bass Guitar: Mike Brignardello / Steve Mackey / Jimmie Lee Sloas
Electric Guitar / Harmonica: Pat Buchanan / Kent Wells / Derek Wells
Drums / Percussion: Nick Buda / Steve Turner
Percussion: Eric Darken
Synthesizer Strings / Synthesizer: Charlie Judge
Electric Guitar: J.T. Corenflos / Steve Gibson / Dann Huff
Drums: Chad Cromwell / Bob Mater / Greg Morrow
Upright Bass: Dennis Crouch / Jay Weaver
Keyboards: Michael Davis / Paul Hollowell
Fiddle: Stuart Duncan / Aubrey Haynie / Jimmy Mattingly
Steel Guitar: Paul Franklin / Tommy White
Mandolin: Aubrey Haynie / Jimmy Mattingly / Danny Roberts
Lap Steel Guitar: Steve Hinson
Harmonica: Jim Hoke / Mickey Raphael
Hammond B-3 Organ: Paul Hollowell
Dobro: Randy Kohrs
Acoustic Guitar: Tom Rutledge / Bryan Sutton / Bobby Terry / Ilya Toshinsky / Kent Wells
Harmonium: John Mock
Banjo: Scott Vestal

Synthesizer: Bobby Wood
Drum Programming Kent Wells
Strings: The Nashville String Machine
Background Vocals: Monty Allen / Rebecca Isaacs Bowman / Sonya Isaacs / Christian Davis / Terry Eldridge / Vicki Hampton / Carl Jackson / Jamie Johnson / Jennifer O'Brien / Val Story / Richard Dennison

Singles Released From This Album:
"Blue Smoke" – December 10, 2013
"Home" – April 22, 2014
"Try" – July 7, 2014
"Unlikely Angel" – February 16, 2015

Album Data:
Highest Chart Position: # 2 on May 30, 2014
Billboard Chart: Hot Country Albums
Number of weeks on chart: 13

Notes / Trivia:
- This album was released on LP and CD on January 31, 2014
- Three of the songs on the album had been previously recorded by Dolly: "Unlikely Angel" was originally written and recorded for the 1996 film of the same name that Dolly appeared in. The version featured in the film was never commercially released. "From Here to the Moon and Back" was previously recorded by Dolly, Jeremy Jordan and Kris Kristofferson for the 2012 film *Joyful Noise* and was also released on the film's soundtrack album."Early Morning Breeze" was originally recorded by Dolly for her 1971 album *Coat of Many Colors* and again for her 1974 album *Jolene*.
- Wal–Mart and QVC offered bonus tracks on their copies. In the UK a version had a bonus disc with 20 tracks called *Blue Smoke: The Best Of Dolly Parton*. This was issued on June 9, 2014 to tie in with the European tour.
- The song "You Can't Make Old Friends," originally released as a Kenny & Dolly duet on Kenny's 2013 album of the same name.
- In the UK, *Blue Smoke* proved to be Dolly's most successful album ever, spending 12 weeks in the top 10 UK Albums Chart, with a peak position of number 2 in the seventh week. It was certified Silver by the BPI (British Phonographic Industry) on July 4, 2014, Gold on July 18, 2014 and Platinum on December 12, 2014. The album has sold over 400,000 copies in the UK as of August 2016.

Pure & Simple
88985 35125 2

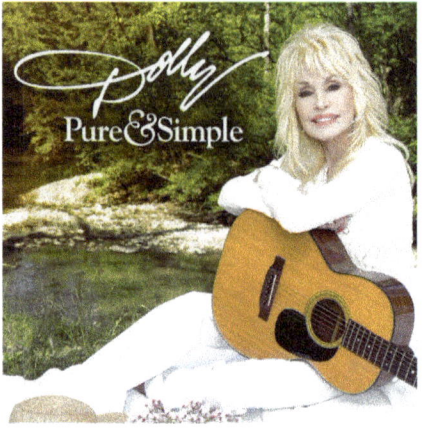

Track Listing:
Pure and Simple / Say Forever You'll Be Mine / Never Not Love You / Kiss It (And Make It All Better) / Can't Be That Wrong / Outside Your Door / Tomorrow Is Forever / I'm Sixteen / Head Over High Heels / Forever Love

Production Information:
Produced by: Dolly Parton with Richard Dennison and Tom Rutledge
Engineers: Patrick Murphy / Tom Rutledge
Mixing Engineer: Patrick Murphy
Mastered by: Sony DADC
Cover Photography: Fran Strine
Art Direction: Jacob Timmons / Sarah Chapman

Musicians:
Piano: Richard Dennison / Paul Hollowell
Electric Piano: Richard Dennison / Richard Dennison
Drums–Percussion: Tom Hoey / Steve Turner
Organ: Paul Hollowell
Synthesizer: Richard Dennison
Steel Guitar: Paul Franklin
Upright Bass: Kevin Grantt
Electric Bass: Steve Mackey
Electric Guitar: Kent Wells / Tom Rutledge
Mandolin / Fiddle: Jimmy Mattingly
Banjo / Acoustic Guitar: Tom Rutledge
String Arrangements: David Davidson
String Programming: Michael Davis
Duet Vocals: Monty Lane Allen / Richard Dennison
Background Vocals: Vicki Hampton / Kristen Wilkinson / Jennifer O'Brien / Jeff Pearles / Richard Dennison
Strings: David Angell / David Davidson / Anthony LaMarchina /

Singles Released From This Album:
"Pure and Simple" – Released: July 8, 2016
"Outside Your Door" – Released: July 29, 2016
"Head Over High Heels" – Released: September 16, 2016

Album Data:
Highest Chart Position: # 1 on September 9, 2016
Billboard Chart: Hot Country Albums
Number of weeks on chart: 22

Notes / Trivia:
- This album was released on CD on August 19, 2016
- The release of this album came in an assortment of versions. The standard version contained the 10–track album. A deluxe version of the album sold through Walmart stores contained two bonus tracks along with a bonus CD featuring ten of Dolly's biggest hits. The UK version of the album contained two bonus tracks and a bonus CD of Parton's 2014 Glastonbury set. A deluxe version of the album was released August 26 exclusively at Cracker Barrel. This came with a 30–page booklet, two bonus tracks from Parton's Glastonbury set, a magnet, and a coupon booklet.
- This album was Dolly's seventh # 1 country album— her first in 25 years.
- Four songs from this album have been previously recorded by Dolly. "Tomorrow Is Forever" was originally recorded on December 2, 1969 as a duet with Porter Wagoner for their 1970 album *Porter Wayne and Dolly Rebecca*. "Say Forever You'll Be Mine" was also originally recorded on August 21, 1972 as a duet with Porter Wagoner for their 1975 album of the same name. "Can't Be That Wrong," with a few lyrical differences, was previously recorded as "God Won't Get You," and released on the soundtrack to Dolly's 1984 film *Rhinestone*.
- The album received Gold certification in Russia for 10,000 copies sold.
- There had been some talk about re–issuing this album and a few others, such as *Backwoods Barbie* originally on CD only on vinyl LP. *Backwoods Barbie* was going to be pressed on pink vinyl to match the cover art. This has not yet happened.

I Believe in You
88985483482

Track Listing:
I Believe in You / Coat of Many Colors / Together Forever / I Am a Rainbow / I'm Here / A Friend Like You / Imagination / You Can Do It / Responsibility / You Gotta Be / Makin' Fun Ain't Funny / Chemo Hero / Brave Little Soldier / A Reading of *Coat of Many Colors* (bonus track)

Production Information:
Produced by: Tom McBryde / Tom Rutledge / Richard Dennison
Executive Producers: Dolly Parton / Paul T. Couch
Recorded at: Westpark Sound, Franklin, Tennessee
Engineers: Tom Reeves / Tom Rutledge
Edited by: Chris Latham / Tom Rutledge / Nathan Smith
Mastered by: John Mayfield
Cover Photography: Trey Fanjoy
Additional photography: Dennis Carney / Jacob Timmons
Original Graphic Design: Jacob Timmons
Album Design: Sarah Chapman
Wardrobe: Robert Behar / Steve Summers
Hair: Cheryl Riddle

Musicians:
Drums: Tom Reeves / Tom Hoey
Keyboards: Tim Hayden
Percussion: Tom Hoey
Guitars: Paul Brannon / Tom Rutledge
Bass: Steve Mackey / Danny O'Lannerghty / Tom Rutledge
Electric Guitars: Kent Wells
Richard Dennison – keyboards
MIDI Guitars: Tom Rutledge
Background Vocals: Vickie Hampton / Richard Dennison / Shelley Jennings / Melodie Kirkpatrick / Shane McConnell / Jennifer O'Brien / The Inner Child Chorus

Singles Released From This Album:
"I Believe in You" – September 15, 2017

Album Data:
Highest Chart Position: # 20 on November 3, 2017
Billboard Chart: Hot Country Albums
Number of weeks on chart: 1

Notes / Trivia:
- This album was released on CD on October 13, 2017
- The album peaked at # 3 on the *Billboard* Kid Albums Chart
- The album was officially made known on Saturday, July 5, 2014, with the release of the title track, "I Believe in You," as a free download on Dolly's official webpage. The release stated, "All families who receive the gift of Imagination Library books were also presented with a free download of Parton's song, "I Believe in You," that she wrote for the Imagination Playhouse at Dollywood. Eleven additional songs will soon be made available for purchase, with 100 percent of sales supporting the longevity of the Dollywood Foundation."
- This is Dolly's first children's album.

A Holly Dolly Christmas
12 Tone

Track Listing:
Holly Jolly Christmas / Christmas Is (featuring Miley Cyrus) / Cuddle Up, Cozy Down Christmas (with Michael Bublé) / Christmas on the Square / Circle of Love* / All I Want for Christmas Is You (with Jimmy Fallon) / Comin' Home for Christmas / Christmas Where We Are (featuring Billy Ray Cyrus) / Pretty Paper (with Willie Nelson) / I Saw Mommy Kissing Santa Claus / You Are My Christmas (featuring Randy Parton) / Mary, Did You Know?

Production Information:
Produced by: Kent Wells / *Richard Dennison / Tom Rutledge
Executive Producer: Dolly Parton
Recorded at: Sound Stage Studios in Nashville, TN / Velvet Apple Studios in Nashville, TN / Little Big Sound in Nashville, TN / Adventure Studios in Nashville, TN / Quad Studios in Nashville, TN / Kent Wells Productions in Franklin, TN / Dark Horse Recording in Franklin, TN / Paragon Studios in Franklin, TN / The Jazz/Pop Sweatshop in Vancouver, BC / Monk Music Studios in East Hampton, NY. / Pedernales Recording Studio in Spicewood, TX
Engineers: Steve Chadie / Joey Crawford / Cynthia Daniels / Jamie Graves / Paul David Hager / Patrick Murphy / Taylor Pollert
Assistant Engineer: Kam Luchterhand / Parker Lyons / Andrew Mayer / Joel McKenney / Adam Wathan
Audio Editing: Kyle Dickinson / Chris Latham / Tyler Spratt / Kevin Willis
Cover Photography: Stacie Huckeba
Art Direction: J.B. Rowland

Singles Released From This Album:
"Comin' Home for Christmas" was originally released as a stand alone single on December 1, 2009 and was included on this album 11 years after initial release.
"Mary Did You Know" – August 21, 2020 (peaked at # 49 on the Billboard Hot Christian Songs chart)
"I Saw Mommy Kissing Santa Claus" – September 15, 2020
"Christmas on the Square" – September 29, 2020
"Cuddle Up, Cozy Down Christmas" – October 2, 2020 (peaked at # 10)
"All I Want For Christmas Is You" – December 3, 2020 (peaked at # 4 on the Billboard Holiday Digital Song Sales chart.)
"Pretty Paper" – December 22, 2020 (peaked at # 12 on the Billboard Holiday Digital Song chart.)

Album Data:
Highest Chart Position: # 1 on October 16, 2020
Billboard Chart: Hot Country Albums

Number of weeks on chart: 13

Notes / Trivia:
- This album was released on CD on October 2, 2020, October 6, 2020 for the Amazon steaming exclusive edition, LP, 8–Track and Cassette on November 13, 2020 and December 4, 2020 for the Digital download streaming (Bonus Version). Vinyl issued in various colors.
- Bonus tracks were available from various outlets. The 8–Track cartridge had "The Wish Book" as the bonus track and the cassette tape had "Three Candles" as the bonus track. Both songs were written by Dolly Parton. These tapes were Amazon exclusives. Another track "I Still Believe" was performed live on Dolly's *A Holly Dolly Christmas* TV Special which aired December 6, 2020 on CBS–TV and drew 6.2 million viewers. The song was a bonus digital only release on December 4, 2020.
- A music video to accompany the release of "Cuddle Up, Cozy Down Christmas" with Michael Bublé was first released onto YouTube on November 7, 2020.
- After the album's initial release several tracks not released as singles charted on the *Billboard* Holiday Digital Song Sales chart. They were: "Circle of Love" peaked at number eight, "Christmas Is" peaked at number 13, "Holly Jolly Christmas" peaked at number 16, "You Are My Christmas" peaked at number 21, and "Christmas Where We Are" peaked at number 34.
- As of December 2020, the album has sold 171,000 copies in the US.
- Target Stores featured an exclusive "Green Sparkle" cover identical to the original red sparkle released.

The Target exclusive album art version

The Amazon 8–Track exclusive

The Amazon cassette tape exclusive

The Photo Gallery

→

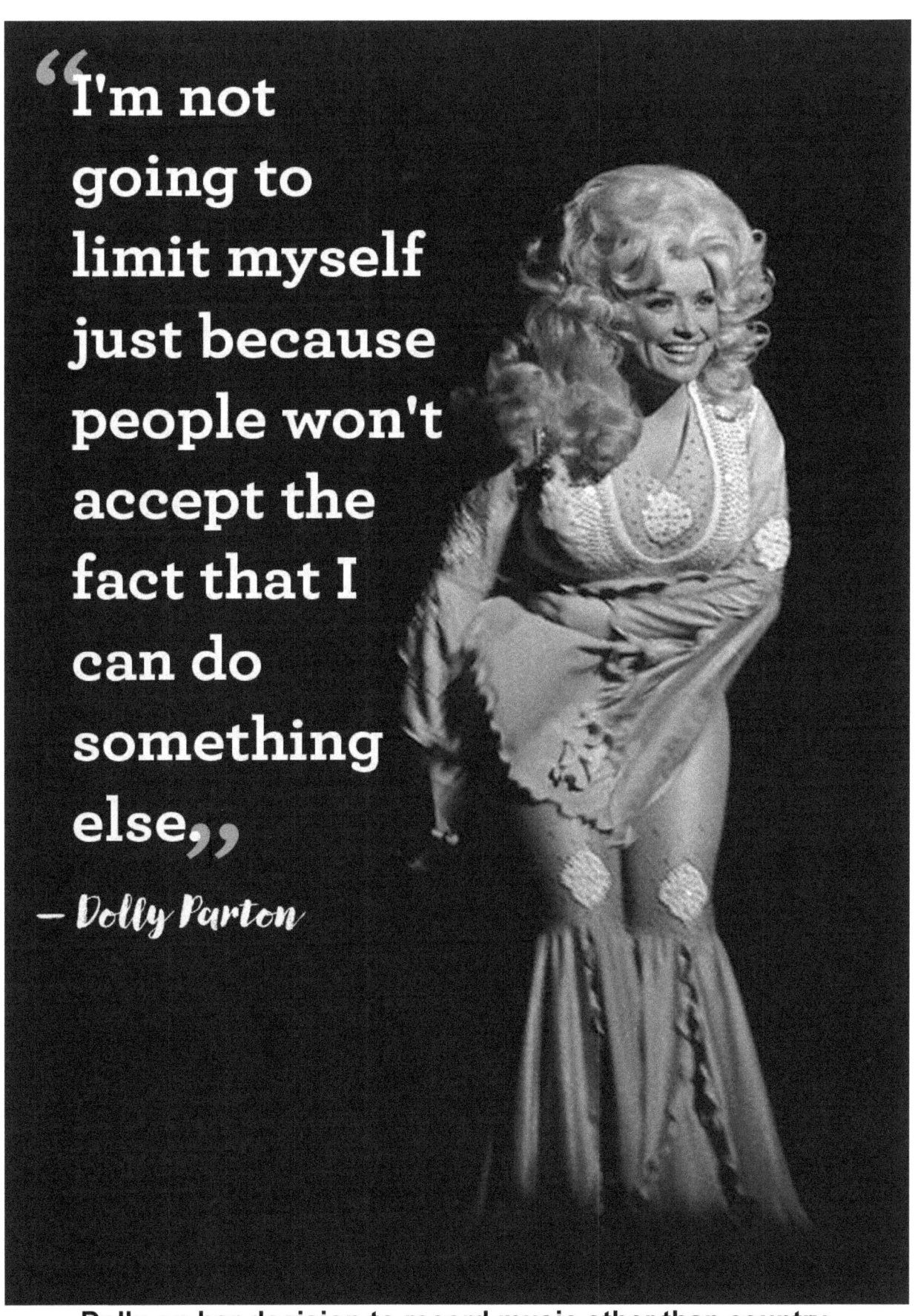

Dolly on her decision to record music other than country.

A 9 to 5 film poster from Japan

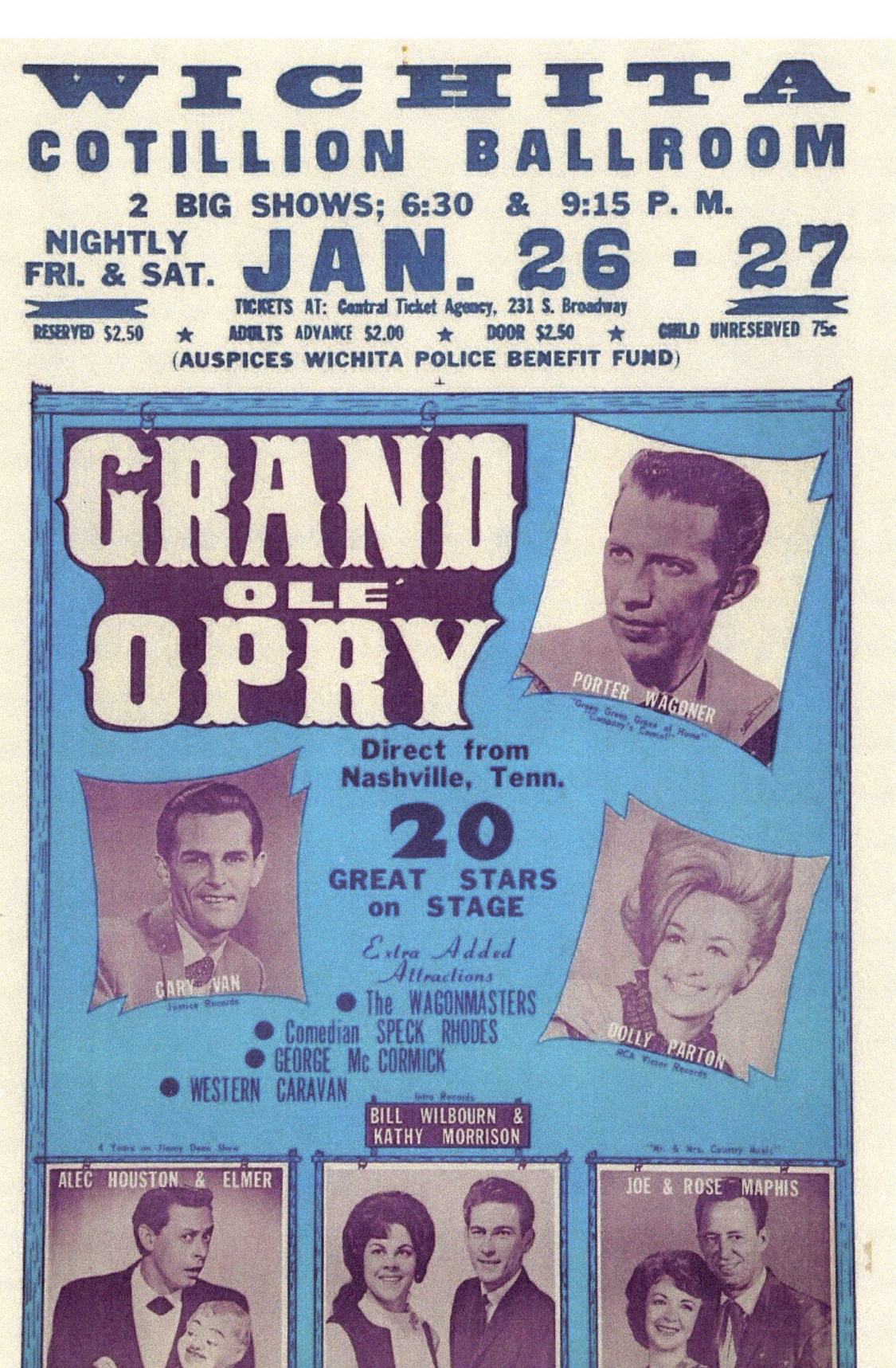

An early concert poster

DOLLY PARTON 1969
WSM Radio

Dolly recording in the 1960's at Fred Foster Sound Studios in Nashville, TN

Promotional ad for Dolly's 1977 album "Here You Come Again" on RCA Records

Dolly doing what she loves!

Trade Ad for Dolly's *Real Love* album

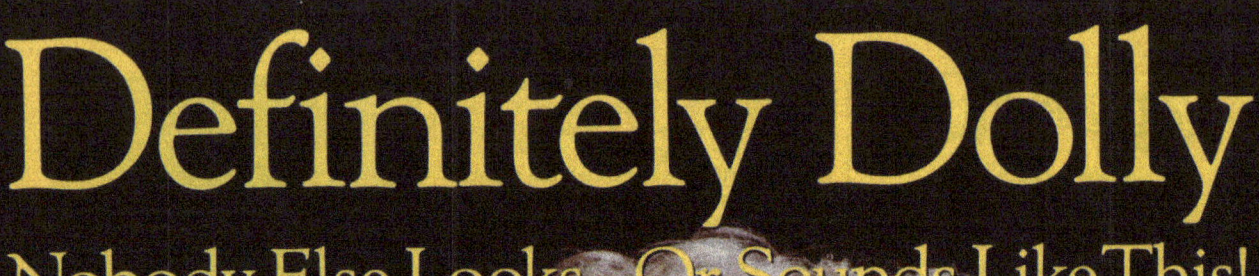

Definitely Dolly
Nobody Else Looks...Or Sounds Like This!

It's definitely Dolly! And she's definitely back home!  "White Limozeen" is the new album produced in Nashville by Ricky Skaggs. First stop: **Why'd You Come In Here Lookin' Like That**, the most "Dolly" single in years!

DOLLY PARTON,
"WHITE LIMOZEEN"
FC/FCT/CK 44384
ON COLUMBIA RECORDS,
CASSETTES AND
COMPACT DISC.

ALSO INCLUDES:
SLOW HEALIN' HEART
TIME FOR ME TO FLY
YELLOW ROSES

© 1989 CBS Records, Inc.

Better Day Tour Book

Some of the great Dolly Parton album covers through the years!

Dolly with Barry Gibb in RCA Victor's Recording Studio, Studio A in Nashville working on the track "Words" from Barry's new album *Greenfields: The Gibb Brothers Songbook, Vol. 1*.
Release date: January 8, 2021

Dolly mid 1970's Promotional shot

**An outtake from a photo session of Dolly with Cher for Cher's 1978 TV Special "Cher: A Special."
Dolly received an Emmy nomination for her appearance.**

The soundsheet that was included with Dolly's doll outfit "Coat of Many Colors." Dolly's mother Avie Lee Parton tells the story of the coat.

The quadraphonic open reel tape of Dolly's 1973 album *Bubbling Over*. Several country artists had their albums issued in the quad format. Somehow quad never really caught on en masse in the early 1970's. Though as recently as 2020 several CD's have been released in a format similar to Quadraphonic. Two such albums are Helen Reddy's *I Am Woman* and *Long Hard Climb (below)*. Both have been reissued together on a Hybrid SACD which also contains a stereo DSD layer for regular CD Players. Both also issued quad originally.

A review magazine featuring *9 to 5*

A gold album award for the sales of more than 500,000 copies of the album *Jolene*.
Not sure where this is from not being an RIAA.

The press kit from CBS for Dolly's album *Rainbow.*

A promotional photo from around
New Harvest...First Gathering

Dolly
*This beautiful little girl
Grew up in East Tennessee.
Now she has found...*

REAL LOVE

Including:

Think About Love

*Tie Our Love
(In A Double Knot)*

We Got Too Much

It's Such A Heartache

Don't Call It Love

*Real Love
(Duet with Kenny Rogers)*

I Can't Be True

*Once In A Very
Blue Moon*

Come Back To Me

*I Hope You're Never
Happy*

*Produced by
David Malloy for
David Malloy
Productions, Inc.*

RCA
Records and Cassettes

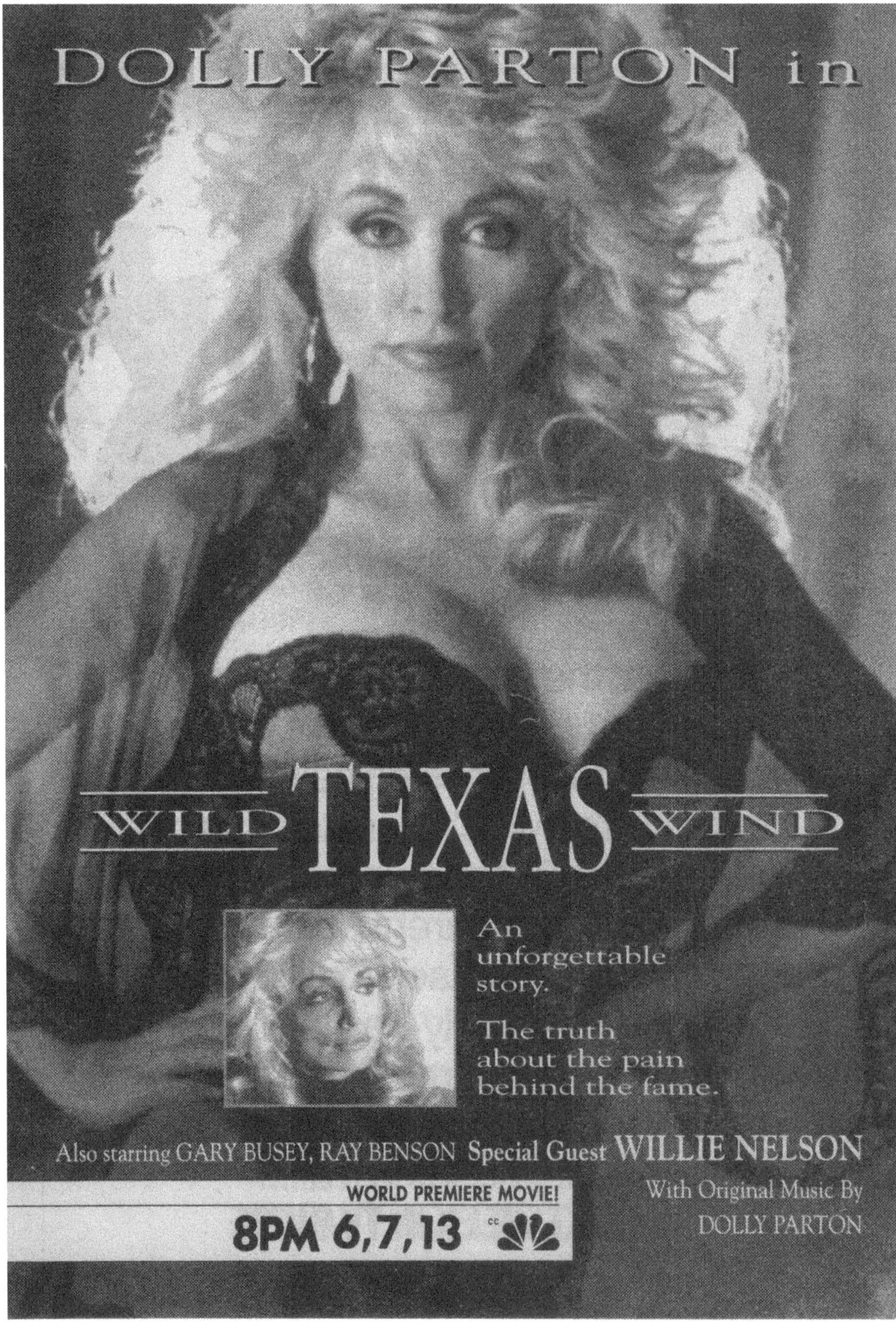

Ad for the TV film *Wild Texas Wind*

Two different ways of promoting albums—
Print ads and TV Specials!

Dolly with Porter Wagoner at what looks to be an industry function.

Dolly with *9 to 5* co–stars Jane Fonda and Lily Tomlin. 1980

A trade ad for the album *Treasures*

Country News Hotline featuring Dolly and Kenny Rogers on the cover. September 1982

A promotional ad for Honky Tonk Angels

Above: RCA Studio A
These two studios are where Dolly recorded most of her RCA material.
Below: RCA Studio B

Dolly in concert sometime in the early 1980's

Dolly in the mid 1970's relaxing and letting her hair down

Dolly has appeared on magazine covers since very early in her career

27 Music Square East
Nashville, Tenn. 37203
(615) 254-8825

CD MASTERING INSTRUCTION CARD			LABEL	RCA Records		
Page 1 of 1 pages DATE 06 / 25 / 90			TIME CODE READINGS ARE EXACT (NO OFFSET)			
PROGRAM TITLE / ARTIST(S) "The Best Of Dolly Parton" / Dolly Parton 5146-2-R11						

Track No.	Index No.	TITLE	TIME	REMARKS	EMP Y/N	TIME CODE h m s f
		1k Tone	:30		N	00 29 26
						01 00 28
1.		Jolene	2:36			01 59 26
						04 37 15
2.		Traveling Man	2:10			04 40 00
						06 50 17
3.		Lonely Comin' Down	3:10			06 53 04
						10 01 28
4.		The Bargain Store	2:39			10 04 06
						12 43 26
5.		Touch Your Woman	2:39			12 46 13
						15 26 06
6.		I Will Always Love You	2:53			15 28 22
						18 22 18
7.		Love Is Like A Butterfly	2:19			18 25 06
						20 44 27
8.		Coat Of Many Colors	3:02			20 47 08
						23 50 03
9.		My Tennessee Mountain Home	3:00			23 52 11
						26 53 03
10.		When I Sing For Him	2:56		↓	26 55 18
						29 52 11

FORMAT Sony 1630   L.P._____ CD XXX   MASTER_____ SAFETY XXX
SAMPLING RATE 44.1   PROOFED Yes
S.M.P.T.E. NDF Ch. 2   PEAK LEVEL_____   ENG. HD

POTENTIAL NEW BOYFRIEND
DOLLY PARTON
RCA

DOLLY PARTON
9 TILL 5
RCA
PB 2133

Dolly
HERE YOU COME AGAIN
POTENTIAL NEW BOYFRIEND
LOVE IS LIKE A BUTTERFLY

RCA
SP - 4944
VICTOR
TWO DOORS DOWN
IT'S ALL WRONG, BUT IT'S ALL RIGHT
Dolly
PARTON
GRABADO EN U.S.A.
IMPRESO EN MEXICO

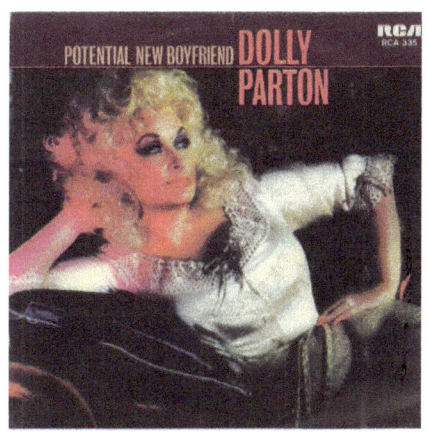

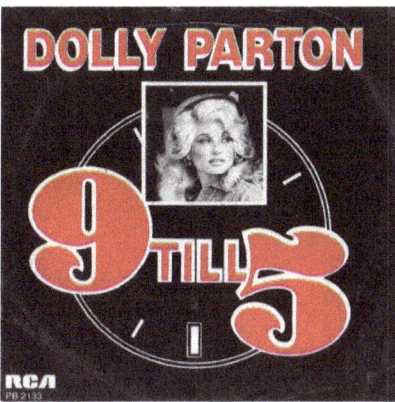

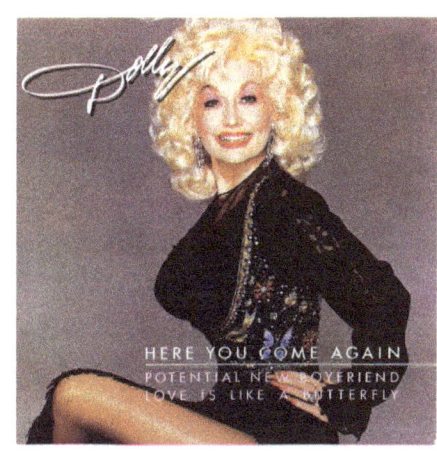

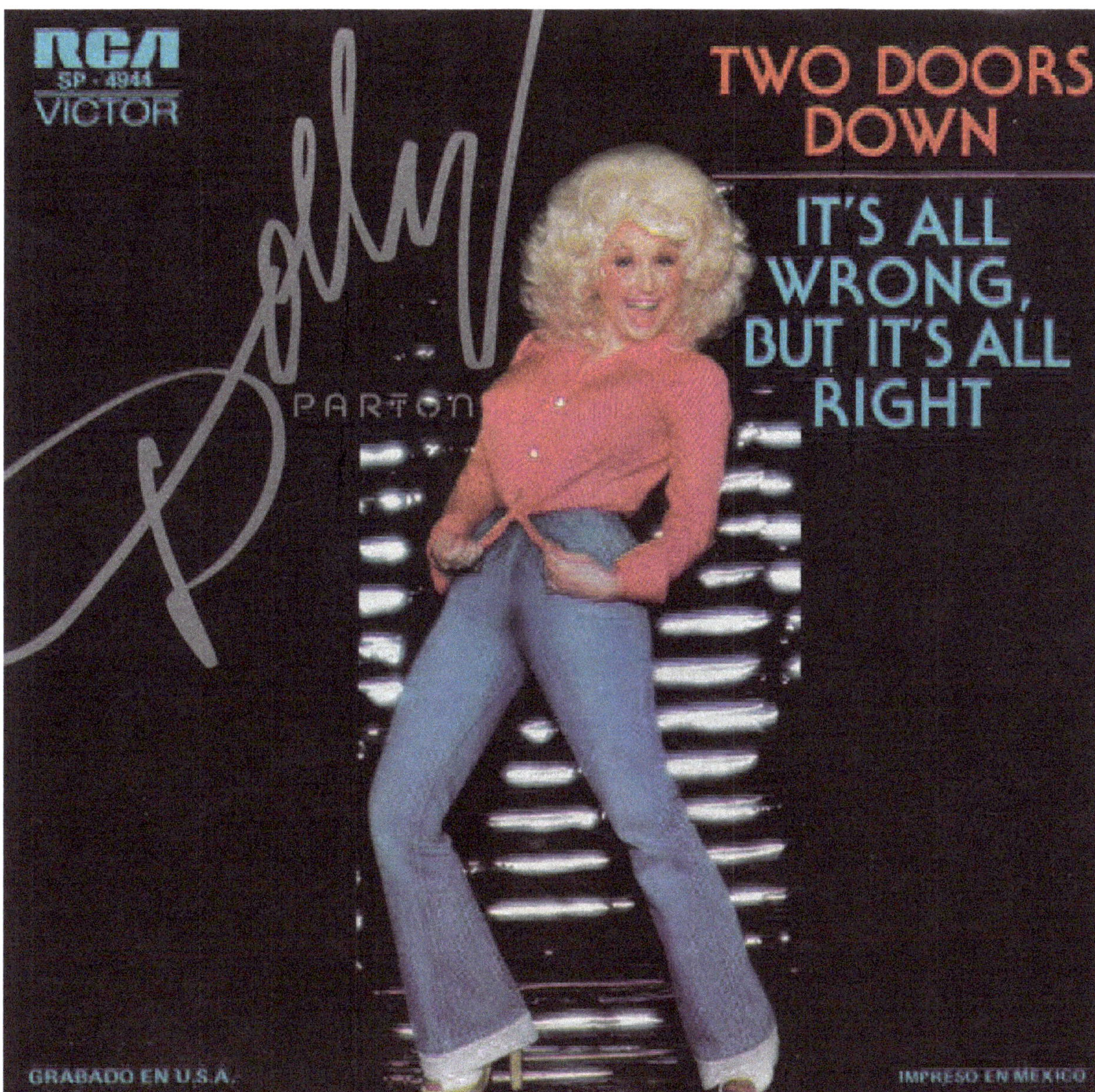

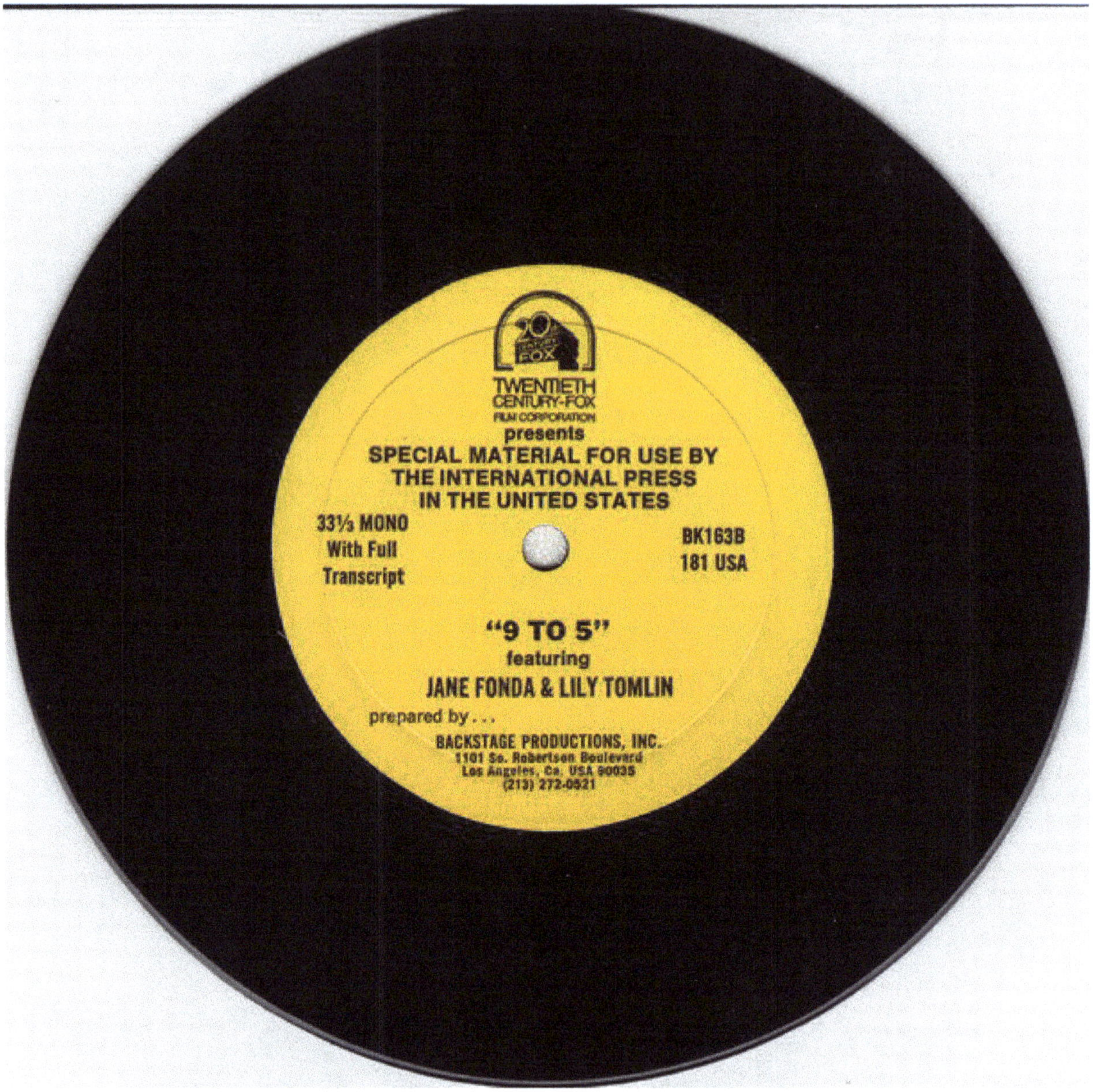

TWENTIETH CENTURY-FOX FILM CORPORATION presents

SPECIAL MATERIAL FOR USE BY THE INTERNATIONAL PRESS IN THE UNITED STATES

33⅓ MONO
With Full Transcript

BK163B
181 USA

"9 TO 5"
featuring
JANE FONDA & LILY TOMLIN

prepared by...
BACKSTAGE PRODUCTIONS, INC.
1101 So. Robertson Boulevard
Los Angeles, Ca. USA 90035
(213) 272-0521

monument
45-1007
PROMOTIONAL COPY
NOT FOR SALE
I'VE LIVED MY LIFE
DOLLY PARTON

MERCURY RECORDS
PROMOTIONAL RECORD
HIGH FIDELITY
71982
YW24124
Tree Pub. Co., Inc. (BMI) 2:18
Produced by Jerry Kennedy
Vocal
** IT'S SURE GONNA HURT **
(Dolly Parton & Bill Owens)
DOLLY PARTON
With The Merry Melody Singers
FOR BROADCAST ONLY · NOT FOR SALE · MERCURY RECORD CORP. · CHICAGO, ILL. · U.S.A.

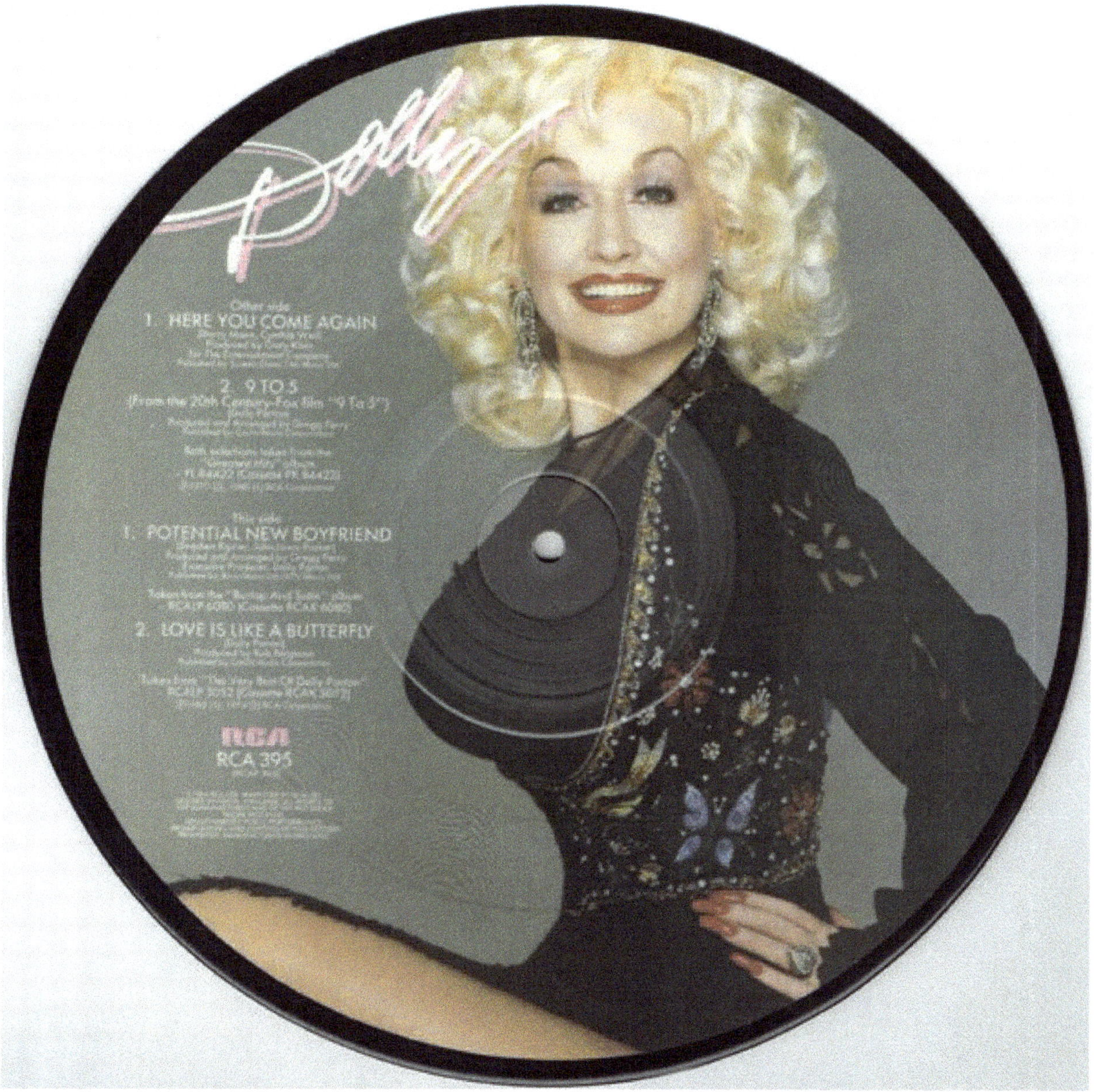

Dolly
1. HERE YOU COME AGAIN
2. 9 TO 5
1. POTENTIAL NEW BOYFRIEND
2. LOVE IS LIKE A BUTTERFLY
RCA
RCA 395

Dolly
REAL LOVE
DUET WITH KENNY ROGERS
RCA
104448
VICTOR
RCA
REAL LOVE
DOLLY PARTON
(Duet with
KENNY ROGERS)

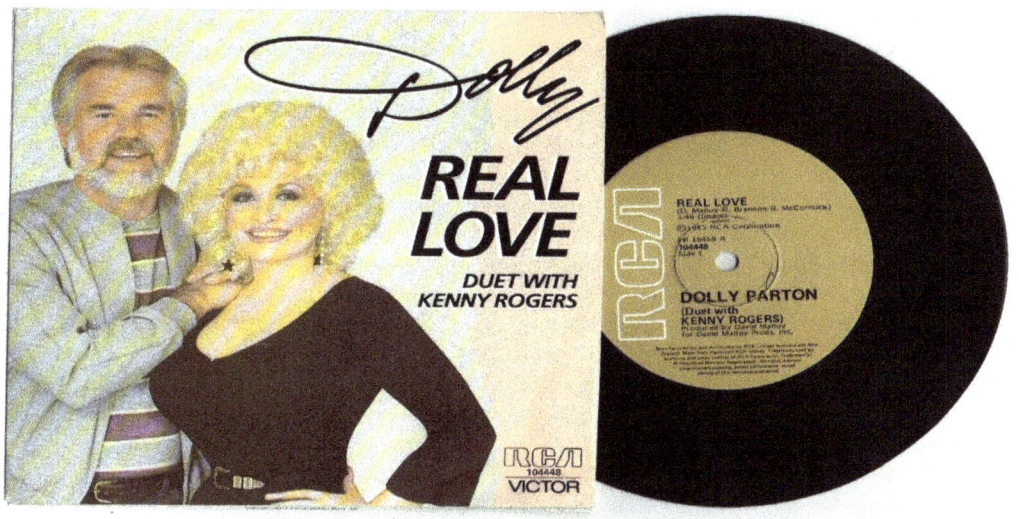

DOLLY PARTON
Two Doors Down
RCA

DOLLY PARTON
5.556
BUSY
SIGNAL
I TOOK HIM FOR GRANTED
LONDON

Dance With
Dolly
Parton
special
disco
mix
BABY I'M
BURNIN'
I WANNA FALL IN LOVE
RCA
PB-1425

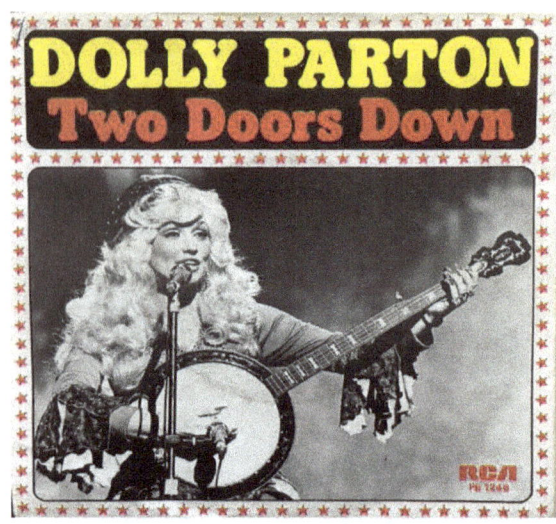

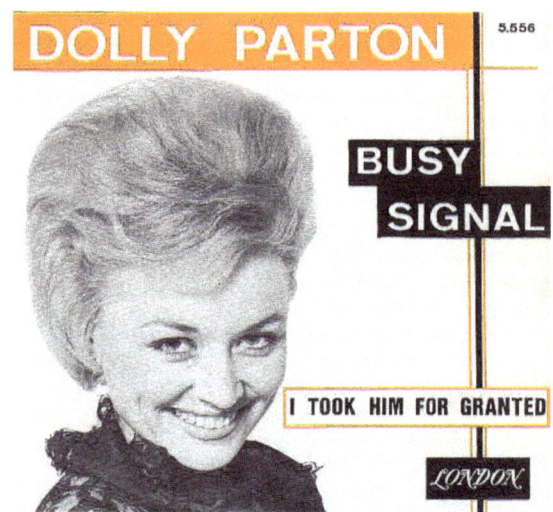

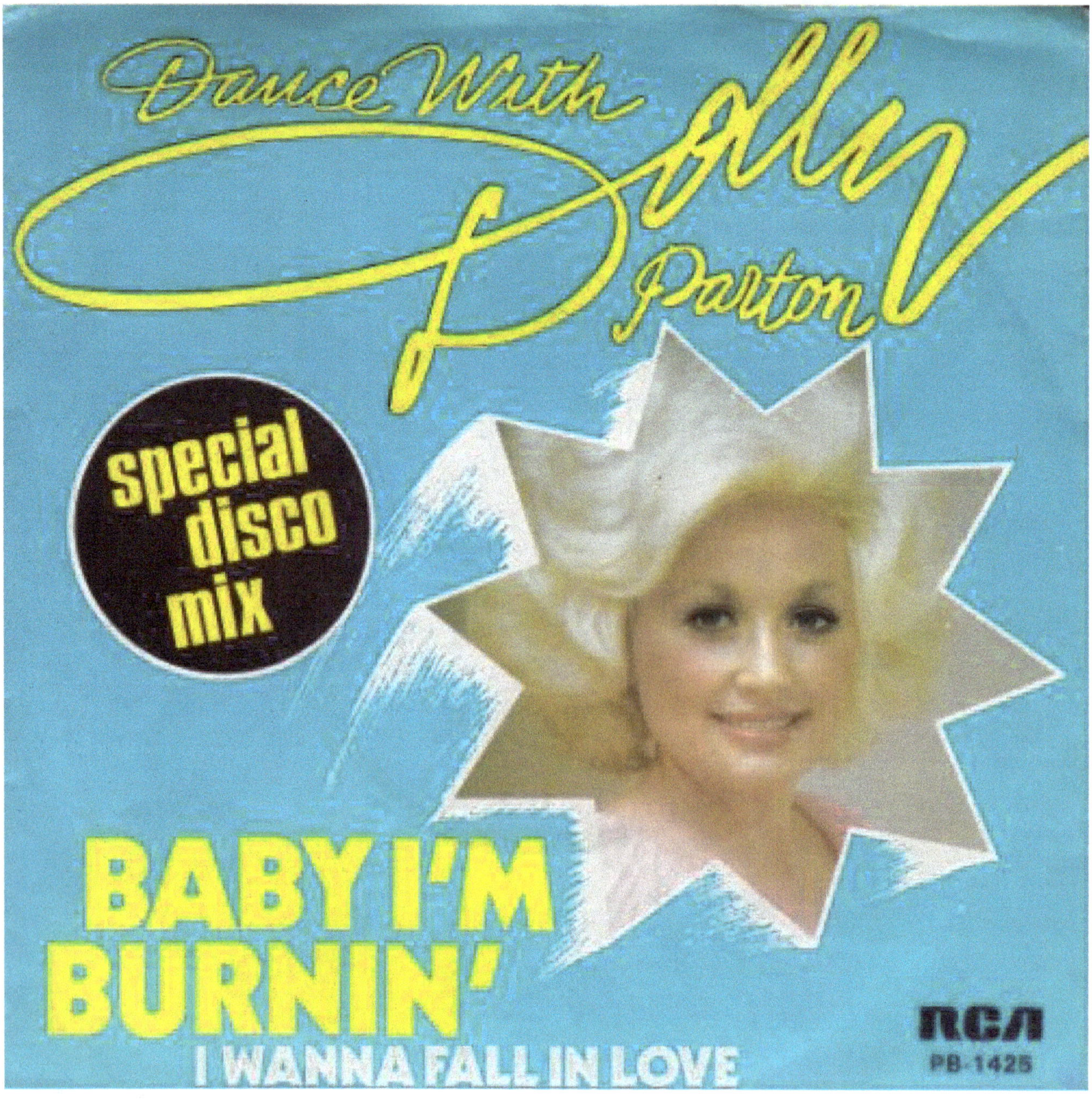

THE RIGHT COMBINATION

Words and Music by PORTER WAGONER

Recorded by PORTER WAGONER and DOLLY PARTON on RCA VICTOR

CHARLES HANSEN MUSIC and BOOKS / 1860 Broadway / New York, New York 10023

OWEPAR PUBLISHING, INC. 95¢

Here You Come Again

Music by BARRY MANN Words by CYNTHIA WEIL
Recorded by DOLLY PARTON on RCA RECORDS

1524HSMX

Columbia Pictures Publications
16333 N.W. 54th Ave., Hialeah, Florida 33014
SCREEN GEMS-EMI MUSIC INC.
and SUMMERHILL SONGS INC.
$1.50

IF TEARDROPS WERE PENNIES

words and music by
CARL BUTLER

as recorded by
PORTER WAGONER
and DOLLY PARTON on RCA

PEER-SOUTHERN PUBLICATIONS
1740 Broadway, New York, N.Y. 10019

The Greatest Gift Of All

As recorded by KENNY ROGERS and DOLLY PARTON

Words and Music by JOHN JARVIS

JOLENE

Words and Music by **DOLLY PARTON**

Recorded by **DOLLY PARTON** on RCA RECORDS

exclusive distributor
SCREEN GEMS-COLUMBIA PUBLICATIONS
a division of
COLUMBIA PICTURES INDUSTRIES, INC.
6744 N.E. 4th Avenue, Miami, Fla. 33138

Includes Dolly Parton Singing "9 To 5"

9 TO 5

―― ORIGINAL MOTION PICTURE SOUNDTRACK ――
MUSIC BY CHARLES FOX

The film "9 To 5" is doing business 'round the clock in all markets!

STOCK THE HIT SOUNDTRACK NOW!

Contact your local RCA Branch for promotional material.

A 20th Century-Fox Film

Manufactured and Distributed by RCA Records

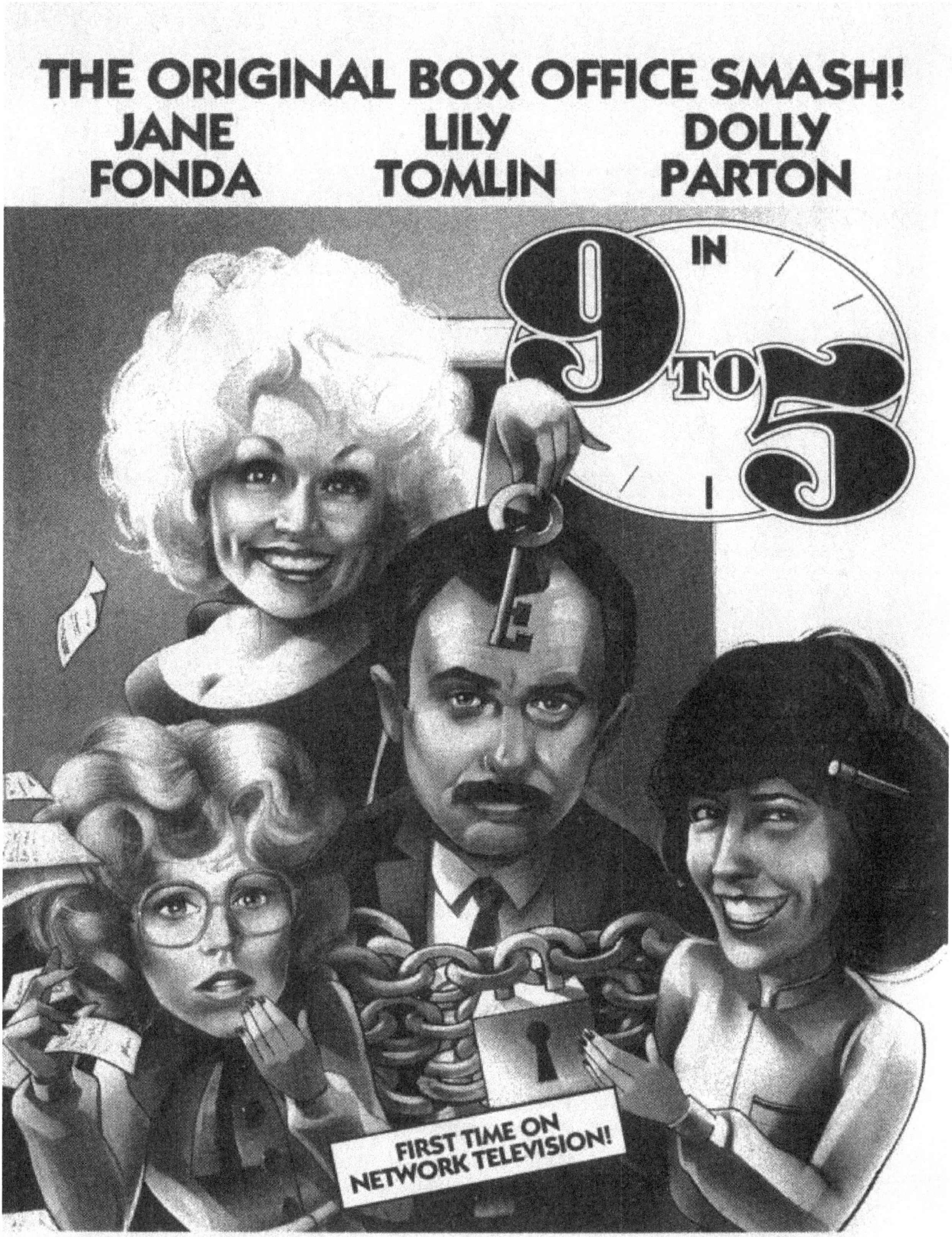

THE ORIGINAL BOX OFFICE SMASH!
JANE FONDA
LILY TOMLIN
DOLLY PARTON
IN
9 TO 5
FIRST TIME ON NETWORK TELEVISION!
Also starring Dabney Coleman, Elizabeth Wilson and Sterling Hayden
A CBS SPECIAL MOVIE PRESENTATION
9PM CBS 15,21,43
FEBRUARY
LOOKS GREAT

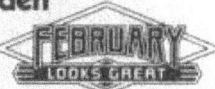

"I had this little doll made of a corncob and Daddy made her a cornsilk wig." – Dolly Parton

AND NOW THERE IS...ONLY ONE
Dolly Parton
LIMITED EDITION COLLECTORS DOLL

Now, the flamboyant and versatile sweetheart of country and pop music–Dolly Parton–has been captured in a doll as exciting as the lady herself!

For years Dolly Parton fans have been wanting a doll of collector's quality that would immortalize their "queen of music and movies".

Ms. Parton recently agreed to have this doll made, and chose the Goldberger Doll people to create it — in the same superior manner that they have made unique dolls for seventy years.

The face had to capture her expression.

There were many initial designs submitted by various artists. However, it was the world renowned sculptor, Neil Estern who made a face that was so much like Dolly's—that everyone expected her to open her mouth and start singing, "9 to 5"!

After the hard part was accomplished, step by step every detail of the doll was attended to...under the watchful eye of Dolly Parton. The hair style had to be pretty and current, the choice of gown had to be theatrical, without being gaudy. Progress was slow, but worth the effort.

The doll had to be remarkable, and worthy of being a limited edition collectible.

Dolly Parton grew up the fourth in a family of twelve children, and her father was a struggling dirt farmer. Her only doll was made of a corncob, so she wanted to be sure that people who bought her doll would get their money's worth. And they surely will!

Dolly Parton IN CONCERT

The Dolly Parton In Concert Doll...
★ Has been meticulously sculpted, down to the beauty mark on her chin.
★ Shows off magnificent painted eyes.
★ Is 18 inches tall.
★ Has long luxuriantly styled, rooted blonde hair.
★ Is dressed in a simulated gold lamé evening gown, her veil cover-up displaying dozens of sparkling ornaments.
★ Comes with presentation stand.

Her arms are raised awaiting your applause. And, we think you will applaud this truly magnificent doll that is so lifelike she will take front-row center in your collection.

CMSA MEMBERS GET 15% OFF!

TO JOIN: Simply check the box in the coupon below and add $12 to the discounted price (you pay $99.40 complete.) You get an extra year of Country Music with your membership.

Mail To: Country Music Society, Dept. JF, 450 Park Ave. So., N.Y., N.Y. 10016

YES, send my **DOLLY DOLL** for $99.95 plus $2.45 shipping, handling and insurance. I understand this is a limited edition of 25,000 and I will receive a Certificate of Authenticity.

Enclosed find: ☐ personal check ☐ money order (no COD's)
☐ I am a Society member so I pay only $84.95 plus $2.45.

My membership ID no. is _____
Name _____
Street _____
City _____ State _____ Zip _____
Charge my ☐ MasterCard ☐ VISA   Expir. Date _____
Card No. _____ Signature _____
☐ Sign me up in the CMSA and send my doll. I've included $12 for one year.

1285-4

Who Hasn't?

A promotional picture from *A Christmas to Remember*
Kenny Roger & Dolly Parton

The green vinyl promotional pressing for *Starting Over Again* from 1980. This copy has a misprint in the title.

Live Albums →

A Real Live Dolly
LSP–4387

Track Listing:
Introduction by Cas Walker – Wasbash Cannon Ball / You Gotta Be My Baby / Tall Man / Medley: Dumb Blonde – Something Fishy – Put It Off Until Tomorrow / My Blue Ridge Mountain Boy / You All Come (Ya'll Come) / Bloody Bones (A Story for Kids) / Don Howser Makes Presentation / Comedy By Speck Rhodes / *Run That By Me One More Time / *Jeannie's Afraid Of The Dark / *Tomorrow Is Forever / *Two Sides To Every Story / *How Great Thou Art
(*With Porter Wagoner)

Production Information:
Produced by: Bob Ferguson
Recorded at: Live at Sevier County High School in Sevierville Tennessee on April 25, 1970.
Engineers: Al Pachucki
Assistant Engineers: Roy Shockley and Bill Vandevort
Cover Photography: Les Leverett

Album Data:
Highest Chart Position: # 32 on August 14, 1970
Billboard Chart: Hot Country Albums
Number of weeks on chart: 4

Notes / Trivia:

- This album was released on LP and 8 Track on June 29, 1970.
- This album was also issued in the Quad format on LP, 8–Track and Open reel tape.
- Eight songs performed that day were edited from the release: "Just Because I'm a Woman," "In the Good Old Days (When Times Were Bad)," "Daddy Come and Get Me," "He's a Go–Getter," "Just the Way I Am," "Coat of Many Colors," "Chicken Every Sunday," and a reprise of "Tall Man."
- April 25, 1970 was the second annual "Dolly Parton Day" in Dolly's hometown of Sevierville and this concert was a benefit show at her Alma Mater to establish a scholarship fund and purchase musical instruments for students at the school.

In Concert With Host Charley Pride
CPL2–1014

Track Listing:
Kaw–Liga – Charley Pride
Mississippi Cotton Picking Delta Town – Charley Pride
Louisiana Man – Charley Pride
Jolene – Dolly Parton
Love Is Like a Butterfly – Dolly Parton
That Girl Who Waits On Tables – Ronnie Milsap
Medley: Slippin' and Slidin' – I'm In Love Again – Johnny B. Goode – Whole Lotta Shakin' Goin' On' – Ronnie Milsap
Kiss An Angel Good Mornin' – Charley Pride
Chaplin in New Shoes – Chet Atkins
The Entertainer (Theme from the motion picture THE STING) – Chet Atkins
Rollin' In My Sweet Baby's Arms – Ronnie Milsap and Dolly Parton
Let's Sing Our Song – Jerry Reed
A Thing Called Love – Jerry Reed
Lord, Mr. Ford – Jerry Reed
Coat of Many Colors – Dolly Parton
The Bargain Store – Dolly Parton
Out of Hand – Gary Stewart
Colonel Bogey – Chet Atkins and Jerry Reed
For The Good Times – Charley Pride
John Henry (Traditional) – Chet Atkins and Jerry Reed

Notes / Trivia

- This 90 minute concert program was broadcast on April 11, 1975 on ABC–TV. Taped at Grand Ole Opry – 2802 Opryland Drive, Nashville, Tennessee.
- This television special was recorded by RCA Records and released as a double album.
- Dolly's version of "Jolene" recorded live during this concert was nominated for a "Best Vocal Performance, Female" Grammy award.
- This 1972–1975 Friday night ABC TV music series was produced by Dick Clark Productions and featured select performances from several concerts each week.

Great Moments at the Grand Ole Opry
CPL2–1904

Track List:
Dialogue – Ralph Emery – Minnie Pearl / Once A Day – Connie Smith / Apache – Sonny James / Galloping On The Guitar – Chet Atkins / Daddy What If – Bobby Bare / I'm Movin' On – Hank Snow / Where No One Stands Alone – Don Gibson / Coat Of Many Colors – Dolly Parton / Highway Headin' South – Porter Wagoner / He'll Have To Go – Jim Reeves / Make Friends – Archie Campbell with Johnny Russell / Just In Case – Ronnie Milsap / Word Games – Billy Walker / Country Sunshine – Dottie West / It's That Time Of The Night – Jim Ed Brown

Production Information:
Re– Issue Producer: Ralph Emery
Recorded by: Al Pachuchi in RCA's "Nashville Sound" Studios, Nashville, TN
Album Design: Pinwheel Studios / Herb Burnette

Notes / Trivia:
- "Stories and Songs Told And Sung By The Stars Of The Grand Ole Opry." Each performer recounts their "Opry Moments" prior to their song.
- Came with a souvenir program CPL2–1904
- Also released on a double length cassette tape: CPK2–1904 and 8–Track CPS2–1904
- Released in a two LP set in Japan as RCA–9125A/9126B
- This is a compilation of recorded work dated between 1972 – 1976 by various original producers. Some recordings are older than 1972 and were recorded in Monophonic.

The Japanese version. The OBI strip is removable.

Souvenir program for *Great Moments at the Grand Old Opry.*

Heartsongs: Live from Home
MME –70050

Track Listing:
Heartsong / "I'm Thinking Tonight of My Blue Eyes" / Mary Of The Wild Moor / In The Pines / My Blue Tears /Applejack / Coat Of Many Colors / Smoky Mountain Memories / Night Train To Memphis / What A Friend We Have In Jesus / Hold Fast To The Right / Walter Henry Hagan / Barbara Allen / Brave Little Soldier / To Daddy / True Blue / Longer Than Always / Wayfaring Stranger / My Tennessee Mountain Home / Heartsong (Reprise) / Cas Walker Theme / Black Draught Theme / PMS Blues

Production Information:
Produced by: Steve Buckingham and Dolly Parton
Recorded at: Dollywood, Pigeon Forge, TN on April 23–24, 1994
Cover Photography: Timothy White

Singles Released From This Album:
"To Daddy" b/w "PMS Blues" – October 10, 1994

Musicians:
Piano: Hargus "Pig" Robbins
Fiddle: Mairead Nimahonaigh / Ciaran Tourish / Jimmy Matthingly / Alison Krauss
Flute: Frankie Kennedy
bouzouki: Ciaran Curran
Guitar: Daithi Gproule / Randy Scruggs / Bruce Watkins / Steve Buckingham / Carl Jackson
Drums: Harry Stinson
Upright Bass: Roy Huskey Jr. / Viktor Krauss
Banjo: Ron Block / Robbie Mercury / David Lindley
Mandolin: Ronnie McCoury / Adam Steffey
Accordion: Dermot Bryne
Uilleann Pipes: Jerry O'Sullivan
Dobro: Jerry Douglas
Bronson Acoustic Steel, Hawaiian Acoustic Steel, Dulcimer, Autoharp, Claw hammer: David Lindley
Vocals:Alison Krauss / Suzanne Cox / Rhonda Vincent / Darrin Vincent / Carl Jackson / Jennifer O'Brien–Enoch / Richard Dennison / Lisa Silver / Louis Nunley / Altan / Mairead Nimahonaigh

Album Data:
Highest Chart Position: # 16 on November 11, 1994
Billboard Chart: Hot Country Albums
Number of weeks on chart: 18

Notes / Trivia:
- This album was released on CD and Cassette on September 27, 1994
- Dolly's original rendition of the song "To Daddy," recorded in 1976, was intended to appear on her *All I Can Do* album, but was ultimately not included on the album; the recording later appeared on her 1995 compilation "The Essential Dolly Parton One." But was released from this 1994 album on a 7" vinyl single.
- For this album, recorded at her theme park, Dollywood, Dolly wanted to pay tribute to her heritage by featuring a mix of her own songs and traditional Appalachian music. The album's design was to showcase Dolly's Appalachian roots and the region's musical descent from the music of places such as Ireland, Scotland, and Wales.
- The budget reissue is missing 1 song which is the title track: "Heartsongs."

Back of the CD case

Live and Well
SUG–CD–3998

Track Listing:
Orange Blossom Special / Train Train / The Grass Is Blue / Mountain Angel / Shine / Little Sparrow / Rocky Top / My Tennessee Mountain Home / Coat of Many Colors / Smoky Mountain Memories / Applejack / Marry Me / Halos and Horns / I'm Gone / Dagger Through the Heart / If / After the Gold Rush / 9 to 5 / Jolene / A Cappella Medley: Islands in the Stream – Here You Come Again – Why'd You Come in Here Lookin' Like That – Two Doors Down / We Irish / Stairway to Heaven / I Will Always Love You

Production Information:
Produced by: Dolly Parton with Gary Davis and the Blueniques
Recorded at: The Celebrity Theater, Dollywood, Pigeon Forge, TN
Mixed at: Southern Sound Studios, Knoxville, TN
Mastered at Soundcurrent Mastering by Seva David–Louis Ball
Cover Photography: Dennis Carney
Album Design: Sue Meyer Design

Musicians:
Acoustic Guitar: Gary Davis / Richard Dennison / Kent Wells
Banjo: Gary Davis
Richard Dennison keyboards, vocals
Randy Kohrs resonator guitar, vocals
Fiddle: Jimmy Mattingly
Mandolin: Brent Truitt
Drums: Steve Turner
Acoustic Bass Guitar: Jay Weaver
Background Vocals: Richard Dennison / Randy Kohrs / Kent Wells

Album Data:
Highest Chart Position: # 22 on October 1, 2004
Billboard Chart: Top Country Albums
Number of weeks on chart: 14

Notes / Trivia:
- This album was released on September 14, 2004.
- Recorded during the *Halos and Horns* tour during the final two concerts on December 12 and 13, 2002 at Dollywood in Pigeon Forge, TN just after Dolly returned home for the European part of the tour.

- During the program, Dolly herself plays many instruments including guitar, harmonica, penny whistle and dulcimer. Both the album and the DVD include Dolly's fun–loving jokes and gab with the crowd and her band.
- A DVD of the concert was released simultaneously with the album, but sold separately .
- This is a two CD set.

Live And Well DVD

Live from London
925–Butterfly 2AV

Track Listing:
Two Doors Down / Jolene / Backwoods Barbie / Coat of Many Colors / Only Dreamin' / Better Get to Livin' / Shinola / Little Sparrow / The Grass is Blue / Do I Ever Cross Your Mind / Here You Come Again / Islands in the Stream / 9 to 5 / I Will Always Love You / Jesus and Gravity

Production Information:
Produced by: Dolly Parton / Steve Summers
Recorded at: The O2 Arena, London, England on July 5th and 6th 2008
Engineers: Mike Fechner
Mixed by: Frank Filipetti
Mastered by: Robert Hadley at The Mastering Lab Ojai, CA
Photos: Fran Strine
Cover Design and Lay out: Jesse Fine
Art Direction: Steve Summers

Album Data:
Highest Chart Position: # 36 on November 27, 2009
Billboard Chart: Hot Country Albums
Number of weeks on chart: 10

Notes / Trivia:
- This set was released on November 10, 2009.
- Two discs— Concert CD and Concert DVD.
- Recorded July 5th and 6th, 2008 at the O2 in London

Cracker Barrel re–released the set with an alternate cover in 2012 with the live DVD and two "live" bonus tracks.

Live from Glastonbury 2014
88985372951

Track Listing:
Fire Medley: Baby I'm Burning – Great Balls of Fire – Girl on Fire / Why'd You Come in Here Lookin' Like That / Jolene / Blue Smoke / Coat of Many Colors / Rocky Top / Mud Song / Banks of the Ohio / Here You Come Again / Two Doors Down / Islands in the Stream / 9 to 5 / Lay Your Hands on Me (with Richie Sambora) / I Will Always Love You

Production Information:
Produced by: Dolly Parton
Co–producers: Richard Dennison / Tom Rutledge
Executive Producers: Mark Cooper / Alison Howe / Ben Challis
Engineers: Mike Felton

Notes / Trivia:
- This album was released on CD and LP on November 25, 2016
- Recorded at and broadcast from the Glastonbury Festival on June 29, 2014
- The festival staff had been trying to book Dolly since their very first event back in 1970, but the timing of her touring schedule and other business did not work out until now, 44 years later! Dolly was very excited to perform at Glastonbury.
- Before the show got underway, Dolly received a very special presentation for album sales surpassing 100 million worldwide.

Compilation albums are usually issued after a performer has amassed enough of a recorded catalog of hits to compile together into an album. A "Greatest Hits," a "Best Of" are also compilation albums. Dolly has had close to 200 compilation albums released world–wide. This next section will show just a small amount of what has been issued in no particular release order. To show them all would take another *entire* book! I always thought the term 'compilation' album was a bit odd since all albums are complied for a selection of tapes from either one or more recording sessions.

Think About Love
AHL-1-9508

Track Listing:
Think About Love / It's Such A Heartache / Tie Our Love (In A Double Knot) / She Don't Love You (Like I Love You) / We Had It All / Do I Ever Cross Your Mind / I Can't Help Myself (Sugar Pie, Honey Bunch) / Even A Fool Would Let Go**

Production Information:
Produced by: David Malloy / Dolly Parton / Val Garay / Gregg Perry / Gary Klein
Executive Producer: Charles Koppelman**
Remixed at: Music Mill, Nashville, TN
Re–Mix engineers: Joe Scaife and Mark Wright
Mastered at: Master Mix, Nashville, TN by Hank Williams
Art Direction: John Coulter Design

Singles Released From This Album:
"We had It All" b/w "Do I Ever Cross Your Mind" – August 18, 1986 (peaked at # 31 on Billboard's Hot Country Singles chart)

Album Data:
Highest Chart Position: # 54 on June 20, 1986
Billboard Chart: Hot Country Albums
Number of weeks on chart: 7

Notes / Trivia:
- This album was released on LP, 8–Track, Cassette and CD on April 15, 1986.
- This eight song album is a 1986 compilation consisting of previously released tracks. A majority of which were remixes or are alternate takes. This album was conceived and released after Dolly had left the label. The project was under the control of Mark Wright, an executive at RCA in Nashville at the time. Of the eight tracks, only three appear to be unaltered from their original release: "It's Such a Heartache", "Tie Our Love (In a Double Knot)" and "Even a Fool Would Let Go." The remaining tracks have all been remixed. "Think About Love" differs dramatically from the version on the *Real Love* album with the addition of the lyric "Think about love" before the bridge, a shortened instrumental section, much louder drum overdubs and a punchier mix overall. This version is actually the single remix and is the version that was played on the radio

during its chart run and released on 45, but it has never been re–released on any CD. "We Had It All" is a completely different vocal take from the version on *The Great Pretender* album. Instead of the piano being the primary instrument, this time the song is driven by an acoustic guitar. This remixed version of "We Had It All" was released as a single in the fall of 1986 and would reach # 31 on the country singles chart in the U.S.

8-Track Cartridge Tape

The Best of Porter & Dolly
LSP-4556

Track Listing:
Just Someone I Used to Know / Daddy Was an Old Time Preacher Man / Tomorrow Is Forever / Jeannie's Afraid of the Dark / The Last Thing on My Mind / The Pain of Loving You / Better Move It on Home / Holding On to Nothin' / Run That by Me One More Time / We'll Get Ahead Someday

Production Information:
Produced by: Bob Ferguson
Recorded at: RCA's "Nashville Sound" Studios, studios A & B, Nashville, TN
Engineers: Al Pachucki / Jim Malloy / Chuck Seitz
Assistant Engineer: Roy Shockley
Cover Photography: Les Leverett
Liner Notes: Paul W. Soelberg, July 1971 (Nashville Publicist)

Album Data:
Highest Chart Position: # 7 on August 20, 1971
Billboard Chart: Hot Country Albums
Number of weeks on chart: 20

Notes / Trivia:
- This album was released on LP and 8-Track on July 19, 1971
- In a review by *Billboard* in the July 31, 1971 issue they said, "This collection of the best performances by Porter Wagoner and Dolly Parton is sure to prove a blockbuster programming and sales item. Their top treatments of "Daddy Was an Old Time Preacher Man," "The Pain of Loving You," "The Last Thing on My Mind" and "Just Someone I Used to Know" are standouts."
- *Cashbox* published its review on July 24, 1971 and said, "One whole lot of sales power in this album from a duo that consistently hits the charts together and apart. The most recent hit here included is "Better Move It on Home" while other titles will be equally familiar to their large following: "Just Someone I Used to Know," "The Pain of Loving You" and "Holding on to Nothin'" just to mention a few. A musical marriage made in country heaven."

**The album was also released in Japan in 1979.
The OBI strip at the left is removable.**

Side 1 label from 1979 Japanese RCA Records release

Dolly Parton Her Greatest Hits and Finest Performances
446-RM-28498

Record One:
9 to 5 / But You Know I Love You / Heartbreaker / Do I Ever Cross Your Mind / Joshua / Old Flames Can't Hold a Candle to You / Here You Come Again / It's All Wrong But It's All Right / Baby, I'm Burning / Two Doors Down / I Really Got the Feeling / I Will Always Love You

Record Two:
Islands in the Stream / Sweet Summer Lovin' / You're the Only One / Lost Forever in Your Kiss / All I Can Do / Please Don't Stop Loving Me / Heartbreak Express / If Teardrops Were Pennies / Touch Your Woman / We Used To / Hey, Lucky Lady / Just Someone I Used to Know

Record Three:
The Right Combination / Making Plans / Tomorrow is Forever / If You Go, I'll Follow You / We'll Get Ahead Someday / Is Forever Longer Than Always / The Last Thing on My Mind / Holding On to Nothing / Better Move It On Home / Yours, Love / Together Always / Say Forever You'll Be Mine

Record Four:
Coat of Many Colors / My Tennessee Mountain Home / Dark As a Dungeon / Daddy Was An Old Time Preacher Man / Washday Blues / Appalachian Memories / Preacher Tom / Sacred Memories / My Blue Ridge Mountain Boy / In the Good Old Days (When Times Were Bad) / Applejack / Tennessee Homesick Blues

Record Five:
Down from Dover / Single Woman / Traveling Man / Where Beauty Lives In Memory / The House of the Rising Sun / Jeannie's Afraid of the Dark / The Seeker / Wings of a Dove / I Believe / There / When I Sing for Him / How Great Thou Art

Record Six:
Mule Skinner Blues (Blue Yodel # 8) / Detroit City / I Walk the Line / D–I–V–O–R–C–E / Release Me (ans Let Me Love Again) / Great Balls of Fire / She Don't Love You (Like I Love You) / We'll Sing in the Sunshine / I Can't Help Myself (Sugar Pie, Honey Bunch) / Downtown / Save the Last Dance for Me

Record Seven:
Love is Like a Butterfly / The Bargain Store / Me and Little Andy / A Cowboy's Ways / Burning the Midnight Oil / Send Me the Pillow You Dream On / Jolene / Sandy's Song / Light of a Clear Blue Morning / Working Girl / Starting Over Again

Notes / Trivia:

- This is a major compilation consisting of 7 full length albums in a hard case box.
- Released in 1985 in the US and 1986 in Canada on LP and cassette tape.
- In 1985 Readers Digest also released a single LP titled Dolly Parton – 12 of Her Biggest Hits with a similar track line up to disc one of this release.

The Great Dolly Parton Vol.1
CDS–1171

Track Listing:
D–I–V–O–R–C–E / Love and Learn / Big Wind / Mule Skinner Blues / Daddy / She Never Met a Man (She Didn't Like) / I Wish I Felt This Way at Home / Love Isn't Free / The Only Way Out / Try Being Lonely / You're Gonna be Sorry / We Had All The Good Things Going

Notes / Trivia:

- This album was released on LP and Cassette in 1979 by Camden in the UK
- Material is from 1969–1974

The cassette issue of the album / CAM 482

The Great Dolly Parton Vol.2
CDS-1184

Track Listing:
Mine / Don't Let It Trouble Your Mind / More Than Their Share / Little Bird / Mama Say a Prayer / In The Ghetto / The Carroll County Accident / But You Loved Me Then / I'm Doing This For Your Sake / Chas / When Possession Get Too Strong

Notes / Trivia:

- This album was released on LP and Cassette in 1980 by Camden in the UK
- Material is from 1969–1970

The cassette issue of the album / CAM 489

Best Of Dolly
5706–1–R

Track Listing:
Don't Call It Love / Save the Last Dance for Me / Real Love" (with Kenny Rogers) / *We Had It All
Tie Our Love (In a Double Knot) / Think About Love / Potential New Boyfriend / *Do I Ever Cross Your Mind / Tennessee Homesick Blues

Production Information:
Produced by: David Malloy / Val Garay / Gregg Perry / Dolly Parton / Mike Post
*Over–dubbed and mixed by: Mark Wright and Joe Scaife
Mastered by: Hank Williams at Master Mix, Nashville
Art Direction: Mary Hamilton
Design: Katherine DeVault Design

Notes / Trivia:

- This album was released on LP, cassette and CD on September 22, 1987.
- This is Best of Vol. 3 though that is not stated on the cover, though it is on the spine of the LP and on the label of the LP, CD and Cassette.
- "Tennessee Homesick Blues" is a song that was written and recorded by Dolly for the 1984 film *Rhinestone*. Released on May 28, 1984 as a single it peaked at # 1 in the US on September 8, 1984 on the Hot Country Songs Chart and it also peaked at # 1 in Canada on the Canadian *RPM* Country Tracks .
- The album, strangely enough, did not chart and almost no promotion was given to it.
- This album contains the remixes of "We Had It All" and "Do I Ever Cross Your Mind" first released on the 1986 compilation album "Think About Love." (AHL–1–9508)

Greatest Hits
AHL-1-4422

Track Listing:
9 to 5 / But You Know I Love You / Heartbreak Express / Old Flames Can't Hold a Candle to You / Applejack / Me and Little Andy / Here You Come Again / Hard Candy Christmas / Two Doors Down / It's All Wrong, But it's All Right / Do I Ever Cross Your Mind / I Will Always Love You

Production Information:
Mastered by: Glenn Meadows at Masterfonics, Nashville, TN
Cover Photography: Ron Slenzak
Back cover / interior gate-fold Photography: Ed Caraeff / Herb Ritts / Ron Slenzak / Richard Avedon / Steve Shapiro / Nick Sangiamo / Dennis Carney / 20th Century Fox / Universal
Art Direction and Design: Phyllis Chotin & Michele Hart / Media Arts

Album Data:
Highest Chart Position: # 7 on November 19, 1982
Billboard Chart: Hot Country Albums
Number of weeks on chart: 96

Notes / Trivia:

- This album was released on LP, 8-Track and Cassette on September 21, 1982
- On the 1983 re-issue one song was changed out. "Islands in the Stream" replaced "Hard Candy Christmas" on side two. The 1983 re-issue did not have a gate-fold cover.
- The album was reissued again in 1989 minus the cuts "Applejack," "Heartbreak Express," "Me and Little Andy" and "Hard Candy Christmas."
- This release was certified gold on October 31, 1983 and certified platinum on October 7, 1986.

The Best Of Dolly Parton
LSP–4449

Track Listing:
Mule Skinner Blues / Down From Dover / My Blue Ridge Mountain Boy / In The Good Old Days (When Times Were Bad) / Gypsy, Joe and Me / In The Ghetto / Just Because I'm A Woman / Daddy Come and Get Me / How Great Thou Art / Just The Way I Am

Production Information:
Produced by: Bob Ferguson
Recorded at: RCA Victor's "Nashville Sound" Studios, Nashville, TN
Engineer: Al Pachucki
Assistant Engineer: Roy Shockley and Bill Vandevort
Cover Photography: Les Leverett

Singles Released From This Album:
"Mule Skinner Blue's" b/w "More Than Their Share" – June 22, 1970 (peaked at # 3 on August 28, 1970)

Album Data:
Highest Chart Position: # 12
Billboard Chart: Hot Country Albums

Notes / Trivia:

- This album was released on LP, 8–Track and Cassette on November 9, 1970.
- The track "Mule Skinner Blues" was recorded on May 4, 1970 just ahead of the sessions for *The Golden Streets of Glory* album. But it is not known if the song was meant for any other album than this *Best of*. Other than this album the track appeared on the 2 LP compilation: "This Is The Nashville Sound" released in 1971.
- The flip side of *Mule Skinner Blues— More Than Their Share,* was taken from the album *The Fairest of Them All* and was recorded October 31, 1969
- Recorded December 18, 1967– May 12, 1970
- This album was certified Gold by the RIAA on June 12, 1978, for sales of over 500,000 copies.
- Dolly earned her first solo Grammy nomination for "Mule Skinner Blues (Blue Yodel No. 8)." It was nominated for *Best Female Country Vocal Performance* at the 13th Annual Grammys.
- This is the authors favorite Dolly Parton "Best Of" collection.

Best of Dolly Parton
AHL-1-1117

Track Listing:
Jolene / Traveling Man / Lonely Comin' Down / The Bargain Store / Touch Your Woman / I Will Always Love You / Love Is Like A Butterfly / Coat of Many Colors / My Tennessee Mountain Home / When I Sing For Him

Production Information:
Produced and Arranged by: Porter Wagoner
Recorded at: RCA Victor's "Nashville Sound" Studios, Nashville, TN
Engineers: Tom Pick / Al Pachucki
Assistant Engineer: Roy Shockley / Mike Shockley
Cover Photography: Dennis Carney
Art Direction: Bob Jones

Album Data:
Highest Chart Position: # 5 on October 10, 1975
Billboard Chart: Hot Country Albums
Number of weeks on chart: 47

Notes / Trivia:

- This album was released on LP, 8-Track and Cassette on July 14, 1975.
- The album's original release included an 11 x 20" poster and a gate-fold cover.

The LP's gate-fold interior photo was used as the CD re-issue cover.

As Long As I Love
SLP–18136

Track Listing:
Why, Why, Why / I Wound Easy / I Don't Want You Around Me Anymore / Hillbilly Willy / This Boy Has Been Hurt / Daddy Won't Be Home Anymore / As Long As I Love / A Habit I Can't Break / I'm Not Worth The Tears / I Don't Trust Me Around You / I Couldn't Wait Forever / Too Lonely Too Long

Production Information:
Produced by: Fred Foster
Recorded at: Monument Recording Studio, Nashville, TN
Engineer: Tommy Strong
Arranger and Conductor: Bill Walker
Cover Photography: Bill Goodwin
Art Direction: Ken Kim

Notes / Trivia:

- This album was released on June 8, 1970 on LP.
- *As Long As I Love* consisted of two tracks previously issued and ten that had been unreleased up to that point.
- *Billboard* published a review on June 20, 1970, which read, "Although Dolly Parton is now on another label, this album should draw considerable attention from her legion of fans. And the selections, such as "I Don't Want You Around Me Anymore," "Too Lonely Too Long," and the title song. "Daddy Won't Be Home Anymore" is another first–rate number."
- In a June 27, 1970 review *Cashbox* printed, "Here are some old Dolly Parton sides that her fans should enjoy. Most of the songs on the set are Dolly's own compositions (some of them are co–cleffings with Bill Owens), and "Why, Why, Why", "I Don't Want You Around Me Anymore," "As Long as I Love," "Too Lonely Too Long," and the other numbers on the set should please many. LP should fare nicely."
- On June 13, 1970 a *Record World* review of the album said; "Dolly's new release on her old label is unique in that all but three tunes are self–penned. If you like the singing of Miss Dolly and the songwriting combo of Owens and Parton, then you'll go for the East Tennessee beauty's new release. Gal shows why she's so firmly established.

16 Biggest Hits
88697 13481 2

Track Listing:
Here You Come Again / 9 to 5 / Jolene / Islands in the Stream (duet with Kenny Rogers) / I Will Always Love You / Coat of Many Colors / The Seeker / Two Doors Down / Single Women / All I Can Do / Heartbreak Express / Don't Call it Love / Love is Like a Butterfly / Rockin' Years (duet with Ricky Van Shelton) / Why'd You Come In Here Lookin' Like That / Romeo (with Billy Ray Cyrus, Tanya Tucker, Mary Chapin Carpenter, Kathy Mattea and Pam Tillis)

Production Information:
Producers: Albhy Galuten / Barry Gibb / Bob Ferguson / David Malloy / Dolly Parton / Gary Klein / Gregg Perry / Karl Richardson / Mike Post / Porter Wagoner / Ricky Skaggs / Steve Buckingham
Compilation produced by: Rob Santos
Original 2009 CD mastered at: Sonopress Arvato
Vinyl Mastered by: Vic Anesini at Sony Music Studios, New York
LP Cover Photography: Mark Sennet / Shooting Star
LP Art Direction: Bob Goodman
LP Design: Pat Moroney / Morony Advertising

Original 2008 CD Data:
Highest Chart Position: # 32 on April 18, 2008
Billboard Chart: Hot Country Albums
Number of weeks on chart: 69

Notes / Trivia:

- This album was originally released on CD in August 2007. Re–issued in January 2011 with different cover art.
- This album was re–issued on LP and CD on July 17, 2020 with the 2011 CD artwork. (LP #19439750711)
- Walmart released a exclusive copy on violet vinyl also using the 2011 CD artwork. This issue came with a code card redeemable at *We Are Vinyl* for a digital download of the album.

Just Between You and Me
LSP–3926

Track Listing:
Because One of Us Was Wrong / The Last Thing on My Mind / Love is Worth Living / Just Between You and Me / Mommie, Ain't That Daddy / Four O Thirty Three / Sorrow's Tearing Down the House (That Happiness Once Built) / This Time Has Got To Be Our Last Time / Before I Met You / Home Is Where the Hurt Is / Two Sides to Every Story / Put It Off Until Tomorrow

Production Information:
Produced by: Bob Ferguson
Recorded at: RCA Victor's "Nashville Sound" Studio, Nashville, TN
Engineer: Jim Malloy

Musicians:
Piano: Hargus "Pig" Robbins
Drums: Jerry Carrigan
Steel Guitar: Pete Drake
Bass: Roy M. Huskey Jr.
Fiddle: Mack Magaha
Rhythm Guitar: George McCormick
Electric Guitar: Wayne Moss
Banjo: Buck Trent
Background Vocals: Anita Carter / Dolores Edgin

Singles Released From This Album:
"The Last Thing on My Mind" b/w "Love is Worth Living" – October 30, 1967 (peaked at # 7 on *Billboard's* Hot Country Songs chart)

Album Data:
Highest Chart Position: # 8 on
Billboard Chart: Hot Country Albums
Number of weeks on chart: 27

Notes / Trivia:
- This album was released on LP on January 15, 1968
- The B–side of the album's single, "Love Is Worth Living," (written by Dolly Parton) was a success in Canada, peaking at # 4 on the *RPM* Country Singles chart.
- The album was recorded in three sessions on October 10, 11 and 12, 1967

- The duo had their first recording session together on October 10, 1967 at RCA Studio A in Nashville recording the title cut of the album *Just Between You and Me*. Dolly's first three sessions for RCA were limited to duets with Porter as she could not record for RCA as a solo artist until her contract with Monument expired.
- Dolly made her first TV appearance with Porter on September 5, 1967 and a little more than a week later the duo first appeared in concert together on September 14, in Lebanon, Virginia. The crowd greeted Dolly with boos and chants for Norma Jean, who had been Porter's previous singing partner since 1961 and who had left Porter's show when she married Jody Taylor, whom she would later divorce.
- Wagoner and Parton made their first Grand Ole Opry appearance together on November 25, 1967.
- A January 27, 1968 *Billboard* review of the album said "The bouncy, uptempo "The Last Thing on My Mind" heads up the list of 12 enjoyable tunes on this LP combining two exciting voices. Soloing or combining, this duo balances out to singing that exceptional. Miss Parton wrote four of the songs. The twangy arrangement is groovy."

Just The Two Of Us
LSP-4039

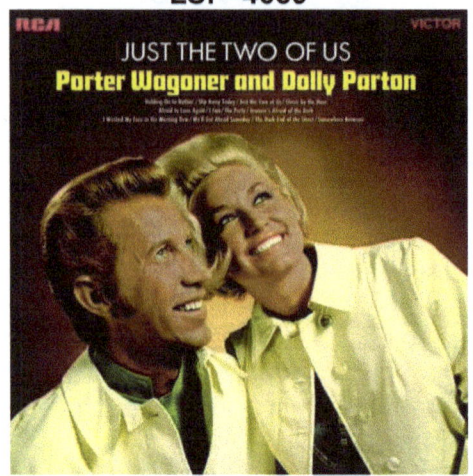

Track Listing:
Closer by the Hour / I Washed My Face in the Morning Dew / Jeannie's Afraid of the Dark / Holding on to Nothin' / Slip Away Today / The Dark End of the Street / Just the Two of Us / Afraid to Love Again / We'll Get Ahead Someday / Somewhere Between / The Party / I Can

Production Information:
Produced by: Bob Ferguson
Recorded at: RCA Victor's "Nashville Sound" Studio, Nashville, TN
Engineer: Al Pachucki

Musicians:
Drums: Jerry Carrigan
Steel Guitar: Pete Drake
Bass: Roy M. Huskey, Jr.
Fiddle: Mack Magaha
Rhythm Guitar: George McCormick
Electric Guitar: Wayne Moss / Jerry Stembridge
Piano: Hargus "Pig" Robbins
Banjo: Buck Trent
Background Vocals: Anita Carter / Dolores Edgin

Singles Released From This Album:
"Holding on to Nothin'" b/w "Just Between You and Me" – March 11, 1968 (peaked at # 7 on the *Billboard* Hot Country Songs chart dated June 1, 1968)
"We'll Get Ahead Someday" b/w "Jeannie's Afraid Of The Dark" – July 1, 1968 (peaked at # 5 on the *Billboard* Hot Country Songs chart dated September 28, 1968)

Album Data:
Highest Chart Position: 5 # on April 5, 1969
Billboard Chart: Hot Country Albums
Number of weeks on chart: 49

Notes / Trivia:
- This album was released on LP on September 9, 1968
- Recording sessions for the album took place at RCA Studio in Nashville, Tennessee, beginning on January 31, 1968. Three additional sessions followed on May 20, 21 and 22, 1968.

- A review *Billboard* published on the album in the September 21, 1968 issue said, "Wagoner and Parton have proved a hot sales combination for the singles charts, and their second LP built around their singles hits, "Holding on to Nothin'," "The Dark End of the Street," and "We'll Get Ahead Someday" is sure to prove a hot piece of album product."
- *Cashbox* also published a review of the album on September 21, 168 saying, "After scoring excellent success with their initial duet LP, as well as with several singles, Porter Wagoner and Dolly Parton launch their second album on the heels of their latest single, "Holding on to Nothin'." Kicking off the set with that track, the twosome also make a winning combination with such additional tracks as "The Dark End of the Street" and "I Washed My Face in the Morning Dew" among others."

Always, Always
LSP–4186

Track Listing:
Milwaukee, Here I Come / Yours Love / I Don't Believe You've Met My Baby / Malena / The House Where Love Lives / Why Don't You Haul Off & Love Me / Always, Always / There Never Was A Time / Good As Gold / My Hands Are Tied / No Reason To Hurry Home / Anything's Better Than Nothing

Production Information:
Produced by: Bob Ferguson
Recorded at: RCA Victor's "Nashville Sound" Studio, Nashville, TN
Engineer: Al Pachucki
Assistant Engineer: Roy M. Shockley

Musicians:
Piano: Hargus "Pig" Robbins / David Briggs
Bass: Bobby Dyson / Roy M. Huskey, Jr.
Drums: Jerry Carrigan
Steel Guitar: Lloyd Green
Electric Guitar: Jerry Stembridge
Fiddle: Mack Magaha
Rhythm Guitar: George McCormick
Guitar: Wayne Moss
Banjo: Buck Trent
Trumpet: Bill McElhiney / Glenn Baxter
Harp: Jean Alrshuler
Background Vocals: June Evelyn Page / Dolores Edgin / Anita Carter / Joseph Babcock / Hurshel Wigginton

Singles Released From This Album:
"Yours Love" b/w "Malena" – February 3, 1969 (peaked at # 9 on the *Billboard* Hot Country Songs chart dated May 10, 1969)
"Always, Always" b/w "No Reason to Hurry Home" – May 19, 1969 (peaked at # 16 on the *Billboard* Hot Country Songs chart dated July 26, 1969)

Album Data:
Highest Chart Position: # 5 on September 19, 1969
Billboard Chart: Hot Country Albums
Number of weeks on chart: 27

Notes / Trivia:
- This album was released on LP and 8–Track on June 30, 1969
- Recording sessions for the album took place at RCA Studios in Nashville, Tennessee, on December 3 and 20, 1968. Three additional sessions took place on April 21, 22 and 23, 1969.
- The song "Why Don't You Haul Off and Love Me" was also recorded by Marie Osmond for MGM Records on December 10, 1973 at Jack Clement Studios in Nashville, but remains unreleased.
- The July 12, 1969 *Billboard* review of the album said, "In the tradition of the country duet, you would have to see far to find another as polished and professional as Porter Wagoner and Dolly Parton—and few of those would be as successful. Here's their hit "Always, Always," and the impactful "Yours Love." Also recommended: "I Don't Believe You've Met My Baby.""
- In a July 12, 1969 *Cashbox* review they said, "Titled after their latest single, this talented twosome offer a powerful package loaded with listening and sales appeal. Set contains twelve oldies and newies, including "Milwaukee, Here I Come," "Why Don't You haul Off & Love Me," "There Never Was a Time," "No Reason to Hurry Home," and "Anything's Better Than Nothing." Expect instant action on this one."

Green Label Promotional copy of Yours Love with Plug

Porter Wayne and Dolly Rebecca
LSP–4305

Track Listing:
Forty Miles From Poplar Bluff / Tomorrow Is Forever / Just Someone I Used To Know / Each Season Changes You / We Can't Let This Happen To Us / Mendy Never Sleeps / Silver Sandals / No Love Left / It Might As Well Be Me / Run That By Me One More Time / I'm Wasting You Time and You're Wasting Mine

Production Information:
Produced by: Bob Ferguson
Recorded at: RCA Victor's "Nashville Sound" Studio, Nashville, TN
Engineer: Al Pachucki
Assistant Engineer: Roy M. Shockley
Cover Photography: Les Leverett

Musicians:
Piano: Hargus "Pig" Robbins
Drums: Jerry Carrigan
Bass: Bobby Dyson / Roy M. Huskey, Jr
Steel Guitar: Pete Drake / Lloyd Green
Rhythm Guitar: George McCormick
Guitar: Wayne Moss / Dale Sellers
Electric Guitar: Jerry Stembridge
Trumpet: Glenn Baxter / Danny Davis / Bill McElhiney
Fiddle: Mack Magaha
Banjo: Buck Trent
Background Vocals: Hurshel Wigginton / Joseph Babcock / Anita Carter / Dolores Edgin / June Evelyn Page

Singles Released From This Album:
"Just Someone I Used to Know" b/w "My Hands Are Tied" – September 29, 1969 (peaked at # 5 on the *Billboard* Hot Country Songs chart dated December 13, 1969 and at # 20 in Canada on the *RPM* Country Singles chart)
"Tomorrow Is Forever" b/w "Mendy Never Sleeps" – January 19, 1970 (peaked at # 9 on the *Billboard* Hot Country Songs chart dated April 4, 1970)
"Tomorrow Is Forever" b/w "Run That by Me One More Time" – (South Africa release only)

Album Data:
Highest Chart Position: # 4 on June 12, 1970
Billboard Chart: Hot Country Albums
Number of weeks on chart: 25

Notes / Trivia:
- This album was released on LP, 8–Track and Cassette on March 9, 1970
- Recording sessions for the album took place at RCA Studios in Nashville, Tennessee, on December 1, 2 and 3, 1969. Two songs on the album were recorded during sessions for 1969's *Always, Always*. "Just Someone I Used to Know" and "Mendy Never Sleeps" were recorded on April 21 and 22, 1969, respectively.
- "My Hands are Tied," flip side to the first single released from the album was recorded April 23, 1969 and was also recorded during sessions for 1969's *Always, Always*.
- "Just Someone I Used to Know" was nominated for Best Country Performance by a Duo or Group at the 12th Annual Grammy Awards. This was Porter's eighth nomination and Dolly's first.
- In the issue of *Billboard* dated March 21, 1970, the magazine said, "This great country duo does "Tomorrow is Forever," their current smash single. In addition to "Forty Miles from Poplar Bluff," "Silver Sandals" and others. It is a powerful package, full of true country flavor."
- In their issue from a week before March 14, 1970, *Cashbox* published a review saying, "Porter Wagoner and Dolly Parton join forces once again and perform an album that's certain to be a smash. The two singers blend their talents on a cluster of good tunes, a number of them the work of Dolly herself (one of these, "Tomorrow Is Forever" is a current single hit for Porter and Dolly). Reserve a spot on the charts for this one."

Green Label Promotional Copy with Plug

Once More
LSP–4388

Track Listing:
Daddy Was An Old Time Preacher Man / I Know You're Married But I Love You Still / Thoughtfulness / Fight and Scratch / Before Our Weakness Gets Too Strong / Once More / One Day at at Time / Ragged Angel / A Good Understanding / Let's Live for Tonight

Production Information:
Produced by: Bob Ferguson
Recorded at: RCA Victor's "Nashville Sound" Studio, Nashville, TN
Engineer: Al Pachucki
Assistant Engineer: Roy M. Shockley
Cover Photography: Les Leverett

Musicians:
Piano: Hargus "Pig" Robbins
Drums: Jerry Carrigan
Steel Guitar: Pete Drake
Bass: Bobby Dyson
Fiddle: Johnny Gimble / Mack Magaha
Guitar: Dave Kirby
Rhythm Guitar: George McCormick
Guitar: Dale Sellers / Jerry Stembridge
Banjo: Buck Trent
Background Vocals: Hurshel Wigginton / Joseph Babcock / Dolores Edgin / June Evelyn Page

Singles Released From This Album:
"Daddy Was An Old Time Preacher Man" b/w "A Good Understanding" – June 29, 1970 (peaked at # 7 on the *Billboard* Hot Country Singles chart and #12 in Canada on the *RPM* Country Singles chart.)

Album Data:
Highest Chart Position: # 7 on October 23, 1970
Billboard Chart: Hot Country Albums
Number of weeks on chart: 24

Notes / Trivia:
- This album was released on LP, 8–Track and Cassette on August 3, 1970
- The album's single, "Daddy Was an Old Time Preacher Man," received a nomination for "Best Country Performance by a Duo or Group" at the 13th Annual Grammy Awards. The single also

- received the Country Award at the 1971 BMI Awards and a Songwriter Achievement Award from the Nashville Songwriters Association International.
- Recording sessions for the album began at RCA Studio in Nashville, Tennessee, on April 21, 1970. Two additional sessions followed on May 5 and 6, 1970.
- On October 14, 1970 Porter and Dolly were presented with the Country Music Association's award for "Best Vocal Duet Group."
- In a review by *Billboard* dated August 15, 1970 they said, "That lilting voice of Dolly Parton's blends perfectly with the lusty sound of Porter Wagoner – as they prove in definitive measure on the hit "Daddy Was an Old Time Preacher Man" – the key sales impetus on this LP. Some outstanding cuts include the tear–jerker "Ragged Angel," the bright and tart "Fight and Scratch," and "Thoughtfulness." Another winning LP from this duo."
- *Cashbox* published a review on August 8, 1970 which said, "Here's the new album release by one of country music's most famous duos, Porter Wagoner and Dolly Parton and it's a powerhouse item all the way. Decker features such tracks as "Daddy Was an Old Time Preacher Man," "I Know You're Married But I Love You Still," "Before Our Weakness Gets Too Strong," "A Good Understanding" and "Let's Live for Tonight." They all get great vocal stylings from the famed duo. Sure to be a biggie in no time."

Two Of A Kind
LSP–4490

Track Listing:
Oh, the Pain of Loving You / Possum Holler / Is It Real? / The Flame / The Fighting Kind / Two of a Kind / All I Need Is You / Curse of the Wild Weed Flower / Today, Tomorrow and Forever / There'll Be Love

Production Information:
Produced by: Bob Ferguson
Recorded at: RCA Victor's "Nashville Sound" Studio, Nashville, TN
Engineer: Al Pachucki
Assistant Engineer: Roy M. Shockley
Cover Photography: Les Leverett

Musicians:
Piano: Hargus "Pig" Robbins / Jerry Smith
Drums: Jerry Carrigan
Steel Guitar: Pete Drake
Bass: Bobby Dyson
Fiddle: Johnny Gimble / Buddy Spicher / Mack Magaha
Guitar: Dave Kirby / Dale Selleras
Mandolin: Mack Magaha
Rhythm Guitar: George McCormick
Trumpet: Donald Sheffield / Glenn Baxter
Banjo: Buck Trent
Background Vocals: Joseph Babcock / Dolores Edgin / June Evelyn Page

Singles Released From This Album:
"Two of a Kind" b/w "Better Move It on Home" – January 26, 1971 (peaked at # 7 on the *Billboard* Hot Country Singles chart on April 10, 1971)

Album Data:
Highest Chart Position: # 13 on May 7, 1971
Billboard Chart: Hot Country Albums
Number of weeks on chart: 14

Notes / Trivia:
- This album was released on LP and 8–Track on February 8, 1971
- Recording sessions for the album took place at RCA Studios in Nashville, Tennessee on December 2, 1970. Three additional sessions followed on December 8, 9 and 14, 1970.

- "There'll Be Love" had been recorded on May 6, 1970 during a session for 1970's *Once More*.
- "Curse of the Wild Weed Flower" is of note for it being an anti–marijuana song, one of the few country songs of the period to discuss drugs. Dolly later re–recorded "Oh, the Pain of Loving You" with Linda Ronstadt and Emmylou Harris, as part of their 1987 album *Trio*, with "Oh" being dropped from the song's title.
- The B side of the album's single, "Better Move It On Home," did not appear on the album though it was recorded during the final sessions on December 14, 1970 along with "Oh the Pain of Loving You" and "Two of A Kind" at RCA Studio A. It was nominated for Best Country Vocal Performance by a Duo or Group at the 14th Annual Grammy Awards. Horns on "Better Move It on Home" overdubbed at RCA Studio B by engineer Chuck Seitz. The track, however, was released on the July 19, 1971 Porter and Dolly "Best of" album.
- On October 10, 1971 Porter and Dolly were once again presented with the Country Music Association's award for "Best Vocal Duet Group."
- The review in *Billboard* published February 20, 1971 said,"The highly successful country duo comes up with another LP destined for top programming and sales, and should soon be riding at the top of the charts. They turned in first–rate performances of "Two of a Kind," The Fighting Kind," "Oh, the Pain of Loving You" and "Curse of the Wild Weed Flower" among others."
- The review from *Cashbox* dated February 13, 1971, which said, "Having already won just about every award possible for a vocal duo, Porter Wagoner and Dolly Parton, certainly "Two of a Kind," are back on the right track again with their first LP release of the new year. Porter and Dolly are capable of delivering soft, moody ballads, or up–tempo rockers with the utmost of sincerity and smoothness. Among the more outstanding tracks are "Oh, the Pain of Loving You," "Is It Real," "Today, Tomorrow and Forever," and the title track, "Two of a Kind," but the entire album is a classic and will be one of their biggest ever."

The Right Combination • Burning The Midnight Oil
LSP–4628

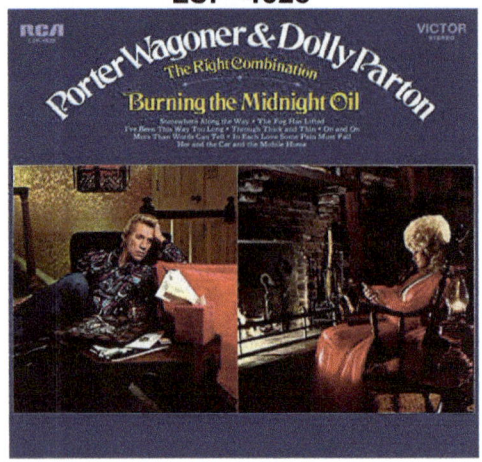

Track Listing:
More Than Words Can Tell / The Right Combination / I've Been This Way Too Long / In Each Love Some Pain Must Fall / Her and the Car and the Mobile Home / Burning The Midnight Oil / Somewhere Along The Way / On and On / Through Thick and Thin / The Fog Has Lifted

Production Information:
Produced by: Bob Ferguson
Recorded at: RCA Victor's "Nashville Sound" Studio, Nashville, TN
Engineer: Al Pachucki
Assistant Engineer: Roy M. Shockley
Cover Photography: Les Leverett

Musicians:
Piano: Hargus "Pig" Robbins / David Briggs
Drums: Jerry Carrigan
Steel Guitar: Pete Drake
Bass: Bobby Dyson
Electric Guitar: Dave Kirby / Jerry Shook
Fiddle: Mack Magaha / Buddy Spicher
Rhythm Guitar: George McCormick / Billy Sanford / Jerry Stembridge
Electric Banjo: Charles Trent
Background Vocals: Joseph Babcock / Dolores Edgin / June Evelyn Page

Singles Released From This Album:
"The Right Combination" b/w "The Pain of Loving You" – May 24, 1971 (peaked at # 14 on the *Billboard* Hot Country Songs chart)
"Burning the Midnight Oil" b/w "More Than Words Can Tell" – October 18, 1971 (peaked at # 11 on the *Billboard* Hot Country Songs chart and # 9 in Canada on the *RPM* Country Singles chart)

Album Data:
Highest Chart Position: # 6 on March 3, 1972
Billboard Chart: Hot Country Albums
Number of weeks on chart: 16

Notes / Trivia:
- This album was released on LP, 8–Track and Cassette on January 3, 1972
- Recording sessions for the album started on April 7 and 8, 1971, at RCA Studios in Nashville,

Tennessee. Two additional sessions followed on September 28 and 30. "Her and the Car and the Mobile Home" was recorded on December 9, 1970, during the session for the 1971 *Two of a Kind* album.
- The Billboard review published January 15, 1972 said, "Porter and Dolly have here an LP that will be a big hit for them in the first few months of 1972. Each of the stars has written a few cuts and their performance of their own material is beautiful. Highlights include "The Right Combination," "More Than Words Can Tell," "The Fog Has Lifted" and "Her and the Car and the Mobile Home" (a comedy spotlight)."
- *Cashbox* also published a review on January 15, 1972 that said, "Judging from their popularity it's indisputable that Porter Wagoner and Dolly Parton have the right combination to open the doors of success. Unlike most other C&W duets who spend most of the time harmonizing with occasional solos, Porter & Dolly are not only adept at their harmonies, they allow each other room for individual expression within the scope of each arrangement. Most unique is the extent to which they feel at ease with each other; the good time dialogue and banter in songs such as "I've Been This Way Too Long" is as much a part of the right combination as the music."

Together Always
LSP-4761

Track Listing:
Together Always / Love's All Over / Christina / Poor Folks Town / Take Away / Ten Four—Over And Out / Lost Forever in your Kiss / Anyplace You Want to Go / Looking Down / You and Me—Her and Him

Production Information:
Produced by: Bob Ferguson
Recorded at: RCA Victor's "Nashville Sound" Studio, Nashville, TN
Engineer: Tom Pick
Assistant Engineer: Roy M. Shockley
Cover Photography: Les Leverett

Musicians:
Drums: Jerry Carrigan
Steel Guitar: Pete Drake
Bass: Bobby Dyson
Fiddle: Johnny Gimble / Mack Magaha / Buddy Spicher
Guitar: Dave Kirby / Billy Sanford / Dale Sellers / Jerry Shook / Jerry Stembridge / Robert Thompson
Rhythm Guitar: George McCormick
Piano: Hargus "Pig" Robbins
Electric Banjo: Buck Trent
Background Vocals: Joseph Babcock / Dolores Edgin / June Evelyn Page

Singles Released From This Album:
"Lost Forever in your Kiss" b/w "The Fog Has Lifted" – March 6, 1972 (peaked at # 9 on the *Billboard* Hot Country Songs chart)
"Together Always" b/w "Love's All Over" – July 31, 1972 (peaked at # 14 on the *Billboard* Hot Country Songs chart)

Album Data:
Highest Chart Position: # 3 on November 24, 1972
Billboard Chart: Hot Country Albums
Number of weeks on chart: 19

Notes / Trivia:
- This album was released on LP, 8–Track and Cassette on September 11, 1972

- Recording sessions for the album took place on April 28, May 1 and 2, 1972, at RCA Studios in Nashville, Tennessee. Six of the album's ten tracks were recorded during sessions for 1972's *The Right Combination • Burning the Midnight Oil*. "Love's All Over," "Take Away" and "You and Me – Her and Him" were recorded on April 7, 1971. "Anyplace You Want to Go," "Looking Down" and "Lost Forever in Your Kiss" were recorded on September 28, 29 and 30, 1971, respectively.
- "Poor Folks Town" was later re–recorded as a solo by Dolly on her 1980 album, *9 to 5 and Odd Jobs*.
- The back jacket features a thank you note from both Porter and Dolly to their fans and each is written out in long hand, not typeset.
- A review dated September 23, 1972 in *Billboard* said, "Two of the most consistent chart winners join forces once again for another top package loaded with programming and sales potency. Duo wrote all the material with highlights that include "Lost Forever in Your Kiss," "Love's All Over," "Ten Four – Over and Out" and of course the current hit single, "Together Always."
- A *Cashbox* review published September 9, 1972 said, "The time is September, 1982, and the scene is an anniversary party. Porter Wagoner and Dolly Parton are celebrating the tenth anniversary of their "Together Always" album; they are celebrating as proof that the album title was accurate and that they would truly remain a team forever. Maybe this fantasy is projecting too far into the future, but if you hear the closeness of Porter and Dolly's music on their new album, then you would not only agree with me, you would make advance reservations for the 1992 anniversary party! Includes "Lost Forever in Your Kiss," "Poor Folks Town" and "Christina."
- The original cover for this album featured Porter and Dolly sitting on what looks to be a split rail fence in the woods. The back jacket design remains the same with them walking hand in hand. The "In the woods" cover is highly sought after and has sold for as much as $900 in mint condition on eBay. This is also thought to be a promotional copy of the album, though it is unusual to use different graphics just for a promotional copy of an album.

We Found It
LSP–4841

Track Listing:
Love City / Between Us / We Found It / Satan's River / I've Been Married (Just As Long As You Have) / I Am Always Waiting / Sweet Rachel Ann / That's When Love Will Mean The Most / Love Have Mercy on Us / How Close They Must Be

Production Information:
Produced by: Bob Ferguson
Recorded at: RCA Victor's "Nashville Sound" Studio, Nashville, TN
Engineers: Tom Pick / Al Pachuchi
Assistant Engineer: Roy M. Shockley
Cover Photography: Les Leverett

Musicians:
Electric Guitar: Jimmy Capps / Jimmy Colvard / Dave Kirby
Rhythm Guitar: Bobby Thompson / Jerry Stembridge
Steel Guitar: Pete Drake
Bass: Bobby Dyson
Banjo: Buck Trent
Fiddle: Johnny Gimble / Mack Magaha
Piano & Harpsichord: Hargus "Pig" Robbins
Drums: Jerry Carrigan
Background Vocals: Joseph Babcock / Dolores Edgin / June Evelyn Page

Singles Released From This Album:
"We Found It" b/w "Love Have Mercy on Us" – February 12, 1973 (peaked at # 30 on the *Billboard* Hot Country Songs chart)

Album Data:
Highest Chart Position: # 20 on April 6, 1973
Billboard Chart: Hot Country Albums
Number of weeks on chart: 10

Notes / Trivia:
- This album was released on LP, 8–Track and Cassette on February 12, 1973
- This album was also issued in the Quad format on 8 track tape cartridge and LP.
- Recording sessions for the album began at RCA Studios in Nashville, Tennessee, on April 28,

1972, yielding only two tracks, of which only "We Found It" made the final cut. Two additional sessions followed on August 21 and 22, producing six of the album's tracks between them. The final session took place on November 29, from which two song were selected to complete the album. One track on the album, "How Close They Must Be," was recorded during the April 7, 1971 session for 1972's *The Right Combination • Burning the Midnight Oil*.

- A February 24, 1973 *Billboard* review of the album: "It's all original material, written individually and collectively by the pair, and they manage to mix love and happiness into a perfect blending. Some of their best material to date, and that says a great deal. "I've Been Married (Just as Long as You Have)," "I Am Always Waiting" and "Sweet Rachel Ann" are the best cuts on the album."

Love and Music
APL-1-0248

Track Listing:
If Teardrops Were Pennies / Sounds of the Night / Laugh the Years Away / You / Wasting Love / Come to Me / Love is Out Tonight / In the Presence of You / I Get Lonesome by Myself / There'll Always Be Music

Production Information:
Produced by: Bob Ferguson
Recorded at: RCA Victor's "Nashville Sound" Studio, Nashville, TN
Engineer: Tom Pick
Assistant Engineer: Roy M. Shockley
Cover Photography: Les Leverett
Album Design: Sandi Bernstein
Art Direction: Acy Lehman

Singles Released From This Album:
"If Teardrops were Pennies" b/w "Come to Me" – June 4, 1973 (peaked at # 8 on the *Billboard* Hot Country Songs chart)

Album Data:
Highest Chart Position: # 8 on November 16, 1973
Billboard Chart: Hot Country Albums
Number of weeks on chart: 23

Notes / Trivia:
- This album was released on LP, 8-Track and Cassette on July 2, 1973
- Recording sessions for the album began at RCA Studios in Nashville, Tennessee, on February 12 and 13, 1973. These two sessions yielded 7 of the album's ten tracks. Two more of the album's tracks were recorded during an April 9 session. "In the Presence of You" was recorded during a November 29, 1972 session for 1973's *We Found It*.
- In a positive review of the album in their July 14, 1973 issue, *Billboard* said, "A collection of love ballads with some of the finest cuts this consistent pair have ever come up with. Aside from the single and one other cut, Dolly and/or Porter wrote every song, and they must have been in romantic moods. Good old fashioned love music, with some timeless lyrics, and it's one everyone will want. There is even a dialog recitation." They went on to say that eight of the ten tunes...have the potential to be around for a long time." They concluded with a note to record dealers, saying that the "...good cover work by Les Leverett sets the mood for the album."

- In another positive review, *Cashbox* said, "Aptly titled, this LP contains a soothing, sincere selection of tunes that touch lightly on love—hearts and flowers abound. And there's nothing wrong with that, as anyone familiar with the phenomenal success accorded Dolly and Porter for their rendering of such sentiments should know! This is the sort of album you put on the phonograph and relax to, love to, and let the troubled world fade away. Dolly penned several delightful tunes. Catch "I Get Lonesome by Myself.""
- The album liner notes were written by Carl and Pearl Butler (nee Jones), writers of the song "If Teardrops Were Pennies" originally a hit in 1951 for country singer Carl Smith. The Butlers were also among the earliest supporters of Dolly, with whom they had worked in Knoxville in the late 1950s, and they helped to get her established in Nashville in the early 1960s. Dolly paid tribute to the Butlers when she included a song they wrote (and had a # 1 hit with in 1962) called, "Don't Let Me Cross Over" on *Treasures, her* 1996 album of covers.

1973 Sheet Music to *If teardrops Were Pennies*

Porter 'n' Dolly
APL–1–0646

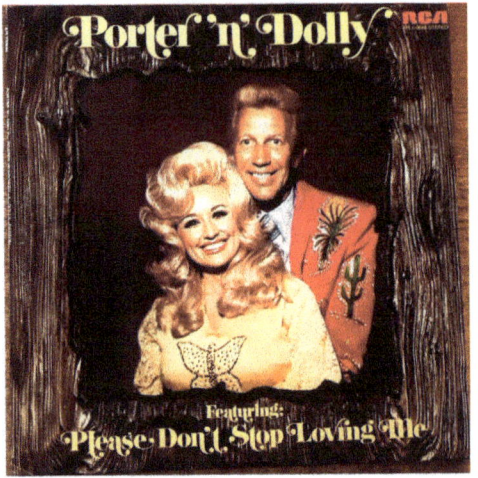

Track Listing:
Please Don't Stop Loving Me / The Fire That Keeps You Warm / Too Far Gone / We'd Have To Be Crazy / The Power of Love / Sixteen Years / Together You and I / Without You / Two / Sounds of Nature

Production Information:
Produced by: Bob Ferguson
Recorded at: RCA Victor's "Nashville Sound" Studio, Nashville, TN
Engineer: Tom Pick
Assistant Engineer: Roy M. Shockley
Cover Photography: Hope Powell
Art Direction: Herb Burnette—Pinwheel Art Studios

Singles Released From This Album:
"Please Don't Stop Loving Me" b/w "Sounds of Nature" – July 15, 1974 (peaked at # 1on the *Billboard* Hot Country Songs chart)

Album Data:
Highest Chart Position: # 8 on October 25, 1974
Billboard Chart: Hot Country Albums
Number of weeks on chart: 25

Notes / Trivia:
- This album was released on LP, 8–Track and Cassette on August 19, 1974
- Recording sessions for the album took place on May 23 and 24, 1974, at RCA Studios in Nashville, Tennessee. These two sessions produced eight of the album's ten tracks. The two other tracks were recorded during sessions for previous albums. "Sounds of Nature" was recorded during a September 30, 1971 session for 1972's *The Right Combination • Burning the Midnight Oil* and "Together You and I" was recorded during the May 1, 1972 session for 1972's *Together Always*.
- Dolly would re–record "The Fire That Keeps You Warm" for her 1976 *All I Can Do* album and "Together You and I" for her 2011 *Better Day* album.
- In their August 31, 1974 review *Billboard* gave the album a positive review noting that all of the album's tracks were written by Wagoner and Parton. They said the album had "some nice ballads, some up–tempo, but all good listening." The reviewer pointed out "We'd Have to Be Crazy," "Two" and "The Power of Love" as the best cuts on the album. They concluded with a

note to record dealers that the album's "...portrait cover will enhance display."
- The August 24, 1974 review by *Cashbox* noted, "Although Porter and Dolly have each assumed their own artistic identities as far as live performing, they are still recording together. This new LP features some excellent material and the inimitable duo are sounding better than ever. The LP is a sparkling collection and Porter and Dolly have always stood as an exceptional duo on the country music scene. "Please Don't Stop Loving Me" is an up–tempo ditty that professes that they need each other. "The Fire That Keeps You Warm" is a heart warming tune that tells of true love."
- The single release from this album was the duo's only #1 together.

Say Forever You'll Be Mine
APL-1-1116

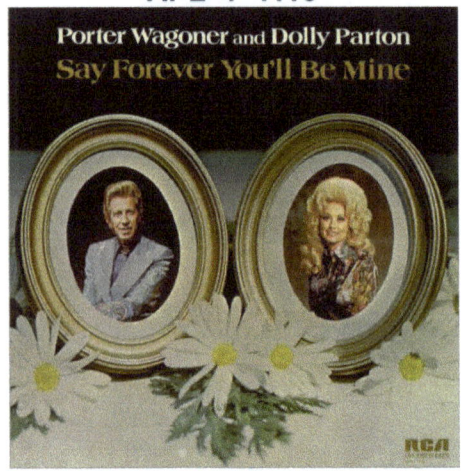

Track Listing:
Say Forever You'll Be Mine / Something to Reach For / Again / Our Love / The Beginning / I Have No Right to Care / If You Were Mine / Love to See Us Through / How Can I (Help You Forgive Me) / Life Rides the Train

Production Information:
Produced and Arranged by: Porter Wagoner
Recorded at: RCA Victor's "Nashville Sound" Studio, Nashville, TN
Engineer: Tom Pick
Assistant Engineer: Roy M. Shockley
Background Vocals: The Lea Jane Singers and The Nashville Edition
Cover Photography: Porter Wagoner and Still Life: Herb Burnette; Dolly Parton: Hope Powell
Art Direction: Herb Burnette—Pinwheel Art Studios

Singles Released From This Album:
"Say Forever You'll Be Mine" b/w "How Can I (Help You Forgive Me)" – June 16, 1975 (peaked at # 5 on the *Billboard* Hot Country Songs chart and # 1 of Canada's *RPM* Chart)

Album Data:
Highest Chart Position: # 6 on November 14, 1975
Billboard Chart: Hot Country Albums
Number of weeks on chart: 15

Notes / Trivia:
- This album was released on LP, 8-Track and Cassette on August 18, 1975
- Only three tracks on the album resulted from new recording sessions, "Our Love," "If You Were Mine," and "Love to See Us Through" were recorded during an April 15, 1975 session at RCA Studios in Nashville, Tennessee. The seven others tracks included on the album date as far back as 1972. "Say Forever You'll Be Mine" is the oldest track included and was recorded on August 21, 1972, during the sessions for 1973's *We Found It*. "I Have No Right to Care" and "How Can I (Help You Forgive Me)" were recorded during the sessions for 1973's *Love and Music* on February 12, 1973. Four other tracks were recorded during sessions for 1974's *Porter 'n' Dolly*. "Something to Reach For" and "Again" were recorded on May 23, 1974, while "The Beginning" and "Life Rides the Train" were recorded May 24, 1974.
- Dolly's younger brother, Randy Parton, wrote the song "If You Were Mine."
- In *Billboard*'s issue dated August 30, 1975, a reviewer said, "As always when the pair get

together, a fine set of love songs giving each a chance to display their vocal wares separately as well as working in their general perfectly succinct harmony. Dolly is enjoying her strongest period of success as a solo yet and Wagoner is a consistent chart maker, yet together they always seem to rise to new heights. Material a bit more on the straight country side than their solo material, with the writing split as usual fairly evenly between the two. Production of Porter is excellent. Instrumentally, fiddle and guitar work in particular shines on this set."

- *Cashbox* also published a review dated August 30 which said, "Running the gamut of most every phase of love, this Porter and Dolly LP includes, "Something to Reach For," "If You Were Mine," "I Have No Right to Care," "The Beginning," "Our Love," "Again," "How Can I (Help You Forgive Me)," "Love to See Us Through" and of course the title song, which is also their current chart climbing single, "Say Forever You'll Be Mine." The sound is gentle and pure country, serving as a perfect foil for the cameo performance of these two great country artists."
- This album would be the last album of new material for Porter and Dolly until August 4, 1980.

Porter & Dolly
AHL-1-3700

Track Listing:
Making Plans / If You Go, I'll Follow You / Hide Me Away / Someone Just Like You / Little David's Harp / Beneath The Sweet Magnolia Tree / Touching Memories / Daddy Did His Best / If You Say I Can / Singing On The Mountain

Production Information:
Produced and Arranged by: Porter Wagoner
Producer: Bob Ferguson (original masters prior to overdubs)
Producer: Jerry Bradley (1979 overdub sessions)
Recorded at: RCA Victor's "Nashville Sound" Studio, Studio A, Nashville, TN
Overdubs recorded at: Fireside Studios, Nashville, TN
Engineers: Tom Pick
Assistant Engineer: Roy M. Shockley
Cover Photography: Porter Wagoner (Hope Powell) and Dolly Parton (Ed Caraeff)
Art Direction: Herb Burnette
Cover Lettering Design: Bill Noss
Special Photo Effects: K&S Photographics

Musicians:
Steel Guitar: Stu Basore
Bass: Bobby Dyson
Electric Guitar: Jim Colvard
Drums: R.E. Hardaway / Jim Isbell
Piano: Hargus "Pig" Robbins / Benny Kennerson / Mike Lawler
Electric Guitar, Acoustic Guitar: Dave Kirby
Electric Guitar, Acoustic Guitar: Fred Newell
Acoustic Guitar: Wayne Moss
Background vocals: Sudie Calloway / Rita Figlio / Curtis Young
String Arrangements: Chuck Cochran

Singles Released From This Album:
"Making Plans" b/w "Beneath The Sweet Magnolia Tree" – June 2, 1980 (peaked at # 2 on the *Billboard* Hot Country Songs chart)
"If You Go, I'll Follow You" b/w "Hide Me Away" – October 13, 1980 (peaked at # 12 on the *Billboard*

Hot Country Songs chart)

Album Data:
Highest Chart Position: # 9 on October 10, 1980
Billboard Chart: Hot Country Albums
Number of weeks on chart: 31

Notes / Trivia:
- This album was released on LP, 8–Track and Cassette on August 4, 1980
- The album is made up of previously unreleased material recorded during Porter and Dolly's duet years from 1967 to 1976, with new studio overdubs. It was released as part of a settlement from legal action Porter took against Dolly following her departure from his band and syndicated television series.
- Two singles were released from the album: "Making Plans" peaked at number two on the *Billboard* Hot Country Singles chart and "If You Go, I'll Follow You" peaked at number 12.
- In 2014, Bear Family Records released *Just Between You and Me: The Complete Recordings, 1967–1976*. It contains the complete duet recordings made by Porter and Dolly during their partnership, including the original masters of the songs from this album, but without the overdubs.
- All ten of the album's tracks were recorded on ten different dates between 1968 and 1976. The two newest tracks on the album, "Touching Memories" and "Someone Just Like You", were the only two tracks from their respective April 22 and 26, 1976 sessions to be released until the 2014 box set. "Hide Me Away" was recorded during a May 24, 1974 session for 1974's *Porter 'n' Dolly*. "If You Say I Can" was the first track to be released from a December 5, 1973 session and is possibly the only surviving track from this session as no other songs recorded that day are included on the 2014 box set. "Beneath the Sweet Magnolia Tree" was recorded during the February 13, 1973 session for 1973's *Love and Music*. "Singing on the Mountain" and "Little David's Harp" were recorded during sessions for 1973's *We Found It* on August 21 and 22, 1972, respectively. "If You Go, I'll Follow You" was the second track to be released from the September 29, 1971 session. "Daddy Did His Best" was recorded during a session on December 2, 1970, for 1971's *Two of a Kind*. The oldest track included on the album, "Making Plans" was the first single released from this album and was recorded on May 22, 1968, during a session for 1968's *Just the Two of Us*. Overdub sessions for the album took place on November 23, December 3, December 7, December 11, and December 14, 1979, at Fireside Studio in Nashville, Tennessee. The producer of these sessions was Jerry Bradley. It is reported that Porter was the owner of Fireside Recording studios. The building is now gone, replaced by apartments, but once stood at 813 18th Ave South in Nashville, which is a block west of the RCA Studios these recordings originated in.
- The cover photo was prepared and produced by K&S Photographics using two separate images, one of Dolly and one of Porter, that had the individual backgrounds carefully removed. Each image was then overlaid manually on a black background with text graphics added on a separate film overlay, then photographed together. Color correction of the final image took place afterwards.

Just Between You and Me: The Complete Recordings 1967 – 1976
BCD 16889 FK

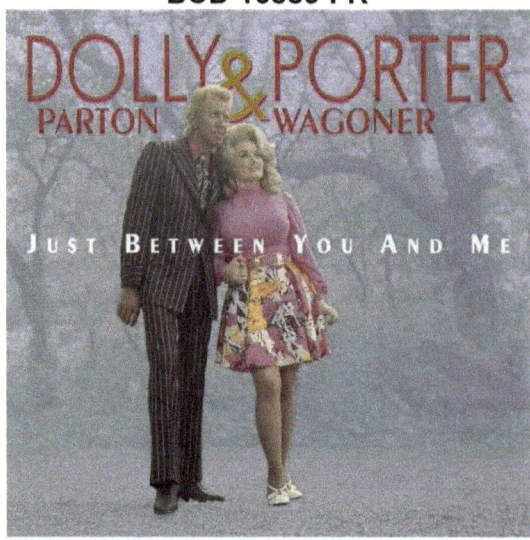

Track Listing:

Disc One: Just Between You and Me / Before I Met You / Two Sides to Every Story / Mommie, Ain't That Daddy / Four O Thirty Three / Love is Worth Living / The Last Thing on My Mind / Sorrow's Tearing Down the House (That Happiness Once Built) / Home is Where the Hurt Is / This Time Has Gotta Be Our Last Time / Put It Off Until Tomorrow / Because One of Us Was Wrong / Slip Away Today / Holding On to Nothin' / Just the Two of Us / Closer by the Hour / Afraid to Love Again / I Washed My Face in the Morning Dew / Jeannie's Afraid of the Dark / The Party / I Can / We'll Get Ahead Someday / The Dark End of the Street / Somewhere Between / Making Plans / Malena / Good As Gold * / One by One * / Good As Gold / Yours Love

Disc Two: Just Someone I Used to Know / No Reason to Hurry Home / Milwaukee, Here I Come / The House Where Love Lives / Why Don't You Haul Off and Love Me / Mendy Never Sleeps / I Don't Believe You've Met My Baby / Anything's Better Than Nothing / Always, Always / My Hands Are Tied / There Never Was a Time / Forty Miles from Poplar Bluff / Each Season Changes You / Daddy Was An Old Time Preacher Man * / Tangled Vines / We Can't Let This Happen to Us / Tomorrow is Forever / Silver Sandals / No Love Left / I'm Wasting Your Time and You're Wasting Mine / Run That by Me One More Time / It Might As Well Be Me / I Know You're Married But I Love You Still / Daddy Was An Old Time Preacher Man / Fight and Scratch / A Good Understanding

Disc Three: Once More / Ragged Angel / Before Our Weakness Gets Too Strong / Let's Live for Tonight / One Day At a Time / Thoughtfulness / There'll Be Love / Daddy Did His Best / Possum Holler / The Fighting Kind / All I Need is You / Curse of the Wild Weed Flower / Today, Tomorrow and Forever / The Flame / Her and the Car and the Mobile Home / Is It Real / Two of a Kind The Pain of Loving You / Better Move It On Home / The Right Combination / Burning the Midnight Oil / Love's All Over / Take Away / You and Me, Her and Him / How Close They Must Be / On and On / More Than Words Can Tell / In Each Love Some Pain Must Fall

Disc Four: Anyplace You Want to Go / Somewhere Along the Way / The Fog Has Lifted / Looking Down / If You Go, I'll Follow You / Waldo the Weirdo * / I've Been This Way Too Long / Lost Forever in Your Kiss / Sounds of Nature / Through Thick and Thin / We Found It / Poor Folks Town / Together You and I / Christina / Together Always / Ten–Four, Over and Out / There's Singing on the Mountain / Say Forever You'll Be Mine / That's When Love Will Mean the Most / Love Have Mercy on Us / Sweet Rachel Ann / Satan's River / I Am Always Waiting / I've Been Married (Just As Long As You Have) / Little David's Harp / Between Us / Love City / In the Presence of You

Disc Five: How Can I (Help You Forgive Me) / Come to Me / Laugh the Years Away / There'll Always Be Music * / I Have No Right to Care / Come to Me * / Beneath the Sweet Magnolia Tree / Love is Out Tonight / If Teardrops Were Pennies / You / There'll Always Be Music / I Get Lonesome by Myself /

Sounds of Night / Wasting Love / All Aboard America / Here Comes the Freedom Train / Too Far Gone / Again / Something to Reach For / The Fire That Keeps You Warm / Without You / Sixteen Years / Carolina Moonshine * / If You Say I Can / The Power of Love / The Beginning / Please Don't Stop Loving Me

Disc Six: Life Rides the Train / Two / Hide Me Away / We'd Have to Be Crazy / Love to See Us Through / If You Were Mine / Our Love / Is Forever Longer Than Always / I Learned It Well * / Touching Memories / In the Morning * / About Susanne, About Your Man * / A Fool Like Me * / Someone Just Like You / Golden Streets of Glory * / Twin Mounds of Clay * / Presentation by Don Howser (live) / Run That by Me One More Time (live) / Jeannie's Afraid of the Dark (live) / Tomorrow is Forever (live) / Two Sides to Every Story (live)

Selections marked * are unreleased or unreleased alternate takes.

Notes / Trivia:

- This six disc set was released on Tuesday, May 26, 2014.
- Dolly and Porter released 13 albums together, had 21 singles on the Billboard Hot Country Singles charts, and 139 duets during that period – they also released a single during the 2000's (a re–recording of the Gospel standard "Drifting too Far From the Shore.") 13 of the tracks here were previously unreleased. Also included is their rare 1973 release of *Here Comes The Freedom Train*.
- This set comes in a 12" x 12" box and includes a 84–page hardcover book written by Alanna Nash with liner notes, photographs and complete recording credits for each track in this collection.

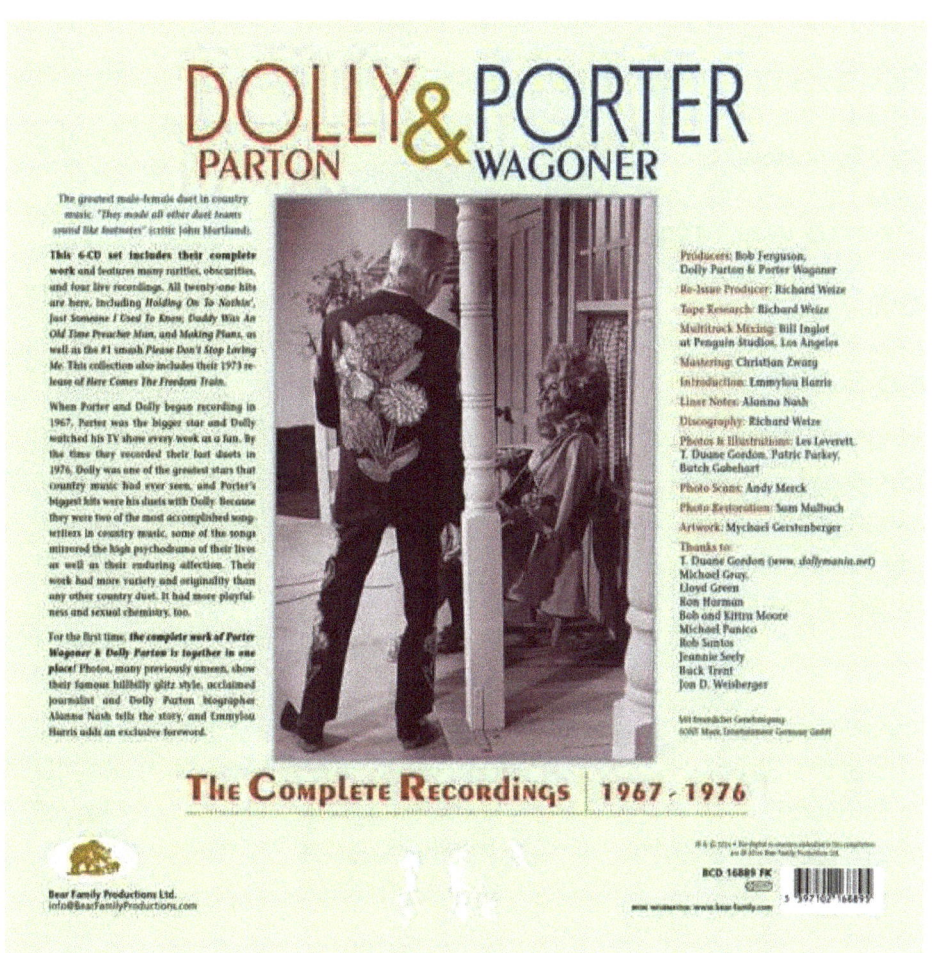

The Recording Sessions of Dolly & Porter
(In Session Order)

1967–1976

No.	Title	Writer(s)	Recording date	Length
1.	"Just Between You and Me"	Jack Clement	October 10, 1967	2:22
2.	"Before I Met You"	Charles L. Seitz, Joe Lewis, Elmer Rader	October 10, 1967	1:56
3.	"Two Sides to Every Story"	Dolly Parton, Bill Owens	October 10, 1967	2:23
4.	"Mommie, Ain't That Daddy?"	Dolly Parton	October 10, 1967	3:15
5.	"Four O Thirty Three"	Bill Owens, Earl Montgomery	October 11, 1967	2:49
6.	"Love Is Worth Living"	Dolly Parton	October 11, 1967	2:44
7.	"The Last Thing on My Mind"	Tom Paxton	October 11, 1967	2:38
8.	"Sorrow's Tearing Down the House (That Happiness Once Built)"	Mel Tillis, Kent Westberry	October 11, 1967	2:27
9.	"Home Is Where the Hurt Is"	Fred MacRae, Marge Barton	October 12, 1967	2:16
10.	"This Time Has Gotta Be Our Last Time"	Bill Owens	October 12, 1967	2:32
11.	"Put It Off Until Tomorrow"	Dolly Parton, Bill Owens	October 12, 1967	2:24
12.	"Because One of Us Was Wrong"	Dolly Parton, Bill Owens	October 12, 1967	2:08
13.	"Slip Away Today"	Curly Putman	January 31, 1968	2:42
14.	"Holding On to Nothin'"	Jerry Chesnut	January 31, 1968	2:31
15.	"Just the Two of Us"	Chesnut	May 20, 1968	2:41
16.	"Closer by the Hour"	Al Gore	May 20, 1968	2:20
17.	"Afraid to Love Again"	Chesnut, Theresa Beaty	May 20, 1968	1:59
18.	"I Washed My Face in the Morning Dew"	Tom T. Hall	May 21, 1968	2:49
19.	"Jeannie's Afraid of the Dark"	Dolly Parton	May 21, 1968	2:50
20.	"The Party"	Dolly Parton	May 21, 1968	2:58
21.	"I Can"	Dolly Parton	May 21, 1968	2:09
22.	"We'll Get Ahead Someday"	Mack Magaha	May 22, 1968	1:59
23.	"The Dark End of the Street"	Dan Penn, Chips Moman	May 22, 1968	2:19
24.	"Somewhere Between"	Merle Haggard	May 22, 1968	2:17
25.	"Making Plans (Original Master)" (Previously Unreleased)	Johnny Russell, Voni Morrison	May 22, 1968	2:14
26.	"Malena"	Dolly Parton	December 3, 1968	2:27

No.	Title	Writer(s)	Recording date	Length
27.	"Good as Gold (Alternate Version)" (Previously Unreleased)	Paul Martin	December 3, 1968	2:53
28.	"One by One" (Previously Unreleased)	Johnnie Wright, Jack Anglin, Jim Anglin	December 3, 1968	2:43
29.	"Good as Gold"	Paul Martin	December 20, 1968	2:33
30.	"Yours Love"	Harlan Howard	December 20, 1968	2:34

No.	Title	Writer(s)	Recording date	Length
1.	"Just Someone I Used to Know"	Clement	April 21, 1969	2:25
2.	"No Reason to Hurry Home"	Dolly Parton	April 21, 1969	2:29
3.	"Milwaukee, Here I Come"	Lee Fikes	April 21, 1969	2:16
4.	"The House Where Love Lives"	Leona Reese	April 21, 1969	2:05
5.	"Why Don't you Haul Of & Love Me?"	Wayne Raney, Lonnie Glosson	April 22, 1969	1:55
6.	"Mendy Never Sleeps"	Dolly Parton	April 22, 1969	2:09
7.	"I Don't Believe You've Met My Baby"	Autry Inman	April 22, 1969	2:13
8.	"Anything's Better Than Nothing"	Marie Wilson	April 23, 1969	2:18
9.	"Always, Always"	Joyce McCord	April 23, 1969	2:39
10.	"My Hands Are Tied"	Dolly Parton	April 23, 1969	2:36
11.	"There Never Was a Time"	Myra Smith, Margaret Lewis	April 23, 1969	2:30
12.	"Forty Miles from Poplar Bluff"	Frank Dycus	December 1, 1969	2:52
13.	"Each Season Changes You"	Ruth Talley	December 1, 1969	2:35
14.	"Daddy Was an Old Time Preacher Man (Alternate Version)" (Previously Unreleased)	Dolly Parton, Dorothy Jo Hope	December 1, 1969	2:46
15.	"Tangled Vines"	Damon Black	December 2, 1969	2:08
16.	"We Can't Let This Happen to Us"	Dorothy Jo Hope	December 2, 1969	2:11
17.	"Tomorrow Is Forever"	Dolly Parton	December 2, 1969	2:50
18.	"Silver Sandals"	Dolly Parton	December 2, 1969	2:42
19.	"No Love Left"	Bill Owens	December 3, 1969	2:03
20.	"I'm Wasting Your Time and You're Wasting Mine"	Dolly Parton	December 3, 1969	2:24
21.	"Run That by Me One More Time"	Dolly Parton	December 3, 1969	2:20
22.	"It Might as Well Be Me"	Dolly Parton, Dorothy Jo Hope	December 3, 1969	2:16

No.	Title	Writer(s)	Recording date	Length
23.	"I Know You're Married But I Love You Still"	Don Reno, Magaha	April 21, 1970	2:25
24.	"Daddy Was an Old Time Preacher Man"	Dolly Parton, Dorothy Jo Hope	April 21, 1970	3:04
25.	"Fight and Scratch"	Dolly Parton	April 21, 1970	2:38
26.	"A Good Understanding"	Dolly Parton	April 21, 1970	2:44

No.	Title	Writer(s)	Recording date	Length
1.	"Once More"	Dusty Owens	May 5, 1970	2:34
2.	"Ragged Angel"	Dolly Parton	May 5, 1970	2:09
3.	"Before Our Weakness Gets Too Strong"	Louis Owens	May 5, 1970	2:43
4.	"Let's Live for Tonight"	Reno	May 5, 1970	2:12
5.	"One Day at a Time"	Joe Babcock	May 6, 1970	2:34
6.	"Thoughtfulness"	Bill Owens	May 6, 1970	2:28
7.	"There'll Be Love"	Dolly Parton, Porter Wagoner	May 6, 1970	2:39
8.	"Daddy Did His Best (Original Master)" (Previously Unreleased)	Chesnut	December 2, 1970	2:49
9.	"Possum Holler"	Dallas Frazier	December 2, 1970	2:19
10.	"The Fighting Kind"	Dolly Parton	December 2, 1970	2:33
11.	"All I Need Is You"	Betty Jean Robsinson	December 8, 1970	3:10
12.	"Curse of the Wild Weed Flower"	Dolly Parton, Louis Owens	December 8, 1970	2:18
13.	"Today, Tomorrow and Forever"	Bill Owens	December 8, 1970	2:45
14.	"The Flame"	Dolly Parton	December 9, 1970	2:57
15.	"Her and the Car and the Mobile Home"	Dave Kirby, Don Stock	December 9, 1970	2:40
16.	"Is It Real?"	Dolly Parton	December 9, 1970	2:56
17.	"Two of a Kind"	Dolly Parton, Porter Wagoner	December 14, 1970	2:40
18.	"Oh, the Pain of Loving You"	Dolly Parton, Porter Wagoner	December 14, 1970	2:07
19.	"Better Move It on Home"	Ray Griff	December 14, 1970	2:16
20.	"The Right Combination"	Porter Wagoner	April 7, 1971	2:57
21.	"Burning the Midnight Oil"	Porter Wagoner	April 7, 1971	1:50
22.	"Love's All Over"	Porter Wagoner	April 7, 1971	3:10
23.	"Take Away"	Porter Wagoner	April 7, 1971	2:28
24.	"You and Me – Her and Him"	Porter Wagoner	April 7, 1971	2:25
25.	"How Close They Must Be"	Porter Wagoner	April 7, 1971	2:29

No.	Title	Writer(s)	Recording date	Length
26.	"On and On"	Eddie Sovine	April 7, 1971	2:08
27.	"More Than Words Can Tell"	Porter Wagoner	April 8, 1971	2:49
28.	"In Each Love Some Pain Must Fall"	Dolly Parton	April 8, 1971	2:06

No.	Title	Writer(s)	Recording date	Length
1.	"Anyplace You Want to Go"	Porter Wagoner	September 28, 1971	2:19
2.	"Somewhere Along the Way"	Dolly Parton	September 28, 1971	3:12
3.	"The Fog Has Lifted"	Porter Wagoner	September 28, 1971	2:23
4.	"Looking Down"	Porter Wagoner	September 29, 1971	2:38
5.	"If You Go, I'll Follow You (Original Master)" (Previously Unreleased)	Dolly Parton, Porter Wagoner	September 29, 1971	2:43
6.	"Waldo the Weirdo" (Previously Unreleased)	Porter Wagoner	September 29, 1971	2:55
7.	"I've Been This Way Too Long"	Dolly Parton	September 30, 1971	2:43
8.	"Lost Forever in Your Kiss"	Dolly Parton	September 30, 1971	3:26
9.	"Sounds of Nature"	Dolly Parton, Porter Wagoner	September 30, 1971	2:21
10.	"Through Thick and Thin"	Bill Owens	September 30, 1971	2:06
11.	"We Found It"	Porter Wagoner	April 28, 1972	2:34
12.	"Poor Folks Town"	Dolly Parton	April 28, 1972	2:44
13.	"Together You and I"	Dolly Parton	May 1, 1972	2:24
14.	"Christina"	Dolly Parton	May 1, 1972	3:05
15.	"Together Always"	Dolly Parton	May 1, 1972	2:18
16.	"Ten Four – Over and Out"	Porter Wagoner	May 2, 1972	3:33
17.	"Singing on the Mountain (Original Master)" (Previously Unreleased)	Porter Wagoner	August 21, 1972	2:27
18.	"Say Forever You'll Be Mine"	Dolly Parton	August 21, 1972	2:49
19.	"That's When Love Will Mean Most"	Porter Wagoner	August 21, 1972	1:59
20.	"Love Have Mercy on Us"	Dolly Parton	August 21, 1972	2:56
21.	"Sweet Rachel Ann"	Dolly Parton	August 21, 1972	2:56
22.	"Satan's River"	Porter Wagoner	August 21, 1972	2:38
23.	"I Am Always Waiting"	Porter Wagoner	August 22, 1972	2:18
24.	"I've Been Married (Just as Long as You Have)"	Dolly Parton, Porter Wagoner	August 22, 1972	2:47
25.	"Little David's Harp (Original Master)" (Previously Unreleased)	Dolly Parton	August 22, 1972	3:08
26.	"Between Us"	Dolly Parton	November 29, 1972	1:50

No.	Title	Writer(s)	Recording date	Length
27.	"Love City"	Dolly Parton	November 29, 1972	2:02
28.	"In the Presence of You"	Porter Wagoner, Tom Pick	November 29, 1972	2:49

No.	Title	Writer(s)	Recording date	Length
1.	"How Can I (Help You Forgive Me)"	Porter Wagoner, Tom Pick	February 12, 1973	1:57
2.	"Come to Me (Alternate Version)" (Previously Unreleased)	Dolly Parton	February 12, 1973	2:19
3.	"Laugh the Years Away"	Howard Tuck	February 12, 1973	2:03
4.	"There'll Always Be Music (Alternate Version)" (Previously Unreleased)	Dolly Parton	February 12, 1973	2:58
5.	"I Have No Right to Care"	Dolly Parton	February 12, 1973	2:46
6.	"Come to Me"	Dolly Parton	February 13, 1973	2:25
7.	"Beneath the Sweet Magnolia Tree (Original Master)" (Previously Unreleased)	Dolly Parton	February 13, 1973	2:28
8.	"Love Is Out Tonight"	Porter Wagoner, Tom Pick	February 13, 1973	2:44
9.	"If Teardrops Were Pennies"	Carl Butler	February 13, 1973	2:10
10.	"You"	Dolly Parton	February 13, 1973	2:25
11.	"There'll Always Be Music"	Dolly Parton	February 13, 1973	3:14
12.	"I Get Lonesome by Myself"	Dolly Parton	February 13, 1973	3:24
13.	"Sounds of Night"	Porter Wagoner	April 9, 1973	2:28
14.	"Wasting Love"	Porter Wagoner	April 9, 1973	1:52
15.	"All Aboard America"	Wagoner, Stephen H. Lemberg	October 12, 1973	3:38
16.	"Here Come the Freedom Train"	H. Lemberg	October 12, 1973	3:56
17.	"Too Far Gone"	Dolly Parton	May 23, 1974	2:15
18.	"Again"	Porter Wagoner	May 23, 1974	2:31
19.	"Something to Reach For"	Dolly Parton	May 23, 1974	2:27
20.	"The Fire That Keeps You Warm"	Dolly Parton	May 23, 1974	2:13
21.	"Without You"	Dolly Parton	May 23, 1974	2:29
22.	"Sixteen Years"	Wagoner, Pick	May 23, 1974	2:54
23.	"Carolina Moonshiner" (Previously Unreleased)	Dolly Parton	May 23, 1974	1:55
24.	"If You Say I Can (Single Master)"	Dolly Parton	December 5, 1973 (Dolly) May 24, 1974 (Porter)	2:28

No.	Title	Writer(s)	Recording date	Length
25.	"The Power of Love"	Porter Wagoner	May 24, 1974	2:26
26.	"The Beginning"	Dolly Parton	May 24, 1974	3:08
27.	"Please Don't Stop Loving Me"	Parton, Wagoner	May 24, 1974	2:47

No.	Title	Writer(s)	Recording date	Length
1.	"Life Rides the Train"	Porter Wagoner	May 24, 1974	2:27
2.	"Two"	Dolly Parton	May 24, 1974	2:41
3.	"Hide Me Away (Original Master)" (Previously Unreleased)	Dolly Parton	May 24, 1974	3:09
4.	"We'd Have to Be Crazy"	Dolly Parton	May 24, 1974	2:35
5.	"Love to See Us Through"	Gore, Dycus	April 15, 1975	2:17
6.	"If You Were Mine"	Randy Parton	April 15, 1975	2:52
7.	"Our Love"	Gore, Dycus	April 15, 1975	2:43
8.	"Is Forever Longer Than Always?"	Wagoner, Dycus	April 15, 1975	2:36
9.	"I Learned It Well" (Previously Unreleased)	Linda Carol Moore	April 22, 1976	2:28
10.	"Touching Memories (Original Master)" (Previously Unreleased)	Porter Wagoner Tom Pick	April 22, 1976	2:28
11.	"In the Morning" (Previously Unreleased)	Dolly Parton	April 22, 1976	2:04
12.	"About Susanne, About Your Man" (Previously Unreleased)	Dolly Parton	April 22, 1976	2:54
13.	"A Fool Like Me" (Previously Unreleased)	Moore	April 29, 1976	2:34
14.	"Someone Just Like You (Original Master)" (Previously Unreleased)	Dolly Parton	April 29, 1976	3:12
15.	"The Golden Streets of Glory" (Previously Unreleased)	Dolly Parton	April 29, 1976	3:00
16.	"Twin Mounds of Clay" (Previously Unreleased)	Howard Lips	April 29, 1976	3:03
17.	"Introduction by Porter (Live)"		April 25, 1970	0:47
18.	"Run That by Me One More Time (Live)"	Dolly Parton	April 25, 1970	2:57
19.	"Jeannie's Afraid of the Dark (Live)"	Dolly Parton	April 25, 1970	2:35
20.	"Tomorrow Is Forever (Live)"	Dolly Parton	April 25, 1970	2:32
21.	"Two Sides to Every Story (Live)"	Unknown		

Dolly Parton • Linda Ronstadt • Emmylou Harris
Trio
WB25491

Track Listing:
The Pain of Loving You / Making Plans / To Know Him is To Love Him / Hobo's Meditation / Wildflowers / Telling Me Lies / My Dear Companion / Those Memories of You / I've Had Enough / Rosewood Casket / Farther Along

Production Information:
Produced by: George Massenburg
Recorded at: The Complex, West Los Angeles, CA
Overdubbed at: Woodland Sound Studios, Nashville, TN / Ocean Way Recording, Los Angeles, CA
Engineers: George Massenburg
Assistant Engineers: Sharon Rice
Analog & Digital Mastering: Doug Sax at The Mastering Lab
Cover Photography: Robert Blakeman
Art Direction & Design: John Kosh & Ron Larson
Costume design by: Manuel

Musicians:
Emmylou Harris: Lead and harmony vocals, acoustic guitar (tracks 1, 5, 7), arrangements (track 11)
Dolly Parton: Lead and harmony vocals
Linda Ronstadt: Lead and harmony vocals
Bill Payne: Acoustic piano (tracks 6, 9, 11), electric piano (track 6), Hammond organ (track 11), harmonium (track 11)
Albert Lee: Acoustic guitar solo (track 1), acoustic guitar (tracks 2, 3, 6, 10, 11), high–strung guitar (tracks 2, 11), mandolin (tracks 5, 7), lead acoustic guitar (track 8)
Steve Fishell: Pedal steel guitar (tracks 1, 6), dobro (track 4), Kona Hawaiian guitar (track 8)
David Lindley: Mandolin (tacks 1, 2, 3, 8), Kona Hawaiian guitar (track 3), autoharp (tracks 5, 7), harpolek (track 5), acoustic guitar (track 6), dulcimer (track 10)
Ry Cooder: Tremolo guitar (track 3)
John Starling: Acoustic guitar (track 4), rhythm acoustic guitar (track 8), arrangements (track 11)
Herb Pedersen: Banjo (track 4), vocal arrangements (tracks 4, 6)
Mark O'Connor: Viola (tracks 1, 2, 5, 7), fiddle (tracks 2, 8), acoustic guitar (track 5), lead acoustic guitar (track 7), mandolin (track 10)
Kenny Edwards: Ferrington acoustic bass (tracks 1, 2, 3, 5, 7, 8, 10), electric bass (track 6)
Leland Sklar: Ferrington acoustic bass (track 4)
Russ Kunkel: Drums (tracks 1, 2, 3, 5, 6, 8)

Marty Krystall: Clarinet (track 8)
Brice Martin: Flute (track 8)
Jodi Burnett: Cello (track 8)
Dennis Karmazyn: Cello solo (track 8)
Novi Novog: Viola (track 8)
David Campbell: Orchestrations and conductor (tracks 6, 8)

Singles Released From This Album:
"To Know Him is To Love Him" b/w "Farther Along" – January 26, 1987 (peaked at # 1 on Hot Country Singles Chart on May 26, 1987 and # 1 on the Canadian RPM Chart)
"Telling Me Lies" b/w "Rosewood Casket" – May 11, 1987 (peaked at # 3 on the Billboard Hot County Singles and # 6 on the Canadian RPM Chart)
"Those Memories of You" b/w "My Dear Companion" – August 31, 1987 (peaked at # 5 on the Billboard Hot Country Singles Chart and # 1 on the Canadian RPM Chart)
"Wild Flowers" b/w "Hobo's Meditation" – March 7, 1988 (peaked at # 6 on Billboard Hot Country Singles and # 8 on Canadian RPM Chart)

Album Data:
Highest Chart Position: # 1 on May 1, 1987
Billboard Chart: Hot Country Albums
Number of weeks on chart: 84

Notes / Trivia:
- This album was released on LP, CD, 8–Track and Cassette on March 2, 1987
- The album was recorded January – November 1986
- Dolly's mother, Avie Lee Parton, arranged the song "Rosewood Casket."
- The album won the Grammy Award for "Best Country Performance by a Duo or Group with Vocal." It was also nominated for "Album of the Year." The song "Telling Me Lies" was also nominated for "Best Country Song." The album won the 1987 Academy of Country Music Award for "Album of the Year" and won "Vocal Event of the Year" at the Country Music Association Awards at the 1988 ceremony.
- In 2021, *Trio* was inducted into the Grammy Hall of Fame.
- The video for "To Know Him is To Love Him" was directed by George Lucas, Linda Ronstadt's lover at that time.
- The song "Telling Me Lies" was nominated for a Grammy award in 1988 for "Country Song of the Year."
- The album was certified platinum on July 14, 1987 for sales of over 1 million copies.

Dolly Parton • Linda Ronstadt • Emmylou Harris
Trio II
Asylum Records 62275–2

Track Listing:
Lover's Return / High Sierra / Do I Ever Cross Your Mind / After The Gold Rush / The Blue Train / I Feel the Blues Movin' In / You'll Never be The Sun / He Rode All the Way to Texas / Feels Like Home / When We're Gone, Long Gone

Production Information:
Produced by: George Massenburg
Co–Producer: John Starling
Recorded at: The Site Recording Studio, 11 Via del Sol, Marin CA 94946
Engineers: George Massenburg
Assistant Engineer: Nathaniel Kunkel / Kevin Scott
Mixed by: George Massenburg
Mastered by: Doug Sax at The Mastering Lab, Los Angeles, CA
Cover Photographs courtesy of: Emmylou Harris / Linda Ronstadt / Dolly Parton
Art Direction: Lyn Bradley / John Kosh

Musicians:
Emmylou Harris: Lead and harmony vocals
Dolly Parton: Lead and harmony vocals
Linda Ronstadt: Lead and harmony vocals, strings (track 4), string arrangements (track 4)
Robbie Buchanan: Acoustic piano (tracks 4, 8, 9), Rhodes (track 5), Hammond B3 organ (track 9)
Helen Voices: Synthesizers (track 4)
Mark Casstevens: Acoustic guitar (tracks 1, 2, 3, 5–9)
Carl Jackson: Acoustic guitar (tracks 1, 2, 3, 6, 10)
Dean Parks: Electric guitar (tracks 5, 8, 9), acoustic guitar (tracks 7, 8), mandolin (track 9)
John Starling: Acoustic guitar (track 10)
David Grisman: Mandolin (tracks 1, 2, 3, 6, 8, 9, 10)
David Lindley: Autoharp (track 1)
Ben Keith: Steel guitar (track 5)
Roy Huskey, Jr.: Bass (tracks 1, 6), double bass (tracks 2, 3, 10)
Leland Sklar: Bass (tracks 5, 8, 9)
Edgar Meyer: Double bass (track 7)
Larry Atamanuik: Drums (track 3)
Jim Keltner: Drums (tracks 5, 6, 8, 9, 10)
Alison Krauss: Fiddle (tracks 2, 3, 6, 10)

Dennis James: Glass harmonica (track 4)
David Campbell: Strings (tracks 4, 7, 9)

Singles Released From This Album:
"High Sierra" – January 1999 (peaked at # 90 on the Canadian *RPM* Country 100 chart)
"After The Gold Rush" – April 1999
"Feels Like Home" – April 1999
"Do I Ever Cross Your Mind" – April 1999

Album Data:
Highest Chart Position: # 4 on March 5, 1999
Billboard Chart: Hot Country Albums
Number of weeks on chart: 37

Notes / Trivia:
- This album was released on CD and Cassette on February 9, 1999
- Reissued on LP in 2016 (Catalog # R1 62275)
- Recorded in 1994
- The album was certified gold on November 15, 2001 for sales of over 500,000 copies.
- The songs on this album were recorded in 1994 but label resistance and conflicting schedules prevented their release. Eventually, Linda Ronstadt remixed five of the album's ten tracks (without Dolly's vocals) to include on her 1995 album, *Feels Like Home. Those songs were*; "Lover's Return", "High Sierra", "After the Gold Rush", "The Blue Train", and "Feels Like Home." In later 1998, after Dolly and Emmylou had left their various labels, it was decided to release the album as originally recorded.
- Childhood photos of Dolly, Emmylou and Linda were used for the album's cover design when a photo shoot proved unworkable due to the busy schedules of the three.
- The album was nominated for the Grammy Award for "Best Country Album." "After the Gold Rush" won the Grammy Award for "Best Country Collaboration with Vocals."
- Scheduling conflicts did not allow for any concert touring, but Dolly, Emmylou and Linda did a television tour to support the album. The trio made appearances on *CBS This Morning*, *The Tonight Show with Jay Leno*, *The Today Show* and *The Late Show with David Letterman* among others.

Dolly Parton • Linda Ronstadt • Emmylou Harris
The Complete Trio Collection

Track Listing:
Disc One: The Pain of Loving You / Making Plans / To Know Him is To Love Him / Hobo's Meditation / Wildflowers / Telling Me Lies / My Dear Companion / Those Memories of You / I've Had Enough / Rosewood Casket / Farther Along
Disc Two: Lover's Return / High Sierra / Do I Ever Cross Your Mind / After The Gold Rush / The Blue Train / I Feel the Blues Movin' In / You'll Never be The Sun / He Rode All the Way to Texas / Feels Like Home / When We're Gone, Long Gone
Disc Three: "Wildflowers" (Alternate Take 1986) / "Waltz Across Texas Tonight" (Unreleased 1994) / "Lovers Return" (Alternate Mix 1994) / "Softly and Tenderly" (Unreleased 1994) / "Pleasant as May" (Unreleased 1986) / "My Dear Companion" (Alternate Take 1986) / "My Blue Tears" (Unreleased 1998) / "Making Plans" (Alternate Take 1986) / "I've Had Enough" (Alternate Mix 1986) / "Grey Funnel Line" (Unreleased 1986) / "You Don't Knock" (Unreleased 1986) / "Where Will the Words Come From?" (Unreleased 1985) / "Do I Ever Cross Your Mind?" (Alternate Take 1994) / "Are You Tired of Me?" (Unreleased 1986) / "Even Cowgirls Get the Blues" / "Mr. Sandman" / "Handful of Dust" (Unreleased 1993) / "Calling My Children Home" (Unreleased 1986) / "In a Deep Sleep" (Unreleased 1986) / "Farther Along" (Alternate Mix 1986)

Singles Released From This Album:
"Do I Ever Cross Your Mind" (Alternate Take 1994) – March 28, 2016
"Wildflowers (Alternate Take 1986) – August 3, 2016
"Calling My Children Home" – August 12, 2016
"Waltz Across Texas Tonight" – August 24, 2016

Album Data:
Highest Chart Position: # 7 on September 30, 2016
Billboard Chart: Hot Country Albums
Number of weeks on chart: 4

Notes / Trivia:
- This album was released on CD on September 9, 2016
- A 2LP set titled *Farther Along*, was released separately on vinyl of the material from disc three.
- Recorded 1978 – 1998
- "Softly and Tenderly" was previously released on Harris' 2007 compilation *Songbird: Rare Tracks and Forgotten Gems*.

- While the album liner notes state "My Blue Tears" is an unreleased recording from 1998, it is actually a recording from 1978 that was originally released on Ronstadt's 1982 album *Get Closer*.
- "Even Cowgirls Get the Blues" was previously released on Harris' 1977 album *Blue Kentucky Girl*, however the version included in this set has Ronstadt and Parton sharing the verses with Harris, whereas in the original album they merely sang the harmony.
- "Mr. Sandman" was previously released on Harris' 1981 album *Evangeline*.

Front and back covers for the 2 LP set *Further Along*.

Loretta Lynn • Dolly Parton • Tammy Wynette
Honky Tonk Angels
CK 53414

Track Listing:
It Wasn't God Who Made Honky Tonk Angels (with special guest Kitty Wells) / Put It Off Until Tomorrow / Silver Threads and Golden Needles / Please Help Me I'm Falling (In Love with You) / Sittin' on the Front Porch Swing / Wings of a Dove / I Forgot More Than You'll Ever Know / Wouldn't It Be Great / That's the Way It Could Have Been / Let Her Fly / Lovesick Blues (with special guest Patsy Cline) / I Dreamed of a Hillbilly Heaven

Production Information:
Produced by: Steve Buckingham / Dolly Parton
Recorded at: Nightingale Studio (Nashville) / Masterfonics (Nashville) / The Doghouse (Nashville)
Engineers: Marshall Morgan / Gary Paczosa
Assistant Engineer: Jason Lehning / Alan Schulman / Toby Seay / Ed Simonton
Tape Editing: Don Cobb
Mastered by: Denny Purcell
Cover Painting: Bruce Wolfe
Art Direction / Design: Bill Johnson / Rollow Welch
Art assistance: Beth Kindig
Production Assistance: Cari Landers

Musicians:
Drums: Eddie Bayers
Guitar / Tic–Tac: Steve Gibson
Fiddle: Rob Hajacos
Upright Bass: Roy Huskey
Vibes: Farrell Morris
Steel Guitar: Weldon Myrick
Bass: Tom Robb
Piano: Hargus "Pig" Robbins
Guitar: Billy Sanford
Mandolin: Adam Steffy
Acoustic Guitar: Bruce Watkins
Harp: Cindy Reynolds Watt
Background vocals: Richard Dennison / Vicki Hampton / Louis Nunley / Jennifer O'Brien–Enoch
Kitty Wells – Guest vocals ("It Wasn't God Who Made Honky Tonk Angels")

"Lovesick Blues" Credits / Musicians:
Producer: Owen Bradley
Vocals: Patsy Cline
Upright Bass: Bob Moore
Electric Guitar: Grady Martin / Hank Garland
Drums: Buddy Harmon
Steel: Jimmy Day
Piano: Floyd Cramer
Tic–Tac piano: Harold Bradley

Singles Released From This Album:
"Silver Threads and Golden Needles" b/w "Let Her Fly" – November 8, 1993 (peaked at # 68 on Billboard's Hot Country Singles Chart dated January 14, 1994)

Album Data:
Highest Chart Position: # 6 on November 19, 1993
Billboard Chart: Hot Country Albums
Number of weeks on chart: 24

Notes / Trivia:
- This album was released on CD and Cassette on November 2, 1993.
- The album's only single "Silver Threads and Golden Needles" was nominated for a Grammy in the category *Best Country Collaboration with Vocals*.
- The album was certified Gold by the RIAA on January 5, 1994, for sales of 500,000 copies.
- "Lovesick Blues" was recorded by Patsy Cline on January 27, 1960 and produced by Owen Bradley. The musicians for this session are noted above.
- Recording on the album started on February 1, 1993.

Single release for *Silver Threads and Golden Needles*

Soundtrack Albums →

9 to 5
20th Century Fox Records / T–627

Track Listing:
9 to 5 (Main Title — Vocal)* / Violet Steals Body / Office Montage / Judy's Fantasy / Hart Tries To Escape / Violet's Fantasy / Easy Time / Dora Lee's Fantasy / Violet's Poisoned The Boss / Ajax Warehouse / The Intruder / Charlie's Bar / 9 to 5 (End Title — Vocal)*
*Performed by Dolly Parton

Production Information:
Album Produced by: Charles Fox, *except produced by: Gregg Perry for RCA Records
The song "9 to 5" was recorded at: Sound Labs, Inc, Los Angeles, CA
Engineer: Armin Steiner
"9 to 5" Mixed at Smoke Tree Ranch Studios, Chatsworth, CA
24 track mixing engineer: Doug Parry

Singles Released From This Album:
"9 to 5" b/w "Sing for The Common Man" – November 3, 1980

Album Data:
Highest Chart Position: # 77 on January 30, 1981
Billboard Chart: Hot Country Albums
Number of weeks on chart: 15

Notes / Trivia:
- This album was released on LP, 8–Track and Cassette on December 8, 1980.
- The song "9 to 5" became one of Dolly's biggest hits of the 1980's and was nominated for several awards, including the Academy Award for Best Song. It went on to win 1981's People's Choice Award for "Favorite Motion Picture Song" and two 1982 Grammy Awards for "Country Song of the Year" and "Female Country Vocal of the Year."
- The song peaked at #47 on the UK singles chart in 1981. It has sold 303,511 digital copies in the UK as of July 2014. As of 2017 it is Dolly's biggest download in the UK, totaling 340,800, while it has also been streamed 8.46 million times
- With "9 to 5", Dolly became only the second woman to top both the U.S. country singles chart and the *Billboard* Hot 100 with the same single (the first being Jeannie C. Riley, who had done so with "Harper Valley PTA" in 1968).
- The album has had only one official CD release on the Intrada label and was limited to 3000 copies in 2008. Copies have recently been seen selling used on–line for between $80 and $170 each.
- The "9 to 5 End Title — Vocal" is different than the opening track.

The Best Little Whorehouse in Texas
MCA-6112

Track Listing:
20 Fans / A Lil' Ole Bitty Pissant Country Place / Sneakin' Around / Watchdog Report / Texas Has A Whorehouse in It / Courtyard Shag / The Aggie Song / The Sidestep / Hard Candy Christmas / I Will Always Love You

Production Information:
Produced by: Gregg Perry
Engineers: Ernie Winfrey (Nashville) / Mike Bradley (Nashville) / Danny Wallin (Los Angeles) / Mickey Crawford (Los Angeles) / Arnie Frager (Los Angeles)
Remix Engineer: Danny Wallin (Los Angeles)
Cover Photography: Herb Ritts
Art Direction: George Osaki
Pressed by: MCA Pressing Plant, Gloversville, NY
Lacquers cut at: Precision Lacquer, Hollywood, CA

Singles Released From This Album:
"I Will Always Love You" b/w "Do I Ever Cross Your Mind" – July 12, 1982 (peaked at # 1 on the Hot Country Songs chart.)
"Hard Candy Christmas" b/w "Act Like A Fool" – October 11, 1982 (peaked at # 8 on the Hot Country Songs chart in January 1983.)

Album Data:
Highest Chart Position: # 5
Billboard Chart: Hot Country Albums

Notes / Trivia:
- This album was released on LP, Cassette and 8–Track on July 12, 1982
- The soundtrack was re–issued on CD in the mid 1980's.
- The film version and the soundtrack version of "Hard Candy Christmas" are different. In the film the woman sing refrains and Dolly Joins them. On the soundtrack Dolly sings alone.
- Dolly sang "Hard Candy Christmas" on Bob Hope's 1988 TV Special.
- Some notable remakes of "Hard Candy Christmas" include Cyndi Lauper's recording for her 2016 album *Detour* as a duet with Alison Krauss. Reba McEntire also recorded the song for her 2016 album *My Kind of Christmas*.

Rhinestone
ABL-1-5032

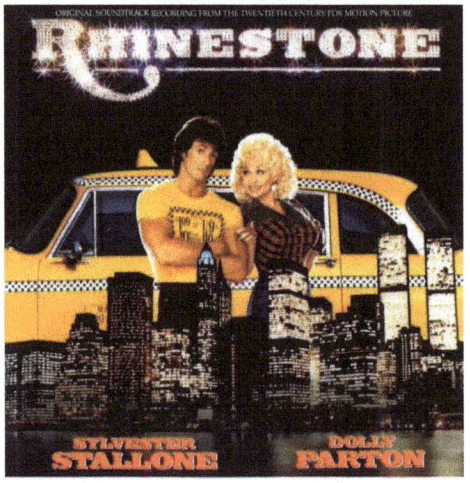

Track Listing:
Tennessee Homesick Blues – Dolly Parton / Too Much Water – Randy Parton / The Day My Baby Died – Rusty Buchanan / One Emotion After Another – Dolly Parton / Going Back To Heaven – Stella Parton and Kim Vassey / What A Heartache – Dolly Parton / Stay Out Of My Bedroom – Sly Stallone and Dolly Parton / Woke Up In Love – Sly Stallone and Dolly Parton / God Won't Get You – Dolly Parton / Drinkin'stein – Sylvester Stallone / Sweet Lovin' Friends – Dolly Parton / Waltz Me To Heaven – Floyd Parton / Butterflies – Dolly Parton / Be There – Dolly Parton and Sly Stallone

Production Information:
Produced by: Dolly Parton
Recorded at: Smoketree Ranch Studios, Chatsworth, CA, August 1983 – January 1984
Engineers: Doug Perry
Assistant Engineer: Ray Sheibley
Cover Photography: Steve Shapiro
Art Direction & Design: Tim Bryant

Musicians:
Drums: Mike Baird / Willie Ornelas
Bass: Dennis Belfield / Leland Sklar
Steel Guitar: John Bidasio
Guitars: John Goux / Herb Pedersen / Steve Watson
Fiddle: David Lindley
Harmonica: Tommy Morgan
Piano: Larry Muhoberac
Banjo: Herb Pedersen
Synthesizers: Pete Robinson / Ian Underwood
Lead Vocals: Dolly Parton / Floyd Parton / Randy Parton / Stella Parton / Kim Vassey / Rusty Buchanan / Sylvester Stallone
Background Vocals: Joey Scarbury / Richard Dennison / Linda Dillard / Randy Parton / Herb Pedersen

Singles Released From This Album:
"Tennessee Homesick Blues" b/w "Butterflies" – May 28, 1984 (peaked at # 1 on Billboard's US Hot Country Songs chart on September 8, 1984 and # 1 on Canada's RPM chart)
"God Won't Get You" b/w "Sweet Lovin' Friends" – August 20, 1984 (peaked at # 10 on Billboard's Hot Country Songs chart and # 8 on Canada's RPM chart)

"Goin' Back to Heaven" b/w "Stay Out of my Bedroom"– October 1984 (did not chart)
"What a Heartache" b/w "Butterflies"– 1984 (Netherlands only release – did not chart)

Album Data:
Highest Chart Position: # 32 on September 8, 1984
Billboard Chart: Hot Country Albums
Number of weeks on chart: 17

Notes / Trivia:

- This album was released on LP, 8–Track, cassette and CD on June 18, 1984.
- Dolly stated in her 1994 autobiography, *My Life and Other Unfinished Business*, that she considers the soundtrack album as some of her best recorded work, though the film was largely regarded as a critical and commercial flop. She's also mentioned "What a Heartache" as a personal favorite of all the songs she has written. She has re–recorded it twice since 1984. The first time was on the 1991 album *Eagle When She Flies* and again on the 2002 album *Halos & Horns*.
- All songs written by Dolly Parton, with the exception of "The Day My Baby Died," words by Phil Alden Robinson and music by Mike Post.

Picture sleeve for "What A Heartache" from The Netherlands

Beverly Hillbillies
Fox Records 07863 66313 2

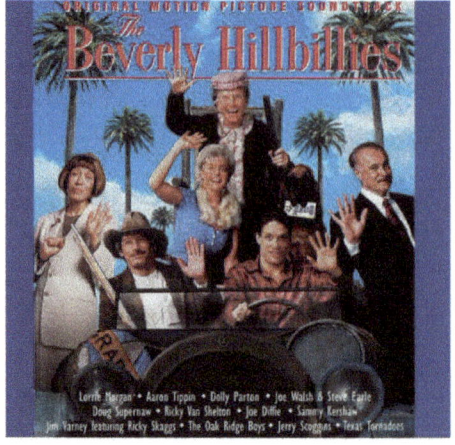

Track Listing:

White Lightnin' (Joe Diffee) / I Ain't Never (The Oak Ridge Boys) / Crying Time (Lorrie Morgan) / I'm Movin' On (Sammy Kershaw) / I'm So Lonely I Could Cry (Aaron Tippin) / Hot Rod Lincoln (Jim Varney Feat. Ricky Skaggs) / Honey Don't (Joe Walsh & Steve Earle) / Together Again (Doug Supernaw) / If You've Got The Money I've Got The Time (Ricky Van Shelton)/ Wasted Days And Wasted Nights (Freddy Fender) / If You Ain't Got Love (Dolly Parton) / The Ballad Of Jed Clampett (Jerry Scoggins)

Notes / Trivia:

- This album was released on cassette and CD on September 28, 1993
- The Dolly Parton 'band' in the film was composed of members of *Rhino Bucket*, the Dwight Yoakam Band (Skip Edwards), and Vern Monnett, Randy Meisner, Texas Tornados and Gary Allan).
- Dolly's appearance reunited her with *9 to 5* co-stars Lily Tomlin and Dabney Coleman.

The cassette tape insert.

Joyful Noise
Sony Music 88691936592

Track Listing:
Not Enough / Man in the Mirror / Maybe I'm Amazed / In Love / Fix Me, Jesus / From Here To The Moon and Back / I'm Yours / Mighty High / That's The Way God Planned It / Higher Medley: I Want To Take You Higher – Forever – Yeah! – Signed, Sealed, Delivered, I'm Yours / He's Everything / Joyful Noise Suite

Production Information:
Produced by: Mervyn Warren

Singles Released From This Album:
"He's Everything" – October 28, 2011
"From Here To The Moon and Back" – July 6, 2012

Album Data:
Highest Chart Position: # 1 on February 3, 2012
Billboard Chart: Soundtracks
Number of weeks on chart: 44

Notes / Trivia:

- This album was released on January 10, 2012

Dumplin'
Dolly Records / RCA / Sony 19075899082

Track Listing:
Here I Am (with Sia) / Holdin' on to You (with Elle King) / Girl in the Movies / Red Shoes / Why (with Mavis Staples) / Dumb Blonde (with Miranda Lambert) / Here You Come Again (with Willa Amai) / Who / Push and Pull (with Jennifer Aniston and Danielle MacDonald) / If We Don't (with Rhonda Vincent and Alison Krauss) / Two Doors Down (with Macy Gray and Dorothy) / Jolene (New String Version)

Production Information:
Produced by: Linda Perry
Executive Producer: Dolly Parton
Recorded at: Greeleaf Studio / Blackbird Studios
Overdubs (strings / Horns) recorded at: Blackbird Studios
Engineers: John McBride / Linda Perry
Assistant Engineer: Luis Flores / Sean Badum
Mixed by: Billy Bish / John McBride at Red Razor Sounds, Atwater Village, CA
Mixing Assistance: Allen Ditto
Mastered by: Emily Lazar at The Lodge
Mastering Assistant: Chris Allgood
Cover Photography: Rob Tshaya
Cover Design: JB Rowland
Hair Stylist: Cheryl Riddle
Wardrobe Design: Steve Summers
String Arrangements: Austin Hoke / Jim Hoke
Horn Arrangements: Jim Hoke

Musicians:
Piano: Willa Amai / Damon Fox
Keyboards: Damon Fox
B3 Organ: Damon Fox
Drums: David Goodstein
Bass: Billy Mohler
Acoustic Guitar: Damon Fox / Eli Pearl / Linda Perry
Electric Guitar: Damon Fox / Eli Pearl
Pedal Steel Guitar: Eli Pearl
Tenor Sax: Jim Hoke
Baritone Sax: Sam Levine

Trombone: Barry Green
Trumpet: Steve Patrick
Fiddle: Alison Krauss
Mandolin: Rhonda Vincent
Strings: David Angell / Avery Bright / David Davidson / Austin Hoke / Kristen Weber / Katelyn Westergard / Kristin Wilkinson / Betsy Lamb / Briana Lee / Emily Nelson
Vocals: Dolly Parton / Willa Amai / Dorothy / Macy Gray / Elle King / Sia / Mavis Staples / Miranda Lambert / Jim Hoke
Background Vocals: Maiya Sykes / Lisa Vitale / Jennifer Aniston / Luke Edgemon / Danielle MacDonald / Linda Perry

Singles Released From This Album:
"Here I Am" – September 14, 2018 (peaked at # 37 on the Billboard Hot Country Songs chart)
"Girl in the Movies" – November 2, 2018
"Jolene" – November 16, 2018

Album Data:
Highest Chart Position: # 16 on December 14, 2018
Billboard Chart: Hot Country Albums
Number of weeks on chart: 4

Notes / Trivia:

- This album was released on November 30, 2018
- Some of the material on the album Dolly had previously recorded: The song "Here I Am" was originally on Dolly's 1971 album *Coat of Many Colors*. "Holdin' on to You" was on Dolly's 1977 album *New Harvest...First Gathering*. "Dumb Blonde" was was on Dolly's 1967 album *Hello, I'm Dolly*. "Here You Come Again" was on Dolly's 1977 album of the same name. "Two Doors Down" was on Dolly's 1977 album *Here You Come Again*. Dolly would re–record the song for its 1978 single release. This 1978 re–recorded version replaced the original on all subsequent releases of the album. "Jolene" has been previously recorded by Dolly six times. Originally it was recorded for her 1974 album of the same name.
- The streaming edition contained 11 bonus tracks. They are: Here You Come Again (Dumplin' Remix) / Jolene (Dumplin' Remix) / 9 to 5 / Dumb Blonde / Two Doors Down / Jolene / Here You Come Again / Holdin' On To You / Just Because I'm A Woman / Better Get To Livin' / High and Mighty (with the Christ Church Choir)

Other Recorded Works

Hits Made Famous By Country Queens
SF-19700

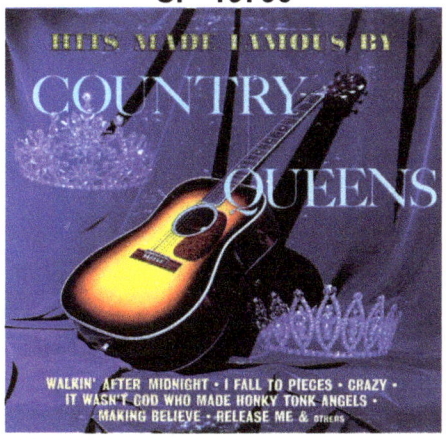

Track Listing:
Side One: Faye Tucker Sings Hits Made Famous by Patsy Cline
Crazy / I Fall To Pieces / Bill Bailey, Please Come Home / Walkin' After Midnight / Since You Went Away
Side Two: Dolly Parton Sings Hits Made Famous by Kitty Wells
It Wasn't God Who Made Honky Tonk Angels / Making Believe / Letter to Heaven* / Release Me / Two Little Orphans / Little Blossom

Production Information:
Produced by: D.L. Miller
Recorded in Nashville, TN

Notes / Trivia:
- This album was released on LP on April 13, 1963.
- This album is a compilation by Faye Tucker and Dolly Parton. The album features Faye singing four selections made famous by Patsy Cline, plus one original song. Parton sings three selections made famous by Kitty Wells, along with two traditional ballads and one original song she wrote*.
- This album was later issued many times over after Dolly became famous. One issue on the original Somerset label (# SF–29400) was titled "Dolly Parton Sings Country Oldies" and on the back the title was "Dolly Parton Sings Country Favorites." Faye is barely mentioned on the back.
- Somerset Records (Stereo Fidelity) were formed around 1959 by Dave Leonard Miller— "D.L. Miller" on the back of many of his albums. Records were pressed at factories in Swarthmore, Pennsylvania and Burbank, California.
- To save money Miller used public domain music and non union musicians to record cover versions of hit songs of the recent time. Miller had his own distribution channels for getting his records distributed in supermarkets and drugstores. The albums were sold in metal racks identical to those holding paperback books. Other were cardboard record holders called "dumps" that could be "dumped" anywhere in a store. Miller's record albums were sold wholesale for $.93 to salesmen who sold them to stores who sold them to the public for $1.98.
- Somerset Records (Stereo–Fidelity) primarily used artist Anthony "Chic" Laganella to create attractive eye catching album covers for all the releases. Miller's philosophy was that recording original "hits" was too unstable, and recording for teenagers and "sophisticates" was unprofitable as the two types bought "fads." Miller said that he did not want to record anything that would not sell ten years in the future.

- The album was remastered in 2016 from original Somerset multi-track master tapes and was made available for streaming and download by Apple Music on May 11, 2018.
- This albums has been reissued and bootlegged many times over the years and as far away as Asia. Some of the reissues are:

"Million Seller Country Hits Made Famous By Country Queens"
Vocals by Dolly Parton & Faye Tucker
Alshire Records– S–5351 (Issued in 1969)

"Dolly Parton sings Kitty Wells / Faye Tucker sings Patsy Cline"
Alshire Records– S–5351 (1978 issue with same catalog # as 1969)
Sides flipped from 1969 issue, tracks reordered, new title and cover design.

"Dolly Parton Sings – Plus Faye Tucker Sings"
Astor Records– S–5351 Australia (Issued in 1978 using the Alshire Records release #)

"Country Queens"
Hua Sheng Record KHS–4133 (year unknown)
This is an Taiwanese Bootleg. Dolly's name appears only on the label, nowhere on the record jacket. The front jacket had Dolly and Faye's names blocked out. The bootleg was also pressed on red vinyl.

Dolly Parton – A Personal Music Dialogue With Dolly Parton
A Personal Music Dialogue with Dolly Parton
New Harvest Radio Show
DJL-1-2314 / RCA-2056

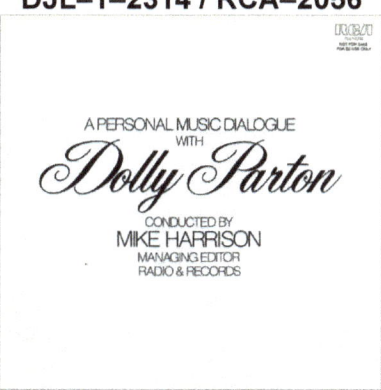

Track List:
Interview / Interview Continued / Higher And Higher Intro. / Your Love Has Lifted Me Higher And Higher / My Love Intro. / My Love / My Girl, My Love / Light Of A Clear Blue Morning Intro. / Light Of A Clear Blue Morning / Holdin' On To You Intro. / Holdin' On To You / Applejack Intro. / Applejack / Applejack Wrap–Up / You Are Intro. / You Are / There Intro. / There / Interview Closing / Where Beauty Lives In Memory

©1977 RCA Records

Notes / Trivia:

- This is a radio only promo and less than 50 copies were thought to have been pressed.
- Marked: For Promotional Use Only. Not For Sale" – Red print on white RCA labels.
- No music appears on this record, only intros and cues for the track to be played.
- Interview conducted by Mike Harrison.

Kenny Roger & Dolly Parton
Once Upon A Christmas
ASL-1-5307

Track Listing:
I Believe In Santa Claus / Medley: Winter Wonderland/Sleigh Ride (Dolly Parton solo) / Christmas Without You / The Christmas Song (Kenny Rogers solo) / A Christmas to Remember / With Bells On / Silent Night (Kenny Rogers solo) / The Greatest Gift of All / White Christmas (Dolly Parton solo) / Once Upon a Christmas

Production Information:
Produced by: David Foster and Kenny Rogers
Recorded at: Lion Share Studios (Los Angeles) / Sunset Sound (Hollywood) / Evergreen Studios (Nashville) / Cecca Sound (Dallas) / Lighthouse Recorders (Los Angeles)
Engineers: Humberto Gatica / Tommy Vicari
Assistant Engineers: Bob Pickering / David Leonard / John Richards / Larry Ferguson / Laura Livingston / Stephen Schmitt / Stephen Shelton / Stuart Furusho / Terry Christian / Tom Fouce / Paul Tye
Mixed by: Humberto Gatica at Lion Share Studios, Los Angeles, CA
Mastered by: Wally Traugott at Capitol Recording Studios, Hollywood, CA
Album pressed at: RCA Records Pressing Plant, Indianapolis. (6550 E. 30th Street Indianapolis, IN 46219)
Cover Photography: Reid Miles (Front & back cover) / Gene Trindl (Interior sleeve)
Art Direction: John Coulter Design

Musicians:
Keyboards / Synthesizer [Programming]: Erich Bulling
Keyboards: Jimmy Cox / John Hobbs / Randy Waldman / David Foster
Guitar: Billy Joe Walker Jr. / Fred Tackett / John Goux / Kin Vassey / Michael Landau / Paul Jackson Jr.
Drums: Ed Greene / John Robinson
Drums / Percussion: Paul Leim
Percussion: Victor Feldman
Bass: Dennis Belfield / Joe Chemay / Neil Stubenhaus

Singles Released From This Album:
"The Greatest Gift of All" b/w "White Christmas" – November 26, 1984 (peaked at number 53 on Hot Country Singles chart .)
Medley: "Winter Wonderland" and "Sleigh Ride" b/w "The Christmas Song" – November 26, 1984
"Christmas Without You" b/w "White Christmas" – November 14, 1984 (UK) / November 25, 1985 (US)
"I Believe in Santa Claus" b/w "Christmas Without You" – November 23, 1987

Album Data:
Highest Chart Position: # 12 on January 11, 1985
Billboard Chart: Hot Country Albums
Number of weeks on chart: 41

Notes / Trivia:

- This album was released on LP, Cassette and CD on October 29, 1984.
- Released to tie in with the CBS–TV Special "A Christmas to Remember" which originally aired on Sunday, December 2, 1984.
- The album received the Canadian Country Music Association Award for Top Selling Album in 1985.
- In 1997, the album was reissued on the BMG Special Products label with an altered track listing. The song order was slightly rearranged and Rogers' two solos were omitted ("The Christmas Song" and "Silent Night"). However, Parton's 1982 recording of "Hard Candy Christmas" from The Best Little Whorehouse in Texas was added.
- The album received gold and platinum certifications on December 3, 1984. Then double platinum on October 25, 1989.

TV Guide clipping December 1984

Bill Owens with Dolly Parton
Dreams Do Come True

Track Listing:
Dreams Do Come True / Fell Off The Wagon Last Night And Hurt My Head / Brand New Man / Honky Tonk Bars / Put It Off Until Tomorrow / Welfare Blues / Don't Let It Trouble Your Mind / Cheap Home Grown Cost Cutter Beer / My Mind's Been Cheating On You / Medley

Notes / Trivia:
- Cassette only release. No catalog number
- It is unknown what tracks Dolly appears on or where this was sold
- Reissued at least once with different cover graphics of Bill and Dolly
- Bill is Dolly's uncle who worked closely with her and helped her start her career.

Sha–Kon–O–Hey! Land of Blue Smoke

Track Listing:
My Mountains, My Home / Hey Howdy Hey / Working on a Dream / Time Flies / Heart of the Smokies / Good Time / Sha–Kon–O–Hey! / Forever Home

Production Information:
Produced by: Dolly Parton / Tony Smith
Mix Engineer: Marv Treutel at Topshelf Studio, Nashville, Tennessee
Mastered at: Benny Quinn Mastering

Musicians:
Background Vocals: Richard Dennison / Vicki Hampton / Jennifer O'Brien

Notes / Trivia:

- This extended play mini album was released on February 11, 2009
- It was was sold exclusively at Dollywood and through the Great Smoky Mountains Association.
- All material written and arranged by: Dolly Parton

Back of the CD packaging

DOLLY PARTON / DONNA FARGO
Compilation

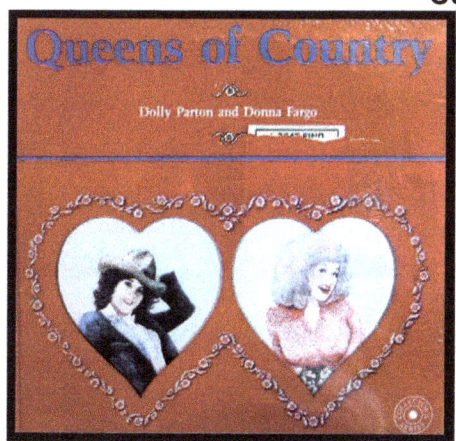 

Two covers of different labels shown here.

Track Listing:

Dolly Parton:
Honky Tonk Angels / Making Believe / Letter to Heaven / Release Me / Little Blossoms / Two Little Orphans

Donna Fargo:
Daddy / Sticks and Stones / Wishful Thinking / All That's Keeping Me Alive

The same or similar tracks are on the following other releases:

Lucky (CLUC–005 / Cassette only release 1983 Australia)
Sundown (SDLP–1001 / SS–O53 / 66053 1983 UK)
Quicksilver (QS–5060 / Intermedia S–10132 1983 US)
Andover / Aura Records (AN–3010 / A–1018 1983 US)
The Collection (OR–0051 CD 1988 UK) (This CD has "Puppy Love" and "Girl Left Alone" added to the other Dolly Parton tracks)

The recordings on all of these releases of Dolly Parton were produced in 1963 and were originally found on the Somerset label out of Burbank, California. The original B side had been songs recorded by Faye Tucker but Donna Fargo has been substituted. These releases are thought to be bootleg, but several could be licensed from Somerset by companies that have since gone out of business. Several other releases not mentioned here for space have been issued with these songs and other singers added to the song line up, but not always to the cover art. One release features Loretta Lynn on the cover, but Lynn Anderson music.

In 1998 a CD release of the Dolly and Donna album was released along with Lynn Anderson songs added by Canadian company Direct Source Special Products # PT76852. That album included the tracks:

Donna Fargo:
Happiest Girl in the Whole USA / Don't Be Angry / Somebody Special / That Was Yesterday / Do I Love You / Funny Face

Dolly Parton:
God Didn't Make Honky Tonk Angels / Making Believe / Letter To Heaven / Release Me / Two Little Orphans / Puppy Love

Lynn Anderson:
Rose Garden / Devil Went Down To Georgia / Rocky Top / Could I Have This Dance / You Needed Me / Blue Bayou

On the Dolly Parton tracks listed above; "God Didn't Make Honky Tonk Angels" should have been listed as "It Wasn't God Who Made Honky–Tonk Angels."

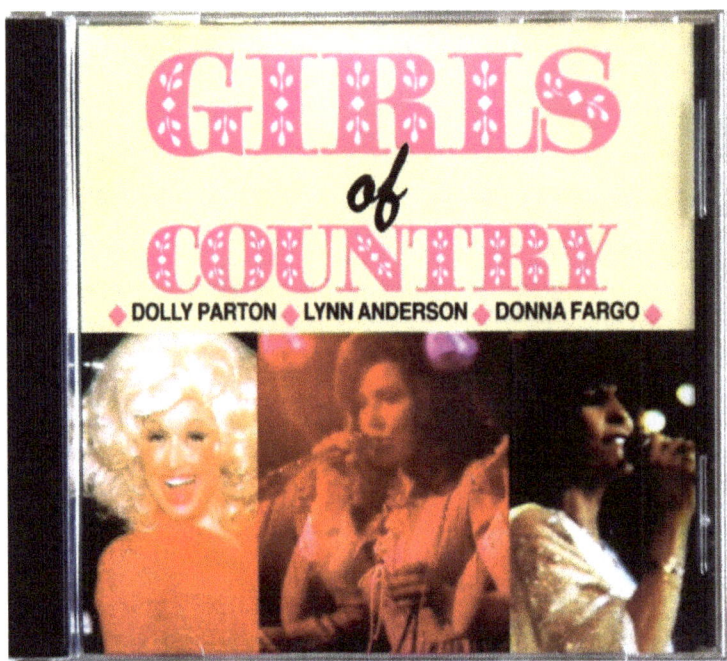

On this release above (which I feel should have been titled "Women of Country") somehow Loretta Lynn's photo was used on the cover, yet Lynn Anderson's music is on the disc. Other than the release number (ARC 36) there is no label information at all.
Doesn't give me a reason to believe in this label!

Though bootlegged many times Dolly's Somerset tracks were released though *Starday* (now Gusto), a legitimate Nashville label, along with George Jones being on the flip side on LP and tape in 1969/1970.

SLP 429 / S–SLP 429 (LP)
Dolly Parton & George Jones

Wild Texas Wind

Track Listing:
1.) Big T (Dolly Parton & Ray Benson)
2.) There's A Ring Around The Moon Tonight (Dolly Parton & Ray Benson)
3.) Say It's True (Dolly Parton & Ray Benson)
4.) Road Happy / On The Road Again (Dolly Parton, Ray Benson & Willie Nelson)
5.) Cover Up A Heart That's Broke (Dolly Parton)
6.) Swingin' Like Tarzan & Jane (Dolly Parton & Ray Benson)
7.) Farther Along (Dolly Parton)
8.) Leave That Cowboy Alone (Dolly Parton & Ray Benson)
9.) Instrumental (Fiddle Interlude)
10.) Wild Texas Wind (Dolly Parton)
11.) Speakin' Of The Devil (Dolly Parton)
12.) I Love A Tall Man (Dolly Parton & Ray Benson)
13.) Songbird (Willie Nelson)
14.) Big T / On The Road Again (Reprise) (Dolly Parton, Ray Benson & Willie Nelson)
15.) Wild Texas Wind Theme (Instrumental Theme Song)

Notes / Trivia:

- This is a bootleg of the TV film soundtrack likely made by a fan. This music has never been officially released by NBC–TV, Sandollar Productions or Dolly Records. This release is sure to have film dialog or other ambient noise from the film.
- "Farther Along" had been recorded by Dolly previously.

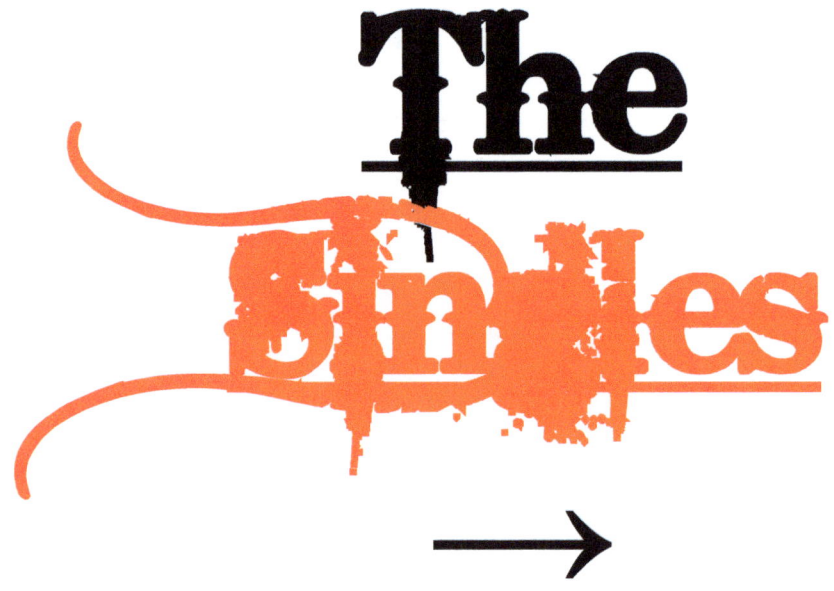

Dolly Parton Singles
PS – Picture Sleeve

1959

Puppy Love / Girl Let Alone – G–1086 (Goldband) (US)

1960

So Little I Wanted, So Little I Got / Forbidden Love – CB–102 (with Bill Owens) (Circle–B Records) (US)

1962

It's Sure Gonna Hurt / The Love You Gave (with the Merry Melody Singers) – 71982 (Mercury) (US)
It's Sure Gonna Hurt / The Love You Gave (with the Merry Melody Singers) – 71982 (Mercury) DJ Copy (US)
It's Sure Gonna Hurt / The Love You Gave (with the Merry Melody Singers) – 71982 (Mercury) Mono (US)

1964

What do You Think About Lovin' / I Wasted My Tears – MN45–869 (Monument) (US)
What do You Think About Lovin' / I Wasted My Tears – MN45–869 (Monument) DJ Copy (US)

1965

Happy, Happy Birthday Baby / Old Enough To Know Better – MN45–897 (Monument) (US)
Happy, Happy Birthday Baby / Old Enough To Know Better – MN45–897 (Monument) DJ Promo (US)

Once You've Left – ©Screen Gems / Columbia Music (single sided promo acetate)

Bill Phillips – It Happens Everytime / Friends Tell Friends – 31848 (DECCA) (US) (Dolly sings background vocals on side two. Dolly also wrote the song with Bill Owens)

1966

Bill Phillips – Put It Off until Tomorrow / Lonely, Lonely Boy – 31901 (DECCA) (US) (Dolly sings background vocals on side one. Dolly also wrote the song)

Don't Drop Out / Control Yourself – MN45 922 (Monument) (US)
Don't Drop Out / Control Yourself – MN45 922DJ (Monument) DJ Copy (US)

Dumb Blonde / The Giving And The Taking – MN–982 (Monument) (Canada)
Dumb Blonde / The Giving And The Taking – MN45–982 (Monument) (US)
Dumb Blonde / The Giving And The Taking – MN45–982DJ (Monument) DJ Copy (US)
Dumb Blonde / The Giving And The Taking – MN45–539 (Monument) (US)

The Little Things / I'll Put It Off Until Tomorrow – MN45–948 (Monument) (US)
The Little Things / I'll Put It Off Until Tomorrow – MN45–948DJ (Monument) DJ Copy (US)

Busy Signal / I Took Him For Granted – MN45–913 (Monument) (US)
Busy Signal / I Took Him For Granted – MN45–913DJ (Monument) DJ Copy (US)

Busy Signal / I Took Him For Granted – LR5.556 (London Records) (Belgium) (PS)

1967

Something Fishy / I've Lived My Life – MN45–1007 (Monument) (US)
Something Fishy / I've Lived My Life – MN45–1007DJ (Monument) DJ Copy (US)
Something Fishy / I've Lived My Life – MN1007 (Monument) (Canada)
I've Lived My Life / I've Lived My Life – MN45–1007 (Monument) White label promotional single (US)

Why, Why, Why / I Could Wait Forever – MN45–1032 (Monument) (US)
Why, Why, Why / I Could Wait Forever – MN45–1032DJ (Monument) DJ Copy (US)
Why, Why, Why / I Could Wait Forever – MN–1032 (Monument) (Canada)

1968

Just Because I'm A Woman / I Wish I Felt This Way At Home – 47–9548 (RCA) (US)
Just Because I'm A Woman / I Wish I Felt This Way At Home – 47–9548 (RCA) DJ Copy / Plug Side (US)
Just Because I'm A Woman / I Wish I Felt This Way At Home – 47–9548 (RCA) Red Label (Canada)

In The Good Old days (When Times Were Bad) / Try Being Lonely – 47–9657 (RCA) (US)
In The Good Old days (When Times Were Bad) / Try Being Lonely – 47–9657DJ (RCA) DJ Copy (US)
In The Good Old days (When Times Were Bad) / Try Being Lonely – 47–9657 (RCA) Red Label (Canada)

I'm Not Worth The Tears / Ping Pong – MN45–1047 (Monument) (US)
I'm Not Worth The Tears / Ping Pong – MN45–1047DJ (Monument) DJ Copy (US)
(Dolly's final single release on her former label)

1969

Daddy / He's A Go–Getter – 74–0132 (RCA) (US)
Daddy / He's A Go–Getter – 74–0132DJ (RCA) DJ Copy / Plug Side / Green Label (US)
He's A Go–Getter / He's A Go–Getter – 74–0132 (RCA) DJ Copy / Plug Side / Green Label (US)

My Blue Ridge Mountain Boy / 'Til Death Do Us Part – 74–0243 (RCA) (US)
My Blue Ridge Mountain Boy / 'Til Death Do Us Part – 74–0243DJ (RCA) DJ copy / plug side / green label (US)
My Blue Ridge Mountain Boy / 'Til Death Do Us Part – 74–0243 (RCA) (Canada)

Daddy Come and Get Me / Chas – 74–9784 (RCA) (US)
Daddy Come and Get Me / Chas – 74–9784 (RCA) (US) DJ Copy / plug side / green label
Daddy Come and Get Me / Chas – 74–9784 (RCA) (Canada)

In The Ghetto / The Bridge – 74–0192 (RCA) (US)
In The Ghetto / The Bridge – 74–0192 (RCA) (US) DJ copy / plug side / green label
In The Ghetto / The Bridge – 74–0192 (RCA) (Canada)
In The Ghetto / The Bridge – 85–1082 (RCA) (Peru)
In The Ghetto / The Bridge – 3–10443 (RCA) (Spain) (PS)
("In The Ghetto" is credited to Scott Davis, not Mac Davis. Songwriter Mac Davis was born Scott Mac Davis)

Just Because I'm A Woman / I'm Running Out Of Love – 42 140 (RCA) (South Africa)

1970

Joshua / I'm Doing This For Your Sake – 47– 9928 (RCA) (US)
Joshua / I'm Doing This For Your Sake – 47– 9928 (RCA) (US) DJ copy / plug side / green label
Joshua / I'm Doing This For Your Sake – 47– 9928 (RCA) (Canada)
Joshua / I'm Doing This For Your Sake – 47– 9928 (RCA) (New Zealand)

Joshua / J.J. Sneed – 2253DJ (RCA) (UK) DJ copy
Joshua / J.J. Sneed – 2253 (RCA) (UK)

Mule Skinner Blues (Blue Yodel No. 8) / More Than Their Share – 47–9863 (RCA) (US)
Mule Skinner Blues (Blue Yodel No. 8) / More Than Their Share – 47–9863DJ (RCA) (US) DJ copy / plug side / green label

Dumb Blonde / Something Fishy – MN45–552 (Monument) (US)

1971

Comin' For To Carry Me Home / Comin' For To Carry Me Home – SPS–45–254 (RCA) (US) DJ copy / Green label promo / mono – stereo
Comin' For To Carry Me Home / Golden Streets of Glory – 47–9971 (RCA) (US)
Comin' For To Carry Me Home / Golden Streets of Glory – 47–9971 (RCA) (Canada)

My Blue Tears / The Mystery of the Mystery – 47–9999 (RCA) (US)
My Blue Tears / The Mystery of the Mystery – 47–9999 (RCA) (US) DJ Copy / plug side / green label
My Blue Tears / The Mystery of the Mystery – 47–9999 (RCA) (Canada)

Coat of Many Colors / Here I Am – 74–0538 (RCA) (US) (PS)
Coat of Many Colors / Here I Am – 42 284 (RCA) (South Africa)
Coat of Many Colors / Here I Am – 74–0538 (RCA) (Canada)
Coat of Many Colours / Here I Am – 102046 (RCA) (Australia)

1972

Washday Blues / Just As Good As Gone – 74–0757 (RCA) (US)
Washday Blues / Just As Good As Gone – 74–0757 (RCA) (US) DJ copy / plug side / green label
Washday Blues / Just As Good As Gone – 74–0757 (RCA) (Canada)

Dumb Blonde / Something Fishy – ZS7 8912 (Monument)

When I Sing For Him / Lord Hold My Hand – 74–0797 (RCA) (US)
When I Sing For Him / Lord Hold My Hand – 74–0797 (RCA) (US) DJ copy / plug side / green label
When I Sing For Him / Lord Hold My Hand – 74–0797 (RCA) (Canada)

Touch Your Woman / Mission Chapel Memories – 74–0662 (RCA) (US) DJ copy / plug side / green label / Mono
Touch Your Woman / Mission Chapel Memories – 74–0662 (RCA) (US)
Touch Your Woman / Mission Chapel Memories – 74–0662 (RCA) (Canada)

My Tennessee Mountain Home /The Better Part Of Life – 74–0868 (RCA) (US)
My Tennessee Mountain Home /The Better Part Of Life – 74–0868 (RCA) (Canada)

Joshua / J.J. Sneed – 2253 (RCA) (UK) (Promo reissue – release date 8/18/1972)

1973

My Tennessee Mountain Home /The Better Part Of Life – 102223 (RCA) (Australia)
Jolene / Love, You're So Beautiful Tonight – APB0–0145 (RCA) (US)
Jolene / Love, You're So Beautiful Tonight – 42–496 (RCA) (South Africa)
Jolene / Love, You're So Beautiful Tonight – APB0–0145 (RCA) (Canada)
Jolene / Love, You're So Beautiful Tonight – 42–496, APBO 0145 (RCA) (Mozambique)
Jolene / Love, You're So Beautiful Tonight – APBO–0145 (RCA) (Portugal) (PS)
Jolene / Love, You're So Beautiful Tonight – 102414 (RCA) (Australia)

Travelin' Man / I Remember – 74–0950DJ (RCA) (US) DJ Copy / plug side / gold label
Travelin' Man / I Remember – 74–0950 (RCA) (US)
Travelin' Man / I Remember – 74–0950 (RCA) (Canada)

Joshua / Harper Valley PTA / Coat of Many Colors / Jeannie's Afraid of The Dark – 20569 (RCA) (Australia) (EP) (PS) (May 1973)

1974

Jolene / Love, You're So Beautiful Tonight – APB0 0145 (RCA) (UK) (release date: 5/17/1974)
Jolene / Love, You're So Beautiful Tonight – APB0 0145 (RCA) (New Zealand) (PS)

I Will Always Love You / Lonely Comin' Down – APB0–0234 (RCA) (US)
I Will Always Love You / Lonely Comin' Down – DJA0–0234 (RCA) (US) DJ copy / mono / gold label
I Will Always Love You / Lonely Comin' Down – APB0–0234 (RCA) (Canada)
I Will Always Love You / Lonely Comin' Down – APB0–0234 (RCA) (South Africa)
I Will Always Love You / Lonely Comin' Down – APB0–0234 (RCA) (New Zealand)

Love is Like A Butterfly / Sacred Memories – PB–10031 (RCA) (US)
Love is Like A Butterfly / Sacred Memories – 42 540 (RCA) (South Africa)
Love is Like A Butterfly / Sacred Memories – PB–10031 (RCA) (Canada)
Love is Like A Butterfly / Sacred Memories – PB–10031 (RCA) (Canada) DJ copy / white label
Love is Like A Butterfly / Sacred Memories – 102498 (RCA) (Australia)
Love is Like A Butterfly / Sacred Memories – PB–10031 (RCA) (New Zealand)

Jolene / My Tennessee Mountain Home – GB–10165 (RCA) (Canada) (Golden Greats Reissue)

1975

The Bargain Store / The Bargain Store – JH–10164 (RCA) (US) DJ copy / white label
The Bargain Store / I'll Never Forget – PB–10164 (RCA) (US)
The Bargain Store / I'll Never Forget – RCA 2566 (RCA) (UK)
The Bargain Store / I'll Never Forget – 102583 (RCA) (Australia)
The Bargain Store / I'll Never Forget – PB–10164 (RCA) (New Zealand)

The Bargain Store / Down From Dover – RCA–2728 (RCA) (UK) (PS)

The Seeker / Love With Feeling – PB–10310 (RCA) (US)
The Seeker / Love With Feeling – JA–10310 (RCA) (US) DJ copy / mono / white label
The Seeker / Love With Feeling – PB–10310 (RCA) (Canada)
The Seeker / Love With Feeling – RCA 2603 (RCA) (UK)
We Used To / My Heart Started Breaking – PB–10396 (RCA) (US)
We Used To / We Used To – JH–10396 (RCA) (US) DJ copy / mono – stereo / white label

We Used To / My Heart Started Breaking – PB–10396 (RCA) (Canada)
We Used To / My Heart Started Breaking – 102716 (RCA) (Australia)

Hey Lucky Lady / Hey, Lucky Lady – JH–10564 (RCA) (US) DJ copy / mono–stereo / white label
Hey Lucky Lady / Most Of All, Why – PB–10564 (RCA) (US)
Hey Lucky Lady / Most Of All, Why – PB–10564 (RCA) (Canada)

1976

Shattered Image / I'm A Drifter – RCA–2764 (RCA) (UK)

Jolene / Love, You're So Beautiful Tonight – APBO–0145 (RCA) (Netherlands) (PS)

Jolene / My Tennessee Mountain Home – GB–10165 (RCA) (US) (Gold Standard Reissue)

Love is Like A Butterfly / Sacred Memories – GB–10504 (RCA) (US) (Gold Standard Reissue)

I Will Always Love You / Lonely Comin' Down – GB–10505 (RCA) (US) (Gold Standard Reissue)

The Seeker / The Bargain Store – GB–10676 (RCA) (US) (Gold Standard Reissue)

Jolene / Coat of Many Colors / Love is Like A Butterfly – RCA 2675 (RCA) (UK) 3 track EP

Jolene / Coate of Many Colors – PPBO–7064 (RCA) (Germany) (PS) (Sleeve has misspelling)

Touch Your Woman / Coat Of Many Colors – 447–0943 (RCA) (US) (Gold Standard Reissue)
Touch Your Woman / Coat Of Many Colors – 447–0943 (RCA) (Canada) (Golden Greats Reissue)

Dumb Blonde / Something Fishy – GS 1912 (Monument) (US) (Re–issue)

All I Can Do / All I Can Do – JH–10730 (RCA) (US) DJ copy / mono–stereo / white label
All I Can Do / Falling Out Of Love with Me – PB–10730 (RCA) (US)
All I Can Do / Falling Out Of Love with Me – PB–10730 (RCA) (French) (PS)

1977

Applejack / You Are – PB–9059 (RCA) (Netherlands) (PS)

You Are / Applejack – PB–9059 (RCA) (UK)

(Your Love Has Lifted Me) Higher and Higher / Applejack – PB–9134 (RCA) (Germany) (PS)

(Your Love Has Lifted Me) Higher and Higher / Light Of A Clear Blue Morning – 102951 (RCA) (Australia)

Light of A Clear Blue Morning / There – PB–10935 (RCA) (US)
Light of A Clear Blue Morning / Light of A Clear Blue Morning – JH–10935 (RCA) (US) DJ copy / mono–stereo / white label
Light of A Clear Blue Morning / There – PB–10935 (RCA) (Canada)
Light of A Clear Blue Morning / Light of A Clear Blue Morning – JB–10935 (RCA) (US) Promo (May 1977) Long version 4:53 / Short Version 3:16
Here You Come Again / Here You Come Again – JH–11123 (RCA) (US) DJ copy / mono–stereo / white label

Here You Come Again / Me And Little Andy – PB–11123 (RCA) (US)
Here You Come Again / Me And Little Andy – PB–11123 (RCA) (Canada)
Here You Come Again / Me And Little Andy – PB–1123 (RCA) (Netherlands) (PS)
Aqui Vienes Nuevamente (Here You Come Again) / El Pequeño Andy Y Yo (Me And Little Andy) – PB–1123 (RCA) (Peru)
Here You Come Again / Me And Little Andy – 103007 (RCA) (Australia)
Here You Come Again / Me And Little Andy – 103007 (RCA) (New Zealand)
Here You Come Again / Me And Little Andy – PB–1123 (RCA) (France) (PS)
Here You Come Again / Me And Little Andy – PB 9182 (RCA) (UK)
Here You Come Again / Me And Little Andy – PB–1123 (RCA) (Germany) (PS)
Here You Come Again / Me And Little Andy – 101.4089 (RCA) (Brazil)

Two Doors Down / Two Door Down – JH–11240 (RCA) (US) DJ copy / mono–stereo / white label
Two Doors Down / It's All Wrong, But It's All Right – PB–11240 (RCA) (US)
Two Doors Down / It's All Wrong, But It's All Right – JB–11248 (RCA) (US) DJ copy
Two Doors Down / It's All Wrong, But It's All Right – PB–11240 (RCA) (Canada)
Two Doors Down / It's All Wrong, But It's All Right – PB–1240 (RCA) (UK)
Two Doors Down / It's All Wrong, But It's All Right – PB–1240 (RCA) (UK) DJ copy
Two Doors Down / It's All Wrong, But It's All Right – 103100 (RCA) (New Zealand)
Two Doors Down / It's All Wrong, But It's All Right – 103100 (RCA) (Australia)

It's All Wrong, But It's All Right / It's All Wrong, But It's All Right (RCA) (US) DJ copy / white label / stereo–mono
It's All Wrong, But It's All Right / It's All Wrong, But It's All Right – JB–11241 (RCA) (US) Promotional Long version 3:19 / Short version 2:42

1978

Baby, I'm Burnin / I Wanna Fall in Love – PB–1425 (RCA) (Belgium) (PS)
Baby, I'm Burnin / I Wanna Fall in Love – PB 1425 (RCA) (Netherlands) (PS)
Baby, I'm Burnin / I Wanna Fall in Love – PB–11420 (RCA) (Canada)
Baby, I'm Burnin / I Wanna Fall in Love – PB–11420 (RCA) (US)
Baby, I'm Burnin / I Wanna Fall in Love – JB–11420 (RCA) (US) DJ copy / white label
Baby, I'm Burnin / I Wanna Fall in Love – PB 9329 (RCA) (UK)
Baby, I'm Burnin / I Wanna Fall in Love – PB 9329 (RCA) (UK) DJ copy / orange label
Cariño, Me Estoy Quemando (Baby, I'm Burnin) / Deseo Enamorarme (I Wanna Fall In Love) PD–11425 (RCA) (Peru)
Baby, I'm Burnin / I Wanna Fall in Love – JD–11425 (RCA) (US) 12" pink vinyl single (PS) DJ copy
Baby, I'm Burnin / I Wanna Fall in Love – PD–11425 (RCA) (US) 12" pink vinyl single (PS)
Baby, I'm Burnin / I Wanna Fall in Love – PC–11425 (RCA) (UK) 12" pink vinyl single
Baby, I'm Burnin / I Wanna Fall in Love – PD–11425 (RCA) (Canada) 12" pink vinyl single (PS)
Baby, I'm Burnin / I Wanna Fall in Love – TDS–035 (RCA) (Australia) 12" pink vinyl single
Baby, I'm Burnin / I Wanna Fall in Love – TDS–035 (RCA) (Australia) 12" black vinyl single

Baby, I'm Burnin / Baby, I'm Burnin – JB 11420 (RCA) (US) DJ copy / Red vinyl / White label

Baby, I'm Burnin / I Really Got The Feeling – JB–11420 (RCA) (US) DJ copy / white label
Baby, I'm Burnin / I Really Got The Feeling – 103268 (RCA) (Australia)
Baby, I'm Burnin / I Really Got The Feeling – 103268 (RCA) (New Zealand)
Baby, I'm Burnin / I Really Got The Feeling – PB–1420 (RCA) (France) (PS)
Baby, I'm Burnin / I Really Got The Feeling – PB–1420 (RCA) (Germany) (PS)

Aquí Vienes Otra Vez (Here You Come Again) / El Pequeño Andy Y Yo (Me And Little Andy) – PB–

1123 (RCA) (Spain) (PS)

Here You Come Again / Me And Little Andy – SS–3126 (RCA) (Japan) (PS)
Here You Come Again / Me And Little Andy – SP–4909 (RCA) (Mexico) (PS)
Here You Come Again / Me And Little Andy – SP–4909 (RCA) (Mexico) (PS) DJ copy / white label

Here You Come Again / Light of A Clear Blue Morning – PB 9204 (RCA) (Italy) (PS)

Two Doors Down / It's All Wrong, But It's All Right – ECK–200729 (RCA) (Ecuador)
Dos Puertas Abajo (Two Doors Down) / Todo Esta Mal, Pero Esta Bien (It's All Wrong, But It's All Right) – SP–4944 (RCA) (Mexico) (PS)
Two Doors Down / It's All Wrong, But It's All Right – PB–1248 (RCA) (Netherlands) (PS)
Two Doors Down / It's All Wrong, But It's All Right – SS–3154 (RCA) (Japan) (PS)

Rompecorazones (Heartbreaker) / Algo Seguro (Sure Thing) – SP–5088 (RCA) (Mexico) (PS)
Heartbreaker / Sure Thing – PB–11296 (RCA) (US)
Heartbreaker / Heartbreaker – JH–11296 (RCA) (US) DJ copy / white label
Heartbreaker / Sure Thing – PB–1296 (RCA) (France) (PS)
Heartbreaker / Sure Thing – PB–1296 (RCA) (Netherlands) (Clear Vinyl) (PS)
Heartbreaker / Sure Thing – PB–11296 (RCA) (Canada)
Heartbreaker / Sure Thing – 103180 (RCA) (New Zealand)
Heartbreaker / Sure Thing – 103180 (RCA) (Australia)

Heartbreaker / Baby, I'm Burnin' / Here You Come Again / Two Doors Down – PC –9401 (RCA) (UK) (PS) 4 track EP

It's Too Late To Love Me Now / With You Gone – 42–889 (RCA) (South Africa)

1979

Baby, I'm Burnin / I Really Got The Feeling – SP–5148 (RCA) (Mexico) (PS)
Baby, I'm Burnin / I Really Got The Feeling – PB–1420 (RCA) (Italy) (PS)
Estoy ardiendo (Baby, I'm Burnin) / Siento las vibraciones (I Really Got The Feeling) – PB–1420 (RCA) (Spain) (PS)

Baby, I'm Burnin / I Wanna Fall in Love – 100.4003 (RCA) (Brazil) (Green Vinyl)
Baby, I'm Burnin / I Wanna Fall in Love – SS–3188 (RCA) (Japan) (PS)
Baby, I'm Burnin / I Wanna Fall in Love – PC–1425 (RCA) (Spain) (PS) 12" single

Start of the Show / Down – PB 4510 (RCA) (Netherlands) (PS)

Star of the Show / Do You Think That Time Stands Still – 103485 (RCA) (Australia)
Star of the Show / Do You Think That Time Stands Still – 103485 (RCA) (New Zealand)

You're The Only One / You're The Only One – JH–11577 (RCA) (US) DJ copy / white label / stereo–mono
You're The Only One / You're The Only One – JH–11577 (RCA) (US) DJ copy / white label / stereo–mono / Orange marble vinyl / orange labels
You're The Only One / Down – PB–11577 (RCA) (US)
You're The Only One / Down – PB–11577 (RCA) (Canada)
You're The Only One / Down – 45S–9002 (RCA) (Venezuela)
You're The Only One / Down – 103387 (RCA) (New Zealand)
You're The Only One / Down – 103387 (RCA) (Australia)

You're The Only One / Down – 42–925 (RCA) (South Africa)
You're The Only One / Down – SS–3214 (RCA) (Japan) (PS)
You're The Only One / Down – SS–3214 (RCA) (Japan) (PS) DJ copy / white label
You're The Only One / Down – PB–1577 (RCA) (UK)
You're The Only One / Help! – 101.4097 (RCA) (Brazil)

Daddy Come And Get Me / Daddy was An Old Time Preacher Man – 42–939 (RCA) (South Africa)

Great Balls of Fire / Great Balls of Fire – JH–11705 (RCA) (US) DJ copy / white label / stereo–mono

Great Balls of Fire / Sweet Summer Lovin' – JB–11705 (RCA) (US) DJ copy / white label / red vinyl
Great Balls of Fire / Sweet Summer Lovin' – PB–11705 (RCA) (US) (Promotional release used to tie-in with Bally's Dolly Parton pinball machine. Hard cardboard 7" picture sleeve as shown in gallery.)
Great Balls of Fire / Sweet Summer Lovin' – PB–11705 (RCA) (US)
Great Balls of Fire / Sweet Summer Lovin' – PB–11705 (RCA) (Canada)
Great Balls of Fire / Sweet Summer Lovin' – 103427 (RCA) (New Zealand)
Great Balls of Fire / Sweet Summer Lovin' – PB 1705 (RCA) (Spain) (PS)
Great Balls of Fire / Sweet Summer Lovin' – 103427 (RCA) (Australia)
Great Balls of Fire / Sweet Summer Lovin' – SS–3233 (RCA) (Japan) (PS)
Great Balls of Fire / Sweet Summer Lovin' – 42–952 (RCA) (South Africa)

Great Balls of Fire / Do You Think That Time Stands Still – PB 9434 (RCA) (UK) (PS) pink translucent vinyl

Great Balls of Fire / Down – PB–9415 (RCA) (Germany) (PS)
Great Balls of Fire / Down – PB–9415 (RCA) (France) (PS)

1980

Starting Over Again / Sweet Agony – PB–11926 (RCA) (US)
Starting Over Again / Starting Over Again – JH–11926 (RCA) (US) DJ copy / white label / stereo–mono / Green translucent vinyl / green labels
Starting Over Again / Sweet Agony – 42 986 (RCA) (South Africa)
Starting Over Again / Sweet Agony – PB–11926 (RCA) (US) DJ copy / yellow labels / stereo
Starting Over Again / Sweet Agony – PB 1926 (RCA) (UK) DJ copy
Starting Over Again / Sweet Agony – 103565 (RCA) (New Zealand)
Starting Over Again / Sweet Agony – 101.4103 (RCA) (Brazil)
Starting Over Again / Sweet Agony – PB 1926 (RCA) (Spain)
Starting Over Again / Sweet Agony – 103565 (RCA) (Australia)

Old Flames Can't Hold A Candle To You / I Knew You When – PB–12040 (RCA) (US)
Old Flames Can't Hold A Candle To You / Old Flames Can't Hold A Candle To You – JH–12040 (RCA) (US) DJ copy / white label / stereo–mono
Old Flames Can't Hold A Candle To You / Old Flames Can't Hold A Candle To You – JH–12040 (RCA) (US) DJ copy / white label / red print / stereo–mono
Old Flames Can't Hold A Candle To You / I Knew You When – PB–12040 (RCA) (Canada)

But You Know I Love You / Poor Folks Town – PB–12200 (RCA) (US)
But You Know I Love You / Poor Folks Town – JB–12200 (RCA) (US) DJ copy / white labels / stereo
But You Know I Love You / Poor Folks Town – JB–12200 (RCA) (US) DJ copy / pink labels / stereo
But You Know I Love You / Poor Folks Town – PB–12200 (RCA) (Canada)
But You Know I Love You / Poor Folks Town – 103774 (RCA) (Australia)

9 to 5 / Sing For The Common Man – PB–12133 (RCA) (US) (PS)
9 to 5 / Sing For The Common Man – PB–12133 (RCA) (Canada) (PS)
9 to 5 / Sing For The Common Man – PB–2133 (RCA) (Portugal) (PS)
9 to 5 / Canta Para El Hombre De La Calle (Sing For The Common Man) PB–2133 (RCA) (Spain) (PS)
9 to 5 / 9 to 5 – PB–12133 (RCA) (US) DJ copy / tan label / stereo–mono
9 to 5 / 9 to 5 – PB–12133 (RCA) (US) DJ copy / pink label / stereo–mono / blue translucent vinyl
9 to 5 / Sing For The Common Man – PB–2133 (RCA) (Sweden) (PS)
9 to 5 / Sing For The Common Man – PB–2133 (Olympia / RCA) (Sweden) (PS) Promotional release for Olympia Typewriters. (No catalog # on record label)
9 to 5 / Sing For The Common Man – 103730 (RCA) (Australia)
9 to 5 / Sing For The Common Man – PB–2133 (RCA) (Portugal) (PS)
9 to 5 / Sing For The Common Man – RCA 25 (RCA) (UK)
9 to 5 / Sing For The Common Man – PB 8709 (RCA) (France) (PS)
De 9 a 5 (9 to 5) / Sing For The Common Man – CA–11087 (RCA) (El Salvador)
De 9 a 5 (9 to 5) / Sing For The Common Man – CA–11087 (RCA) (El Salvador) Red vinyl release
9 to 5 / Sing For The Common Man – PB–2133 (RCA) (Netherlands) (PS)
9 to 5 / Sing For The Common Man – PB–2133 (RCA) (Germany) (PS)
9 to 5 / Sing For The Common Man – 42–1030 (RCA) (South Africa)
9 to 5 / Sing For The Common Man – 42–1030 (RCA) (Zimbabwe)
9 to 5 / Sing For The Common Man – RS 2149 (RCA) (Bolivia)
9 to 5 / Sing For The Common Man – 103730 (RCA) (New Zealand)

"9 To 5" Featuring Dolly Parton (with theme song) / "9 To 5" Featuring Jane Fonda & Lily Tomlin – BK163A (181USA) (20th Century Fox Productions) (US) (Special material for use by the International Press in the United States) (Prepared by: Backstage Productions, Inc. 1101 So. Robertson Blvd, LA 90035)

House of The Rising Sun / Working Girl – PB–12282 (RCA) (US)
House of The Rising Sun / Working Girl – JB–12282 (RCA) (US) DJ copy / light yellow label
House of The Rising Sun / Working Girl – JB–12282 (RCA) (US) DJ copy / Gold label
House of The Rising Sun / Working Girl – PB–12282 (RCA) (Canada)
House of The Rising Sun / Working Girl – PB–2282 (RCA) (Germany) (PS

Me and Little Andy / Cowgirl and the Dandy – PB 9526 (RCA) (UK)

1981

9 to 5 / Sing For The Common Man – PB–2133 (RCA) (Spain) (PS)
9 to 5 / Sing For The Common Man – RPS–30 (RCA) (Japan) (PS)
9 to 5 / Sing For The Common Man – RPS–30 (RCA) (Japan) (PS) DJ copy / white label
9 to 5 / Sing For The Common Man – 101.4110 (RCA) (Brazil) (PS)
Dalle 9 Alle 5 (9 to 5) / Sing For The Common Man – PB 2133 (RCA) (Italy) (PS)
Dalle 9 Alle 5 (9 to 5) / Sing For The Common Man – PB 2133 (RCA) (Italy) DJ copy / white label
9 to 5 / Canción Para Un Hombre Común (Sing For The Common Man) – XRPBO 1047 (RCA) (Peru)

Como Eliminar A Su Jefe (Violet's Poisoned The Boss) / Cancion Para Un Hombre Comun (Sing For The Common Man) – E–0088 (RCA) (Argentina) (Side one actually translates to: How to eliminate your boss)

9 to 5 / Applejack – PB–60147 (RCA) (Portugal) (PS)
9 to 5 / House of The Rising Sun – DB–8665 (RCA) (France)

But You Know I Love You / Poor Folks Town – PB–2200 (RCA) (Netherlands) (PS)
Pero Tu Sabes Que Te Quiero (But You Know I Love You) / Pobre Gente De Pueblo (Poor Folks Town) – PB–2200 (RCA) (Spain) (PS)
Pero Tu Sabes Que Te Quiero (But You Know I Love You) / Pobre Gente De Pueblo (Poor Folks Town) – PB–2200 (RCA) (Spain) (PS) DJ copy / white labels / stereo
Jolene / Here You Come Again – PB–9814 (RCA) (Netherlands) (PS)

I Will Always Love You / Fool for Your Love – 42 1074 (RCA) (South Africa)

1982

Single Women / Single Women – JK–13057 (RCA) (US) DJ copy / white labels / stereo
Single Women / Single Women – JK–13057 (RCA) (US) DJ copy / red vinyl / white labels / stereo
Single Women / Barbara on Your Mind – PB–13057 (RCA) (US)
Single Women / Barbara on Your Mind – PB–13057 (RCA) (Canada)
Single Women / Barbara on Your Mind – 103954 (RCA) (Australia)
Single Women / Barbara on Your Mind – 103954 (RCA) (New Zealand)

Dumb Blonde / Something Fishy – WS8 03460 (Monument) (US) Reissue

Everything's Beautiful In Its Own Way (w/ Willie Nelson) / Here Comes That Rainbow Again (Kris Kristofferson solo) – MNT A 2983 (Monument) (Netherlands) (PS)
Everything's Beautiful In Its Own Way (w/ Willie Nelson) / Here Comes That Rainbow Again (Kris Kristofferson solo) – MNT A 2983 (Monument) (UK) (PS)
Everything's Beautiful In Its Own Way (w/ Willie Nelson) / Here Comes That Rainbow Again (Kris Kristofferson solo) – MNT A 2983 (Monument) (UK) (PS) DJ copy / white label

Everything's Beautiful In Its Own Way (w/ Willie Nelson) / Everything's Beautiful In Its Own Way (w/ Willie Nelson) – WS4 03408 (Monument) (US) DJ copy / white label
Everything's Beautiful In Its Own Way (w/ Willie Nelson) / Put It Off Until Tomorrow (w/ Kris Kristofferson) – WS4 03408 (Monument) (US)
Everything's Beautiful In Its Own Way (w/ Willie Nelson) / Put It Off Until Tomorrow (w/ Kris Kristofferson) – WS4 03408 (Monument) (Canada)
Everything's Beautiful In Its Own Way (w/ Willie Nelson) / Put It Off Until Tomorrow (w/ Kris Kristofferson) – K 9070 (Monument) (New Zealand)

Heartbreak Express / Heartbreak Express – PB–13234–A – JK–13234 (RCA) (US) DJ copy / green vinyl / green labels / stereo
Heartbreak Express / Act Like A Fool – PB–13234 (RCA) (US)
Heartbreak Express / Act Like A Fool – JB–13234 (RCA) (US) DJ copy / white labels / stereo
Heartbreak Express / Act Like A Fool – 104006 (RCA) (Australia)
Heartbreak Express / Act Like A Fool – 104006 (RCA) (New Zealand)

I Will Always Love You / I Will Always Love You – JK–13260 (RCA) DJ copy / white labels / stereo
I Will Always Love You / Do I Ever Cross Your Mind – JB–13260 (RCA) (US) DJ copy / yellow translucent vinyl / pink labels / stereo
I Will Always Love You / Do I Ever Cross Your Mind – PB–13260 (RCA) (US) (PS)
I Will Always Love You / Do I Ever Cross Your Mind – PB–13260 (RCA) (Canada) (PS)
I Will Always Love You / Do I Ever Cross Your Mind – (RCA) (Jamaica)
I Will Always Love You / Do I Ever Cross Your Mind – PB–3260 (RCA) (Germany) (PS)
I Will Always Love You / Do I Ever Cross Your Mind – 104040 (RCA) (Australia)
Siempre te amaré (I Will Always Love You) / Do I Ever Cross Your Mind – PB–3260 (RCA) (Spain) (PS)

I Will Always Love You / Do I Ever Cross Your Mind – RCA 270 (RCA) (UK) (PS)
I Will Always Love You / Do I Ever Cross Your Mind – PB–3260 (RCA) Netherlands) (PS)

Hard Candy Christmas / Hard Candy Christmas – JK–13361 (RCA) (US) DJ copy / white labels / stereo
Hard Candy Christmas / Hard Candy Christmas – JK–13361 (RCA) (US) DJ copy / red vinyl / pink labels / stereo
Hard Candy Christmas / Me and Little Andy – PB–13361 (RCA) (US)
Hard Candy Christmas / Me and Little Andy – PB–13361 (RCA) (Canada)

1983

You Are / Jealous Heart – PB–60109 (RCA) (Netherlands) (PS)
You Are / Jealous Heart – TRS 492 (RCA) (South Africa)

You're Gonna Love Yourself (In The Morning) (Willie Nelson & Brenda Lee) / What Do You Think About Loving (Dolly Parton & Brenda Lee) – WS4 03781 (Monument) (US)

You're Gonna Love Yourself (In The Morning) (Willie Nelson & Brenda Lee) / What Do You Think About Loving (Dolly Parton & Brenda Lee) – WS1 03781 (Monument) (Canada)

Potential New Boyfriend (Short version) / Potential New Boyfriend (Long version) – JK 13514 (RCA) (US) DJ copy / blue translucent vinyl / pink labels / stereo
Potential New Boyfriend (Short version) / Potential New Boyfriend (Long version) – JK 13514 (RCA) (US) DJ copy / yellow translucent vinyl / yellow labels / stereo
Potential New Boyfriend / One Of Those Days – JB–13514 (RCA) (US) DJ copy / yellow label
Potential New Boyfriend / One Of Those Days – PB–13514 (RCA) (US)
Potential New Boyfriend / One Of Those Days – RCA 335 (RCA) (UK) (PS)
Potential New Boyfriend / One Of Those Days – TRS 461 (RCA) (South Africa)
Potential New Boyfriend / One Of Those Days – 104152 (RCA) (Australasia)
Potential New Boyfriend / One Of Those Days – PB–13514 (RCA) (Canada)
Potential New Boyfriend / One Of Those Days – RCA–335 (RCA) (Netherlands) (PS)
Potential New Boyfriend / One Of Those Days – 104152 (RCA) (New Zealand)
Potential New Boyfriend / One Of Those Days – PB 3514 (RCA) Germany (PS)
Potential New Boyfriend (Long version) / Potential New Boyfriend (Instrumental) / Potential New Boyfriend (Short version) TDS–148 (RCA) (Australia) 12" version
Potential New Boyfriend (Long version) / Potential New Boyfriend (Instrumental) / Potential New Boyfriend (Short version) PW–13545 (RCA) (Canada) 12" version
Potential New Boyfriend (Long version) / Potential New Boyfriend (Instrumental) / Potential New Boyfriend (Short version) PW–13545 (RCA) (US) 12" version
Potential New Boyfriend (Long version) / Potential New Boyfriend (Instrumental) / Potential New Boyfriend (Short version) JW–13545 (RCA) (US) DJ copy / white label / 12" version
Potential New Boyfriend (Long version) / Potential New Boyfriend (Instrumental) / Potential New Boyfriend (Short version) JW–13545 (RCA) (US) DJ copy / pink label / yellow translucent vinyl / 12" version

Islands in the Stream (Kenny Rogers & Dolly Parton) / Midsummer Night (Kenny Rogers Solo) – PB–60107 (RCA) (Netherlands) (PS) (From Kenny Rogers RCA LP *Eyes That See In The Dark*)
Islands in the Stream (Kenny Rogers & Dolly Parton) / Midsummer Night (Kenny Rogers Solo) – PB–60107 (RCA) (Scandinavia) (PS) (From Kenny Rogers RCA LP *Eyes That See In The Dark*)
Islands in the Stream (Kenny Rogers & Dolly Parton) / Midsummer Night (Kenny Rogers Solo) – RCA378 (RCA) (UK) (PS) (From Kenny Rogers RCA LP *Eyes That See In The Dark*)
Islands in the Stream (Kenny Rogers & Dolly Parton) / Midsummer Night (Kenny Rogers Solo) –

PB49477 (RCA) (Germany) (PS) (From Kenny Rogers RCA LP *Eyes That See In The Dark*)
Islands in the Stream (Kenny Rogers & Dolly Parton) / Midsummer Night (Kenny Rogers Solo) – PB 61237 (RCA) (France) (PS) (From Kenny Rogers RCA LP *Eyes That See In The Dark*)
Islands in the Stream (Kenny Rogers & Dolly Parton) / Midsummer Night (Kenny Rogers Solo) – PB–60107 (RCA) (Ireland) (From Kenny Rogers RCA LP *Eyes That See In The Dark*)
Islands in The Stream (Kenny Rogers & Dolly Parton) / Islands in The Stream (Kenny Rogers & Dolly Parton) – JH–13615 (RCA) (US) DJ copy / white label / mono–stereo pressing
Islands in The Stream (Kenny Rogers & Dolly Parton) / I Will Always Love You (Kenny Rogers solo) – PB–13615 (RCA) (US) (PS)
Islands in The Stream (Kenny Rogers & Dolly Parton) / I Will Always Love You (Kenny Rogers solo) – PB–13615 (RCA) (Jamaica)
Islands in The Stream (Kenny Rogers & Dolly Parton) / I Will Always Love You (Kenny Rogers solo) – PB–13615 (RCA) (Barbados)
Islands in The Stream (Kenny Rogers & Dolly Parton) / I Will Always Love You (Kenny Rogers solo) – PB–13615 (RCA) (Portugal) (PS)
Islands in The Stream (Kenny Rogers & Dolly Parton) / I Will Always Love You (Kenny Rogers solo) – PB–3615 (RCA) (Spain) (PS)
Islands in The Stream (Kenny Rogers & Dolly Parton) / I Will Always Love You (Kenny Rogers solo) – XFPBO–1063 (RCA) (Philippines)
Islands in The Stream (Kenny Rogers & Dolly Parton) / I Will Always Love You (Kenny Rogers solo) – RUS–058 (RCA) (El Salvador)
Islands in The Stream (Kenny Rogers & Dolly Parton) / I Will Always Love You (Kenny Rogers solo) – TRS–473 (RCA) (South Africa) (PS)
Islands in The Stream (Kenny Rogers & Dolly Parton) / I Will Always Love You (Kenny Rogers solo) – 104180 (RCA) (Australia)
Islands in The Stream (Kenny Rogers & Dolly Parton) / I Will Always Love You (Kenny Rogers solo) – PB–60107 (RCA) (Germany) (PS)
Islands in The Stream (Kenny Rogers & Dolly Parton) / Islands In The Stream – JR–13662 (RCA) (US) white label 12" promotional single

Just Because I'm A Woman (Dolly Parton) / What's He Doing In My World (Eddy Arnold) – W893 (RCA) (Jamaica)

Save The Last Dance For Me / Save The Last Dance For Me – JK–13703 (RCA) (US) DJ copy / pink labels / stereo
Save The Last Dance For Me / Save The Last Dance For Me – JK–13703 (RCA) (US) DJ copy / white labels / stereo
Save The Last Dance For Me / Save The Last Dance For Me – JK–13703 (RCA) (US) DJ copy / green vinyl / pink labels / stereo
Save The Last Dance For Me (Long version) / Save The Last Dance For Me (Instrumental) / Save The Last Dance For Me (Short version) PW–13712 (RCA) (US)
Save The Last Dance For Me (Long version) / Save The Last Dance For Me (Instrumental) / Save The Last Dance For Me (Short version) PW–13712 (RCA) (US) DJ copy / white labels / stereo
Save The Last Dance For Me / Elusive Butterfly – PB–13703 (RCA) (US)
Save The Last Dance For Me / Elusive Butterfly – PB–13703 (RCA) (Canada)
Save The Last Dance For Me / Elusive Butterfly – 104228 (RCA) (New Zealand)
Save The Last Dance For Me / Elusive Butterfly – PB 3703 (RCA) (Germany) (PS)
Save The Last Dance For Me / Elusive Butterfly – 104228 (RCA) (Australia)
Save The Last Dance For Me / Elusive Butterfly – PB 3703 (RCA) (Netherlands) (PS)
Save The Last Dance For Me / Elusive Butterfly – PB–13703 (RCA) (Barbados)

1984

Tu Y Yo (You and I) Kenny Rogers Solo / Islas En El Arroyo (Islands in The Stream) (Kenny Rogers & Dolly Parton) – Peru–17159 (RCA) (Peru) (From Kenny Rogers RCA LP *Eyes That See In The Dark*)

God Won't Get You / God Won't Get You – JK–13883 (RCA) (US) DJ copy / tan labels / stereo
God Won't Get You / God Won't Get You – JK–13883 (RCA) (US) DJ copy / pink labels / red text / stereo – mono

God Won't Get You / Sweet Loving Friends (w/ Sylvester Stallone) – PB–13883 (RCA) (US)

Here You Come Again / Potential New Boyfriend / Love Is Like A Butterfly – RCA 395 (RCA) (UK) (PS) 3 Track EP

Here You Come Again / Potential New Boyfriend / Love Is Like A Butterfly – RCA 395 (RCA) (UK) (PS) 3 Track EP / poster sleeve

Here You Come Again / 9 to 5 / Potential New Boyfriend / Love Is Like A Butterfly – RCA 395 (RCA) (UK) (PS) 4 Track EP / 10" picture disc

Heartbreaker / Sandy's Song – PB–60129 (RCA) (Netherlands) (PS)

Downtown / Downtown – JK–13756 (RCA) (US) DJ copy / white label / red text
Downtown / Downtown – JK–13756 (RCA) (US) DJ copy / pink label / red text
Downtown / Downtown – JK–13756 (RCA) (US) DJ copy / tan label

Downtown / The Great Pretender – PB–13756 (RCA) (US) (PS)
Downtown / The Great Pretender – PB–13756 (RCA) (Canada)
Downtown / The Great Pretender – DB–61424 (RCA) (France)
Downtown / The Great Pretender – 104273 (RCA) (Australia)

Tennessee Homesick Blues (with audience) / Tennessee Homesick Blues / JB–13819 (RCA) (US) DJ copy / blue translucent vinyl / yellow label
Tennessee Homesick Blues (with audience) / Tennessee Homesick Blues– PB–13819 (RCA) (US) DJ copy / gold label

Tennessee Homesick Blues / Butterflies – PB–13819 (RCA) (US)
Tennessee Homesick Blues / Butterflies – 104294 (RCA) (Australia)
Tennessee Homesick Blues / Butterflies – 104294 (RCA) (New Zealand)
Tennessee Homesick Blues / Butterflies – PB–13819 (RCA) (Canada)

What A Heartache / Butterflies – PB–60179 (RCA) (Netherlands) (PS)

She Don't Love You / The Great Pretender – 104308 (RCA) (New Zealand)

Goin' Back To Heaven (Stella Parton & Kim Vassey) / Goin' Back To Heaven (Stella Parton & Kim Vassey) – JK–13924 (RCA) (US) DJ copy / white label
Goin' Back To Heaven (Stella Parton & Kim Vassey) / Stay Out Of My Bedroom (Dolly Parton & Sylvester Stallone) – PB–13924 (RCA) (US)
Goin' Back To Heaven (Stella Parton & Kim Vassey) / Stay Out Of My Bedroom (Dolly Parton & Sylvester Stallone) – PB–13924 (RCA) (Canada)
Medley: Winter Wonderland – Sleigh Ride / Medley: Winter Wonderland, Sleigh Ride – JK–13944 (RCA) (US) yellow label / green text

Medley: Winter Wonderland – Sleigh Ride / Medley: Winter Wonderland, Sleigh Ride – JK–13944 (RCA) (US) tan label
Medley: Winter Wonderland – Sleigh Ride / The Christmas Song (Kenny Rogers) – PB–13944 (RCA) (US)

The Greatest Gift of All (w/Kenny Rogers) / White Christmas – PB–13945 (RCA) (US)
The Greatest Gift of All (w/Kenny Rogers) / White Christmas – PB–13945 (RCA) (Canada)
The Greatest Gift of All (w/Kenny Rogers) / White Christmas – JK–13945 (RCA) (US) DJ copy / gold label / red text
The Greatest Gift of All (w/Kenny Rogers) / White Christmas – PB–3945 (RCA) (Netherlands) (PS)

I Believe In Santa Claus / Christmas Without You – 5352–7–RDJ (RCA) (US) DJ copy / white label
I Believe In Santa Claus / Christmas Without You – 5352–7–R (RCA) (US)
I Believe In Santa Claus / Christmas Without You – 5352–7–RDJ (RCA) (Canada) DJ copy / white label
I Believe In Santa Claus / Christmas Without You – 5352–7–R (RCA) (Canada)
I Believe In Santa Claus / Christmas Without You – 104627 (RCA) (Australia)
I Believe In Santa Claus / Christmas Without You – 104627 (RCA) (New Zealand)

Christmas Without You (w/ Kenny Rogers) / Christmas Without You (w/ Kenny Rogers) – PB–14261 (RCA) (US) tan label
Christmas Without You (w/ Kenny Rogers) / Christmas Without You (w/ Kenny Rogers) – PB–14261 (RCA) (US) White label
Christmas Without You (w/ Kenny Rogers) / A Christmas To Remember (w/ Kenny Rogers) – PB–14261 (RCA) (US) (PS)
Christmas Without You (w/ Kenny Rogers) / A Christmas To Remember (w/ Kenny Rogers) – PB–14261 (RCA) (Canada) (PS)

Christmas Without You / White Christmas – PB 61534 (RCA) (France) (PS)
Christmas Without You / White Christmas – RCA 465 (PB 60211) (RCA) (UK) (PS)

1985

Don't Call It Love (with sax solo) / Don't Call It Love (without sax solo) – JB–13987 (RCA) (US) DJ copy / tan label
Don't Call It Love / Don't Call It Love (without sax solo) – JB–13987 (RCA) (US) DJ copy / tan label / blue translucent vinyl
Don't Call It Love / Don't Call It Love (without sax solo) – JK–13987 (RCA) (US) DJ copy / pink label / red vinyl / red text
Don't Call It Love / We Got Too Much – PB–13987 (RCA) (US)
Don't Call It Love / We Got Too Much – PB–13987 (RCA) (Canada)

Real Love (w/ Kenny Rogers) / Don't Call It Love – 123–1045 (RCA) (Ecuador)
Real Love (w/ Kenny Rogers) / Don't Call It Love – GB–14346 (RCA) (US) Gold Standard Reissue

Real Love (w/ Kenny Rogers) / Real Love (w/ Kenny Rogers) – JK–14058 (RCA) (US) DJ copy / pink label
Real Love (w/ Kenny Rogers) / I Can't Be True – PB–14058 (RCA) (US) (PS)
Real Love (w/ Kenny Rogers) / I Can't Be True – PB–14058 (RCA) (Canada)
Real Love (w/ Kenny Rogers) / I Can't Be True – 104448 (RCA) (Australia) (PS)
Real Love (w/ Kenny Rogers) / I Can't Be True – 104448 (RCA) (New Zealand) (PS)
Real Love (w/Kenny Rogers) / Come Back To Me – PL 45035 (RCA) (Europe) (PS)

Think About Love /Think About Love – JK–14218 (RCA) (US) DJ copy / orange label / stereo
Think About Love /Think About Love – JK–14218 (RCA) (US) DJ copy / white label / stereo
Think About Love / Come Back To Me – PB–14218 (RCA) (US)
Think About Love / Come Back To Me – PB–14218 (RCA) (Canada)
Think About Love / Come Back To Me – PD–24 (RCA) (Zimbabwe)
Think About Love / Come Back To Me – 104494 (RCA) (New Zealand)
Think About Love / Come Back To Me – 104494 (RCA) (Australia)

Think About Love / Love Is Like A Butterfly – DP–1 (RCA) (UK) DJ copy / white label

Think About Love / We Got Too Much – PD–2336 (RCA) (South Africa) (PS)

Think About Love / Baby, I'm Burnin' – PB49729 (RCA) (Germany) (PS)

Think About Love / I Can't Be True – PB 49995 (RCA) (UK) (PS)

Tie Our Love In A Double Knot – PD–27 (RCA) (Zimbabwe)

Tomorrow is Forever / Just Because I'm A Woman – PD–28 (RCA) (Zimbabwe)

We Had It All / We Had It All – 5001–7–RDA (RCA) (US) DJ copy / tan label
We Had It All / Do I Ever Cross Your Mind – 5001–7–R (RCA) (US)
We Had It All / Do I Ever Cross Your Mind – 5001–7–RAA (RCA) (US) DJ Copy / tan label

Tie Out Love (In A Double Knot) /Tie Out Love (In A Double Knot) – JK–14297 (RCA) (US) DJ copy / pink label / red text
Tie Out Love (In A Double Knot) /Tie Out Love (In A Double Knot) – JK–14297 (RCA) (US) DJ copy / white label
Tie Out Love (In A Double Knot) /Tie Out Love (In A Double Knot)
Tie Out Love (In A Double Knot) / I Hope You're Never Happy – PB–14297 (RCA) (US)

Jolene / Down From Dover – PB–49971 (RCA) (Netherlands) (PS)

We Used To / Travelin' Man – PB–60217 (RCA) (Netherlands) (PS)

1986

Almost In Love / The Love I Used To Call Mine – PB–49887 (RCA) (Germany) (PS)
Jolene / The Bargain Store – OG–9603 (RCA) (UK) (PS)

Puppy Love / Girl Let Alone – G–1086 (NR–16791) (Goldband) (US) (PS) (This copy said to be a bootleg, though I don't think so)

1987

Wildflowers / Wildflowers (Dolly Parton / Emmylou Harris / Linda Ronstadt) – 7–27970 (WB) (US) DJ copy
Wildflowers / Hobo's Meditation (Dolly Parton / Emmylou Harris / Linda Ronstadt) – 7–27970 (WB) (US)
Wildflowers / Hobo's Meditation (Dolly Parton / Emmylou Harris / Linda Ronstadt) – 7–27970 (WB) (Canada)
I Will Always Love You / Love is Like A Butterfly – OG–9667 (Old Gold) (Europe) (Licensed from RCA)

Telling Me Lies / To Know Him Is To Love Him (Dolly Parton / Emmylou Harris / Linda Ronstadt) – 7–21955
Telling Me Lies / Telling Me Lies (Dolly Parton / Emmylou Harris / Linda Ronstadt) – 7–28371 (WB) (US) DJ copy
Telling Me Lies / Rosewood Casket (Dolly Parton / Emmylou Harris / Linda Ronstadt) – 7–28371 (WB) (US)
Telling Me Lies / Rosewood Casket (Dolly Parton / Emmylou Harris / Linda Ronstadt) – 92 83717 (WB) (Canada)
Telling Me Lies / Rosewood Casket (Dolly Parton / Emmylou Harris / Linda Ronstadt) – 7–28371 (WB) (Canada)
Telling Me Lies / Rosewood Casket (Dolly Parton / Emmylou Harris / Linda Ronstadt) – 7–28371 (WB) (Australia)

Telling Me Lies (Edit) / Telling Me Lies (LP Version) (Dolly Parton / Emmylou Harris / Linda Ronstadt) – PRO–CD–2735 (WB) Promo CD single

Those Memories of You / Those Memories of You (Dolly Parton / Emmylou Harris / Linda Ronstadt) – 7–28248 (WB) (US)
Those Memories of You / My Dear Companion (Dolly Parton / Emmylou Harris / Linda Ronstadt) – 7–28248 (WB) (US) (PS)
Those Memories of You / My Dear Companion (Dolly Parton / Emmylou Harris / Linda Ronstadt) – 92 82487 (WB) (Canada)
Those Memories of You / My Dear Companion (Dolly Parton / Emmylou Harris / Linda Ronstadt) – 92 82487 (WB) (Canada) DJ copy

Those Memories of You / Rosewood Casket (Dolly Parton / Emmylou Harris / Linda Ronstadt) – 928 281–7 (WB) (Germany) (PS)

The River Unbroken / The River Unbroken – 38–07665 (CBS) (US) (PS) DJ copy / white label
The River Unbroken / More Than I Can Say – 38–07665 (CBS) (US) (PS)
The River Unbroken / More Than I Can Say – 38–07665 (CBS) (Canada) (PS)
The River Unbroken / More Than I Can Say – 651202 6 (CBS) (UK) (PS)
The River Unbroken / More Than I Can Say – 651202 7 (CBS) (UK) (PS)
The River Unbroken / More Than I Can Say – 651202 7 (CBS) (Netherlands) (PS) Red CBS label
The River Unbroken / More Than I Can Say – 651202 7 (CBS) (Australia) (PS)
The River Unbroken / More Than I Can Say – 651202 7 (CBS) (Spain) (PS)

To Know Him Is To Love Him / To Know Him Is To Love Him (Dolly Parton / Emmylou Harris / Linda Ronstadt) – 9 28492–7 (WB) (US) DJ copy
To Know Him Is To Love Him / Further Along (Dolly Parton / Emmylou Harris / Linda Ronstadt) – 928492–7 (WB) (US) (PS)
To Know Him Is To Love Him / Further Along (Dolly Parton / Emmylou Harris / Linda Ronstadt) – 928492–7 (WB) (Canada) (PS)
To Know Him Is To Love Him / Further Along (Dolly Parton / Emmylou Harris / Linda Ronstadt) – W8492 (WB) (UK) (PS)
To Know Him Is To Love Him / Further Along (Dolly Parton / Emmylou Harris / Linda Ronstadt) – 928492–7 (WB) (Europe) (PS)
To Know Him Is To Love Him / Further Along (Dolly Parton / Emmylou Harris / Linda Ronstadt) – P–2217 (WB) (Japan) (PS)
To Know Him Is To Love Him / Further Along (Dolly Parton / Emmylou Harris / Linda Ronstadt) – 7–28492 (WB) (Australia) (PS)
I Know You By Heart (w/ Smokey Robinson) / I Know You By Heart – 38–07727 (CBS) (US) DJ copy / white label

I Know You By Heart (w/ Smokey Robinson) / Could I Have Your Autograph – 38–07727 (CBS) (US) (PS)
I Know You By Heart (w/ Smokey Robinson) / Could I Have Your Autograph – 38–07727 (CBS) (Canada)
I Know You By Heart (w/ Smokey Robinson) / Could I Have Your Autograph – DOLLY1 (CBS) (UK) (PS)
I Know You By Heart (w/ Smokey Robinson) / Could I Have Your Autograph – DOLLY Q1 (CBS) (UK) (PS / poster)
I Know You By Heart (w/ Smokey Robinson) / Could I Have Your Autograph – 6514347 (CBS) (Australia)
I Know You By Heart (w/ Smokey Robinson) / Could I Have Your Autograph – 651434 7 (CBS) (Netherlands) (PS)

Make Love Work / Make Love Work – 38–07995 (CBS) (US) DJ copy

Make Love Work / Two Lovers – 38–07995 (CBS) (US)

1988

I Know You By Heart (w/ Smokey Robinson) / Make Love Work / Could I Have Your Autograph – DOLLY T1 (CBS) (UK) 12" EP

I Know You By Heart (w/ Smokey Robinson) / Make Love Work / Could I Have Your Autograph – 651434 2 (CBS) (UK) 3" mini CD single (PS)

1989

Slow Healing Heart / Slow Healing Heart 38–73498 (CBS) (US) DJ copy
Slow Healing Heart / Take Me Back To The Country – 38–73498 (CBS) (US)

Why'd You Come In Here Lookin' Like That / Why'd You Come In Here Lookin' Like That – 38–68760 (CBS) (US) DJ copy
Why'd You Come In Here Lookin' Like That / Wait "Til I Get You Home (w/ Mac Davis) – 38–68760 (CBS) (US)
Why'd You Come In Here Lookin' Like That / Wait "Til I Get You Home (w/ Mac Davis) – DOLLY2 (UK) (PS)
Why'd You Come In Here Lookin' Like That / Wait "Til I Get You Home (w/ Mac Davis) – 654903 7 (CBS) (Australia)
Why'd You Come In Here Lookin' Like That / Wait "Til I Get You Home (w/ Mac Davis) – 654903 7 (CBS) (UK) (PS)
Why'd You Come In Here Lookin' Like That CSK 1588 (CBS) (US) Promo CD single
Why'd You Come In Here Lookin' Like That / Wait "Til I Get You Home (w/ Mac Davis) – 38T 68760 (CBS) (US) cassette single (PS)

Yellow Roses / Yellow Roses – 38–69040 (CBS) (US) DJ copy
Yellow Roses / Wait "Til I Get You Home (w/ Mac Davis) – 38–69040 (CBS) (US)
Yellow Roses / Wait "Til I Get You Home (w/ Mac Davis) – 38T 69040 (CBS) (US) Cassette single (PS)

He's Alive / He's Alive – ZSS–1929A (CBS) (US) DJ copy / white label
He's Alive / He's Alive – 38–73200 (CBS) (US) DJ copy
He's Alive / He's Alive – CS7–01929 (CBS) (US) DJ copy / small hole pressing
He's Alive / What Is It My Love – 38–73200 (CBS) (US)

Time For Me To Fly / Time For Me To Fly – 38–73226 (CBS) (US) DJ copy
Time For Me To Fly / The Moon, The Stars And Me – 38–73226 (CBS) (US)

White Limozeen / White Limozeen – 38–73341 (CBS) (US) DJ copy
White Limozeen – CSK 73341 (CBS) Promo CD single (US)
White Limozeen / The Moon, The Stars And Me – 38–73341 (CBS) (US)

Jolene / My Tennessee Mountain Home – GB–10165 (RCA) (US) (Gold Standard Reissue)

All I Can Do / Falling Out Of Love with Me – PB–10730 (RCA) (US) (Gold Standard Reissue)

Here You Come Again / Two Doors Down – GB–11505 (RCA) (US) (Gold Standard Reissue)
(Note: This single contains the re–recording of "Two Doors Down" from January 13, 1978)

Baby, I'm Burnin' / Heartbreaker – GB–11993 (RCA) (US) (Gold Standard Reissue)

9 to 5 / Old Flames Can't Hold A Candle to You – GB–12316 (RCA) (Canada) (Golden Greats Reissue)

1990

Love Is Strange Dolly Parton & Kenny Rogers / Love Is Strange Dolly Parton & Kenny Rogers – 7–19760 (Reprise Records) (US) DJ copy
Love Is Strange (Album version) Dolly Parton & Kenny Rogers / Walk Away (Album version) (Kenny Rogers) – 7–19760 (Reprise Records) (US)
Love Is Strange (Album version) Dolly Parton & Kenny Rogers / Walk Away (Album version) (Kenny Rogers) – 5439–19760–7 (Reprise Records) (Europe) (PS)
Love Is Strange (Album version) Dolly Parton & Kenny Rogers / Walk Away (Album version) (Kenny Rogers) – 543919760–7 (Reprise Records) (Australia)
Love Is Strange (Album version) Dolly Parton & Kenny Rogers / Walk Away (Album version) (Kenny Rogers) 9 19760–4 (Reprise Records) (US) Cassette single (PS)

Christmas Without You / White Christmas – PB 49227 (RCA) (Europe) (PS)
Christmas Without You / White Christmas – PD 49227 (RCA) (Europe) (PS) CD single

1991

Rockin' Years (w/ Ricky Van Shelton) 38–73711 (CBS) (US) DJ copy
Rockin' Years (w/ Ricky Van Shelton) / What A Heartache – 38–73711 (CBS) (US)
Silver and Gold / Runaway Feeling – 38–73826 (CBS) (US)

Eagle When She Flies – CSK 74011 (CBS) Promo CD single (US)
Eagle When She Flies / Wildest Dreams – 38–74011 (CBS) (US)

Country Road – CSK 74183 (CBS) Promo CD single (US)
Country Road / Best Woman Wins (w/ Lorrie Morgan) – 38–74183 (CBS) (US)

1992

I Will Always Love You – RDJ62460–2 (RCA / BMG) Promo CD

Light Of A Clear Blue Morning / Blue Grace – HR–64745–4 (Hollywood Records) (US) Cassette single
Light Of A Clear Blue Morning – PRCD–8564–2 (Hollywood Records) (US) Promo CD

Burning (w/ Les Taylor) – PRCD–10203–2 (Hollywood Records) (US) Promo CD
Straight Talk (single mix) / Straight Talk (LP mix) – PRCD–10129–2 (Hollywood Records) (US) Promo CD
Straight Talk / Burning to Burned – HR–64776–4 (Hollywood Records) (US) Cassette single
Straight Talk / Light Of A Clear Blue Morning – 10128–4 (Hollywood Records) (US) Cassette single
Straight Talk (7" version) / Livin' A Lie / Straight Talk (Album version) D11194 (Hollywood Records) (Australia) CD single / PS
Straight Talk / Burning to Burned / Livin' A Lie – 146162–3 (Hollywood Records) (Benelux) CD single / PS

1993

Romeo (Featuring: Billy Ray Cyrus / Kathy Mattea / Pam Tillis / Tanya Tucker) CSK 74876 (CBS) (US) Promo CD
Romeo (Featuring: Billy Ray Cyrus / Kathy Mattea / Pam Tillis / Tanya Tucker) / High and Mighty – 38 74876 (CBS) (US) (PS)
Romeo (Featuring: Billy Ray Cyrus / Kathy Mattea / Pam Tillis / Tanya Tucker) / High and Mighty – COL 659155 1 (CBS) (UK) CD single (PS)
Romeo (Featuring: Billy Ray Cyrus / Kathy Mattea / Pam Tillis / Tanya Tucker) / High and Mighty – COL 659155 1 (CBS) (US) Cassette single (PS)

More Where That Came From / I'll Make Your Bed – 38–74954 (CBS) (US)
More Where That Came From / I'll Make Your Bed – 38T74954 (CBS) Cassette single
More Where That Came From (Special Remix) / More Where That Came From (Original Version) – CSK 5175 (CBS) (US) Promo CD

Full Circle – CSK 77083 (CBS) (US) Promo CD
Full Circle / What Will Baby Be – 38–77083 (CBS) (US)

You've Lost That Lovin' Feelin' – Neil Diamond and Dolly Parton / Save The Last Dance For Me –Neil Diamond solo – CSK 5411 (CBS) (US) Promo CD (PS) (From the CBS Neil Diamond album: *Up on The Roof – Songs from The Brill Building*)
You've Lost That Lovin' Feelin' – Neil Diamond and Dolly Parton / Save The Last Dance For Me – Neil Diamond solo – 01–659637–17 (CBS) (Europe) Promo CD (PS) (From the Neil Diamond album: *Up on The Roof – Songs from The Brill Building*)

The Day I Fall In Love – (Love Theme From Beethoven's 2nd) – Dolly Parton & James Ingram – CSK 5590 (US) Promotional CD single (PS)
The Day I Fall In Love (Love Theme From Beethoven's 2nd) – Dolly Parton & James Ingram / The Day I Fall In Love (Love Theme From Beethoven's 2nd) (Instrumental) / Opening (Snoozing with Beethoven) – 660028 2 (Europe) Maxi–CD single (PS)
The Day I Fall In Love (Love Theme From Beethoven's 2nd) – Dolly Parton & James Ingram / The Day I Fall In Love (Love Theme From Beethoven's 2nd) (Instrumental) – COL 660028 1 (Europe) CD single (PS)
The Day I Fall In Love (Love Theme From Beethoven's 2nd) – Dolly Parton & James Ingram / The Day I Fall In Love (Love Theme From Beethoven's 2nd) (Instrumental) – COL 660028 1 (France) CD single (PS)
The Day I Fall In Love (Love Theme From Beethoven's 2nd) – Dolly Parton & James Ingram / The Day I Fall In Love (Love Theme From Beethoven's 2nd) (Instrumental) – COL 660028 1 (Australia) CD single (PS)
The Day I Fall In Love (Love Theme From Beethoven's 2nd) – Dolly Parton & James Ingram / The Day I Fall In Love (Love Theme From Beethoven's 2nd) (Instrumental) – COL 660028 4 (US) Cassette single (PS)

Silver Threads and Golden Needles – Dolly Parton / Tammy Wynette / Loretta Lynn 38–77294 (CBS) (US) Promo

Silver Threads and Golden Needles – Dolly Parton / Tammy Wynette / Loretta Lynn 38–77294 (CBS) (US)

1994

When You Tell Me That You Love Me – Julio Iglesias and Dolly Parton – CSK 6256 (CBS) (US) Promo CD (From the 1994 CBS Julio Iglesias album *Crazy*)

When You Tell Me That You Love Me – Julio Iglesias and Dolly Parton / L–O–V–E (Julio Iglesias solo) – CSK 6256 (CBS) (US) Promo CD (PS) (From the CBS Julio Iglesias album *Crazy*)

When You Tell Me That You Love Me – Julio Iglesias and Dolly Parton / L–O–V–E (Julio Iglesias solo) / I Keep Telling Myself (Julio Iglesias solo) – COL 660685 2 (CBS) (Europe) Maxi–single CD (PS)

When You Tell Me That You Love Me (duet with Julio Iglesias and Dolly Parton) – SAMPCD 2360 1 (CBS) (Spain) Promo CD (PS)

To Daddy / PMS Blues – 38–77723 (CBS) (US)

1995

I Will Always Love You (featuring Vince Gill) (CBS) (US) Promo CD
I Will Always Love You (featuring Vince Gill) / Speakin' of The Devil – 38–78079 (CBS) (US)

1996

Just When I Needed You Most (Radio Edit) / Just When I Needed You Most (LP Version) RT5P–1003 (RT/BE) HDCD / Single / Promo
Just When I Needed You Most / For The Good Times – RTS7 56041 (RT/BE) (US) Pink label

Peace Train (Single Double Edit) / Peace Train (Single Edit) – RT5P–1006 (RT/BE) (US) CD Single Promo

Two Doors Down (Boy Wonder Radio Edit) / Two Doors Down (Cyphonix Radio Mix) / Peace Train (Sparky's Piano Mix) / Two Doors Down (Boy Wonder Mix) / Two Doors Down (Cyphonix Extended Mix) – PDJ143DS (Pro DJ International) (Australia) (CD Maxi–Single)

1997

Peace Train (Holy Roller Radio Edit) / Peace Train (Original Album Version) / Peace Train (Holy Roller Mix Extended) / Peace Train (Junior's Arena Anthem) / Peace Train (Paul's TGV Mix) – PDJ7394DS – (Australia) Extended Maxi–single CD (PS)
Peace Train (Holy Roller Radio Edit) / Peace Train (Original Album Version) / Peace Train (Holy Roller Mix Extended) / Peace Train (Junior's Arena Anthem) / Peace Train (Paul's TGV Mix) – PDJ7394DS – (New Zealand) Extended Maxi–single CD (PS)
Peace Train (Holy Roller Radio Edit) / Peace Train (Junior's Radio Edit) / Peace Train (Original Album Version) – Ark 21 (EMI) (Europe) Maxi–single CD

Peace Train (Holy Roller Mix Extended) / Peace Train (Junior's Arena Anthem) / Peace Train (Julian's Morning Passage Mix) / Peace Train (Paul's TGV Mix) / Peace Train (Holy Roller Radio Edit) / Peace

Train (Original Album Version) – 61868 44000 2 5 (Flip It Records / Universal) (US) Maxi–single CD (PS)

Peace Train (Holly Roller Single Edit) / Peace Train (Junior Vasquez Extended Remix) – RR 2196–2 Roadrunner Records (Netherlands) CD single (PS)

Peace Train (Junior's Arena Anthem) / Peace Train (Paul's TGV Mix) / Peace Train (Holy Roller (Radio Edit) / Peace Train (Julian's Morning Passage Mix) / Peace Train Peace Train (Holy Roller Mix (Extended) – 61868 44000 1 8 (Flip It Records) (US) 2 12" vinyl album set

Peace Train (Da Slammin Tapage Remix) / Peace Train (Da Slammin Bibi Dub) / Peace Train (Holy Roller RLP Extended Mix) / Peace Train (Dee's Bitchie Zone Mix) / Peace Train (3000 Beats) / Peace Train (Train Apella) – RR 2196–6 (Roadrunner Records) (France) 2 12" vinyl album set

Peace Train (Da Slammin Tapage Remix) / Peace Train (Da Slammin Bibi Dub) / Peace Train (Holy Roller (Radio Edit) / Peace Train (3000 Beats) / Peace Train (Train Apella) – RR 2196–6 (Roadrunner Records) (France) 2 12" vinyl set (PS)

Peace Train (Junior's Arena Anthem) / Peace Train (Holy Roller Radio Edit) / Peace Train (Paul's TGV Mix) – 7243884 717 (Universal Records) (UK) 12" single

Knockin' On Heaven's Door – Dolly Parton w/Ladysmith Black Mambazo / Yitho Umlilo Ovuthayo (Ladysmith Black Mambazo) – 7243 8945782 (Van Record Company) (Netherlands) CD single (PS)

You Are / Jealous Heart – BMG– 4321 (BMG Special Markets) (Germany)

I Will Always Love You / Lonely Comin' Down – COL–4746 (BMG Special Markets) (US)

Jolene / My Tennessee Mountain Home – COL–04765 (BMG Special Markets) (US)

1998

Peace Train (The Diddy Man Vox Dub) / Peace Train (Original Album Version UK Edit) / Peace Train (Rhythm Infusion Dub) – BNCE–TS 004 (Bounce Music) (UK) 12" Vinyl

Peace Train Sparky's Full On Piano Mix (Radio Edit) / Peace Train Peace Train Sparky's Funky Mix (Radio Edit) / Peace Train Holy Roller Mix (UK Radio Edit) / Peace Train (The Diddyman Vox Dub) – BUCV005 (Bounce Music) (UK) 12" Promo / White Label
Peace Train (Sparky's Full On Piano Mix) / Peace Train (Sparky's Funky Mix) / Peace Train (The Diddyman Vox Dub) / Peace Train (Junior Vasquez Edit) – BUCV 005 (Bounce Music) (UK) 12" White label rubber stamped text

Peace Train (The Diddyman Vox Dub) / Peace Train (Wayne G's Heavenly Dub) / Peace Train (Rhythm Infusion Dub) – BUCV 004 (Bounce Music) (UK) 12" White label rubber stamped text
Peace Train (Sparky's Funky Mix Radio Edit) / Peace Train(Sparky's Funky Club Mix) / Peace Train (Holy Roller Mix) / Peace Train (Sparky's Piano Mix Radio Edit) / Peace Train (Sparky's Piano Club Mix) / Peace Train (Junior Vasquez Edit) – BNCE–CD 004 Bounce Music (UK) 2 CD maxi–single set (PS)

Peace Train (Radio Edit) / Peace Train (Holy Roller Mix Radio Edit) / Peace Train (Holy Roller Mix Extended) / Peace Train (Junior's Arena Anthem) / Peace Train (Julian's Morning Passage Mix) / Peace Train (Paul's TGV Mix) / Peace Train (Original Album Version) – ORCDM 53479 (Orange Records) Scandinavia Maxi–single CD (PS)

Peace Train Sparky's Full On Piano Mix (Radio Edit) / Peace Train Sparky's Funky Mix (Radio Edit) / Peace Train Holy Roller Mix (UK Radio Edit) / Peace Train (The Diddyman Vox Dub) – BUCD006 (Bounce Music) (UK) CD single / promo

Honky Tonk Songs – DRN5P–72061 (Decca / Blue Eye) (US) CD promo single (PS)
Honky Tonk Songs / Paradise Road – DRNS7–72061 (Decca / Blue Eye) (US) 7" vinyl (PS)
Honky Tonk Songs / Paradise Road – DRNDS–72061 (Decca / Blue Eye) (US) CD single (PS)
Honky Tonk Songs / Paradise Road – DRNCS–72061 (Decca / Blue Eye) (US) Cassette single (PS)

The Salt in my Tears – DRN5P–72080 (Decca / Blue Eye) (US) / Promo CD
The Salt in my Tears / Hungry Again – DRNS7 72080 (Decca / Blue Eye) (US)

High Sierra – Emmylou Harris / Dolly Parton / Linda Ronstadt – apcd–1252 (Asylum Records) (US) Promo CD

1999

After The Gold Rush / Feels Like Home / Do I Ever Cross Your Mind – Emmylou Harris / Dolly Parton / Linda Ronstadt – apcd–1294 Promo CD. (These three tracks were released as singles at the same time in April 1999)

A Few Old Memories / Train, Train – SUG–CD–3900 (Sugar Hill Records) Promo CD

Your Kisses Are Charity – Culture Club and Dolly Parton – VSCDX 1736 (Virgin Records) CD single

2001

I Will Always Love You / You Are – amc 14.031 (Belgium) CD single (PS)

A Tender Lie – SUG–CD–3927S7 (Sugar Hill Records) (US) Promo CD single

Shine (Radio edit) –SANPR091 (Sanctuary Records) (US) Promo CD single (PS)

2002

If / Dagger Through The Heart / Dagger Through The Heart (video) / If / Sugar Hill / Shine (Video) – SANX139–139X (Sanctuary Records) (UK) Enhanced 2 CD set w/ PC video content

Dagger Through The Heart – SUG–CD–3946S11 (Sugar Hill/Blue Eye Records) (US) Promo CD single

Dagger Through The Heart / If –DOLLYPRO #03 (Sugar Hill/Blue Eye Records) (Australia) Radio Promo CD single

2004

Light of A Clear Blue Morning (Edit) – 867–2 (Blue Eye Records) (US) Promotional CD single

2005

Travelin' Thru – 74 PE1156 (IFC Films) (US) Promotional CD single / Single track CD "For Your Consideration" Best Original Song promotional CD-R (recordable), from the film *TRANSAMERICA*. This was likely for Academy Award / Grammy / Golden Globe or perhaps some other award show usage.

Thank God I'm A Country Boy (Single Version) (Roy Rivers and Dolly Parton) / Thank God I'm A Country Boy (Roy Rivers and Dolly Parton) (Album Version) / Thank God I'm A Country Boy (Roy Rivers and Dolly Parton) (Karaoke) / Hi Mom, It's Me (Roy Rogers solo) – 426001922016 (AGR Television) (Germany) Maxi single CD

If I Were A Carpenter / Where Have All The Flowers Gone / Me and Bobby McGee / Where Do The Children Play – SUG–CD–7012 (Sugar Hill) (US) (PS)

When I Get Where I'm Going – Brad Paisley and Dolly Parton (Single Edit) / When I Get Where I'm Going (Brad Paisley and Dolly Parton) (Single Edit) / When I Get Where I'm Going (Brad Paisley and Dolly Parton) – 82876–74465–2 (Arista Nashville) (US) (From Brad Paisley's album *Time Well Wasted*)
Single track CD also included with a booklet of the same name by Rivers Rutherford & George Teren

2006

Tomorrow is Forever – Solomon Burke and Dolly Parton – SMASCD082 (Shout! Factory / Snapper Music) (Europe) (From Solomon Burke's album *Nashville*) Promotional CD single

2008

Jesus & Gravity (Radio Edit) – 334581 (Dolly Records) (US) Promotional CD single

9 to 5 / 9 to 5 (Love To Infinity Radio Mix) / 9 to 5 (Love To Infinity Club Mix) – (Sony / BMG) A Promo UK CD–R disc. Also released in WAV and MP3 formats. (Europe / UK)

9 to 5 (Love To Infinity Radio Mix – 3:34) / 9 to 5 (Love To Infinity Club Mix – 6:47) – (Sony / BMG) (UK) A Promo UK CD–R disc. Also released in WAV and MP3 formats.

2009

Boots and Sand –Yusuf with Paul McCartney & Dolly Parton – 2713654 (Island Records) (Europe / UK) 7" limited edition single / (PS) Also released in WAV and MP3 formats.

2010

Two Doors Down / Jolene / 9 to 5 / Here You Come Again / I Will Always Love You – 88843 04520 2 (Masterworks) (US) EP CD / Recorded Live at The 02 Arena London in 2008 (Case with insert)

2014

Home / Blue Smoke – 8843 04940 7 (Dolly Records / Masterworks) (US) 7" limited edition blue vinyl / A Record Store Day exclusive release.

Home – (Dolly Records) (UK) promotional CD single

Try – (Dolly Records) (UK) promotional CD single (*Try* is the theme song for Dolly's literacy program The Imagination Library)

2015

Unlikely Angel – (Sony Music) (UK) promotional CD single

2017

The Story – (CBS) (Europe) This track available as FLAC / MP3 format

Puppy Love / Girl Let Alone – (Yep Roc Records) – SI YEP 2495 – April 22, 2017 – A Record Day Release exclusive

2018

Here I Am – Sia and Dolly Parton (from the *Dumplin'* Original Motion Picture Soundtrack) (US) (Dolly Records / RCA Records) This track available as FLAC / MP3 format downloads.

Girl in the Movies – (from the *Dumplin'* Original Motion Picture Soundtrack) (US) (Netflix) Single track CD "For Your Consideration" Best Original Song promotional.

2019

Faith (Original Mix) – Galantis & Dolly Parton Feat. Mr. Probz – 075679832863 (Big Beat Records) This track available as MP3 format.

God Only Knows – For King & Country and Dolly Parton – (Curb Records / World Entertainment) This track available as an AAC download.

There Was Jesus – Zach Williams and Dolly Parton – (Essential Records) This track available as MP3 format download. (From Zach Williams Rescue Story album) This track won Zach Williams his 2nd Grammy and Dolly her 11th Grammy during the 63rd Annual presentation on March 14, 2021.

2020

Peace Train (Junior's 7") / Peace Train (Junior's Arena Anthem With Reprise) / Peace Train (Junior's Arena Anthem) / Peace Train (Junior's Arena Dub) / Peace Train (Junior's Instrumental) / Peace Train (Junior's Riff Dub) / Peace Train (Junior's Tribal Beats) – (Polydor Records) This was released as 7 downloadable "FLAC" files on June 26, 2020. Also released as downloadable "WAV" files same day.

When Life Is Good Again – (Butterfly Records) This track available as an AAC download.

Pink – Dolly Parton / Monica / Jordin Sparks / Rita Wilson / Sara Evans (Brighter Day Records) This track available as an AAC download.

2021

Words – Barry Gibb & Dolly Parton – (Capitol / EMI Records)
(Dolly appears on Barry Gibb's 2020 album *Greenfields: The Gibb Brothers Songbook, Vol. 1*. The track was recorded in Nashville at RCA Recording Studio (Studio A) at 30 Music Square West where Dolly recorded so many of her hits.) This track available as MP3 format download. Available: 1/2/2021

5 to 9 – (Butterfly Records) This track available as an AAC download.

Singles with Porter Wagoner
PS – Picture Sleeve

1967

The Last Thing on My Mind / Love Is Worth Living – 47–9368 (RCA) (US) white label promo / plug side
The Last Thing on My Mind / Love Is Worth Living – 47–9368 (RCA) (US)
The Last Thing on My Mind / Love Is Worth Living – 47–9368 (RCA) (Canada) Red RCA label

1968

Somewhere Between / Just The Two of Us – 42–664 (RCA) (Zimbabwe)
Somewhere Between Just The Two of Us – 42–664 (RCA) (South Africa)

Someday We'll Get Ahead / Jeannie's Afraid Of The Dark – 47–9577 (RCA) (US) Green label promo
Someday We'll Get Ahead / Jeannie's Afraid Of The Dark – 47–9577 (RCA) (US)

Holding On To Nothin' / Just Between You and Me – 47–9490 (RCA) (US) Green label promo
Holding On To Nothin' / Just Between You and Me – 47–9490 (RCA) (US)
Holding On To Nothin' / Just Between You and Me – 47–9490 (RCA) (Canada) Red RCA label

1969

Yours Love / Malena – 74–0104 (RCA) (US) Green label promo
Yours Love / Malena – 74–0104 (RCA) (US) Orange RCA label

Always, Always / No Reason To Hurry Home – 74–0172 (RCA) (US) Green label promo / plug side
Always, Always / No Reason To Hurry Home – 74–0172 (RCA) (US) Orange RCA Label
Always, Always / No Reason To Hurry Home – 74–0172 (RCA) (Canada) Orange label promo

Just Someone I Used To Know / My Hands Are Tied – 74–0247 (RCA) (US)
Just Someone I Used To Know / My Hands Are Tied 74–0247 (RCA) (US) Green label promo / plug side

1970

Someday We'll Get Ahead / Jeannie's Afraid Of The Dark – 447–0900 (RCA) (Canada)

Tomorrow is Forever / Mendy Never Sleeps – 47–9799 (RCA) (US) Green label promo / plug side
Tomorrow is Forever / Mendy Never Sleeps – 47–9799 (RCA) (US)
Tomorrow is Forever / Mendy Never Sleeps – 47–9799 (RCA) (Canada)

Daddy Was An Old Time Preacher Man / A Good Understanding – 47–9875 (RCA) (US) Green label promo / plug side
Daddy Was An Old Time Preacher Man / A Good Understanding – 47–9875 (RCA) (US)
Daddy Was An Old Time Preacher Man / A Good Understanding – 47–9875 (RCA) (Canada)

1971

Two of a Kind / Better Movie It on Home – 47–9958 (RCA) (US)
Two of a Kind / Better Movie It on Home – 47–9958 (RCA) (Canada)
Two of a Kind / Better Movie It on Home – 47–9958 (RCA) (US) Green label promo / stereo
Two of a Kind / Better Movie It on Home – 47–9958 (RCA) (Canada) Green label promo / stereo

The Right Combination / The Right Combination – PSP-45-261-PS-45-261 (RCA) Green label promo / mono-stereo pressing

The Right Combination / The Pain of Loving You – 47-9994 (RCA) (US)

Just Someone I Used To Know / The Pain of Loving You – TRS-200 (RCA) (Rhodesia)

Burning the Midnight Oil / More Than Words Can Tell – 74-0565 (RCA) (US)
Burning the Midnight Oil / More Than Words Can Tell – 74-0565 (RCA) (Canada)
Burning the Midnight Oil / More Than Words Can Tell – 74-0565 (RCA) (US) Gold label Issue
Burning the Midnight Oil / More Than Words Can Tell – 74-0565 (RCA) (US) Green label promo / mono pressing

1972

Forty Miles From Poplar Bluff / No Love Left / Each Season Changes You / Run That By Me One More time / Silver Sandals / We Can't Let This Happen To Us – 7-4305 (RCA) (7" Jukebox record with PS. Select songs from *Porter Wayne and Dolly Rebecca* LP.)

Lost Forever in Your Kiss / The Fog Has Lifted – 74-0675 (RCA) (US) Green label promo / plug side / mono pressing
Lost Forever in Your Kiss / The Fog Has Lifted – 74-0675 (RCA) (US)
Lost Forever in Your Kiss / The Fog Has Lifted – 74-0675 (RCA) (Canada)
Lost Forever in Your Kiss / The Fog Has Lifted – 42-350 (RCA) (South Africa)

Lost Forever in Your Kiss / Touch your Woman – SS-2192 (RCA) (Japan) (PS)

Together Always / Loves All Over – 74-0773 (RCA) (US) Green label promo / plug side / mono pressing
Together Always / Loves All Over – 74-0773 (RCA) (US)

Tomorrow Is Forever / Run That By Me One More Time – 42-402 (RCA) (South Africa)

Lost Forever In Your Kiss / Together Always – 447-0952 (RCA) (US) Gold Standard Reissue / Red RCA label

1973

We Found It / Love Have Mercy On Us – 74-0893 (RCA) (US) yellow label promo / plug side / mono pressing
We Found It / Love Have Mercy On Us – 74-0893 (RCA) (US)
We Found It / Love Have Mercy On Us – 74-0893 (RCA) (Canada)

If Teardrops Were Pennies / If Teardrops Were Pennies – SPS-45-509 (RCA) (US) DJ copy / mono-stereo pressing
If Teardrops Were Pennies / Come To Me – 74-0981 (RCA) (Australia)
If Teardrops Were Pennies / Come To Me – 74-0981 (RCA) (New Zealand) Side one marked "Heads" – Side Two "Tails."
If Teardrops Were Pennies / Come To Me – 74-0981 (RCA) (Canada)
If Teardrops Were Pennies / Come To Me – 42-475 (RCA) (South Africa)

Here Comes The Freedom Train b/w All Aboard America (Porter solo) – Freedom Train – NR5767 (Porter and Dolly recorded "Here Comes the Freedom Train" in 1973, their only non-RCA single, as a fundraiser for a bicentennial train that was going to be traveling America with a museum car featuring the nation's historic documents on display.)

1974

Please Don't Stop Loving Me / Please Don't Stop Loving Me – JH-10010 DJ copy / white label / mono-stereo pressing
Please Don't Stop Loving Me / Sounds Of Nature – PB-10010 (RCA) (US) DJ copy / white label
Please Don't Stop Loving Me / Sounds Of Nature – PB-10010 (RCA) (US)
Please Don't Stop Loving Me / Sounds Of Nature – PB-10010 (RCA) (Canada)
Please Don't Stop Loving Me / Sounds Of Nature – GB-10506 (RCA) (US) Gold Standard reissue / red RCA label

Daddy Was An Old Time Preacher Man / Please Don't Stop Loving Me – GB-50194 (RCA) (USA)
Daddy Was An Old Time Preacher Man / Please Don't Stop Loving Me – GB-50194 (RCA) (Canada)

1975

Say Forever You'll Be Mine / Say Forever You'll Be Mine – JH-10328 (RCA) (US) DJ copy / white label mono pressing
Say Forever You'll Be Mine / How Can I (Help You Forgive Me) – PB-10328 (RCA) (US)
Say Forever You'll Be Mine / How Can I (Help You Forgive Me) – GB-10675 (RCA) (US) Reissue
Say Forever You'll Be Mine / How Can I (Help You Forgive Me) – PB-10328 (RCA) (Canada)
Say Forever You'll Be Mine / How Can I (Help You Forgive Me) – 42-632 (RCA) (South Africa)

1976

Is Forever Longer Than Always / Is Forever Longer Than Always – JH-10652 (RCA) (US) DJ copy / white label / mono-stereo pressing
Is Forever Longer Than Always / If You Say I Can – PB-10652 (RCA) (US)
Is Forever Longer Than Always / If You Say I Can – PB-10652 (RCA) (Canada)
Is Forever Longer Than Always / If You Say I Can – 42-696 (RCA) (South Africa)

1980

Making Plans / Making Plans – JH-11983 (RCA) (US) DJ copy / white label / mono-stereo pressing
Making Plans / Beneath The Sweet Magnolia Tree – PB-11983 (RCA) (US)
Making Plans / Beneath The Sweet Magnolia Tree – PB-11983 (RCA) (Canada)

If You Go, I'll Follow You / If You Go, I'll Follow You – JH-12119 (RCA) (US) DJ copy / white label / mono-stereo pressing
If You Go, I'll Follow You / If You Go, I'll Follow You – JH-12119 (RCA) (US) DJ copy / pink label / mono-stereo pressing
If You Go, I'll Follow You / Hide Me Away – PB-12119 (RCA) (US)
If You Go, I'll Follow You / Hide Me Away – PB-12119 (RCA) (Canada)
If You Go, I'll Follow You / Hide Me Away – 42-1035 (RCA) (South Africa)

1984

If You Leave, I Will Follow You / Making Plans – TRS-201 (RCA) (Zimbabwe)

Dolly Related Singles / Recordings:

These recordings feature Dolly in a duet with the artist(s) or Dolly provides background vocals on the track. *denotes if Dolly wrote the track. Some of these tracks may have been released as singles, but not mentioned in the singles section of this book, but can be found on albums of the mentioned artist.

John Henry III "Mathilda (I Cry and Cry For You)" b/w "Bony Moronie" 1970 Country Blues Records (# C.B.RA 146A–B). Dolly is John's niece and provides back up vocals on the A side as stated on the label. Mathilda (I Cry and Cry For You)" was later re-recorded and released on Monument Records in July 1970 with "You Just Answered The Question" as the B side. (#MN45–1218). Dolly is not listed on the label of the Monument release, so it is uncertain if she appears on that recording, likely not since Dolly was with RCA by that time.

Randy Travis "Do I Ever Cross Your Mind*" (Duet with Randy Travis) 1990

Dottie Rambo "Stand By The River" 2003

Lulu Roman "I Will Always Love You*" 2013

Mindy Smith "Jolene*" 2004

Straight No Chaser "Jolene*" 2013

Mary Sarah "Jolene*" 2014

Emmylou Harris "Light of the Stable" (with Dolly Parton, Linda Ronstadt and Neil Young) 1979

Linda Ronstadt "I Never Will Marry." 1977

Gail Davies "Unwed Fathers" 1985

Ladysmith Black Mambazo "Knockin' on Heaven's Door" 1997

The Nobles "Sleepless Nights" 1998

Mary Kay Place "All I Can Do*" 1976

Kim McLean "Angels & Eagles" 2005

Sonja Isaacs "The Angels Rejoiced" 2003

Pam Gadd "Applejack*" 2009

Rod Stewart "Baby It's Cold Outside" 2004

Asleep at the Wheel "Billy Dale" 1993

Patty Loveless "Bluegrass, White Snow" (with Dolly Parton and Ricky Skaggs) 2002

Rhonda Vincent "Blues Ain't Working On Me" 1996

George Jones "Blues Man, The" 2005

Maura O'Connell "Bright Blue Rose, The" 2009

Kathie Lee Gifford "Circle Game" 2000

Charlie Louvin "Circle of Friends" (with Dolly Parton and Alison Krauss) 2006

Shania Twain "Coat of Many Colors*" (with Dolly Parton, Alison Krauss and Union Station) 2003

Mary Kay Place "Coke and Chips" 1976

Darrell Webb "Cold*" 2005

Herb Pederson "Cora is Gone" 1977

Andy Landis "Corner of the World" 1993

Norah Jones "Creepin' In" 2004

Arlo Guthrie "Dixie Darling" 2002

Ricky Scaggs "Don't Step Over an Old Love" 1983

Alison Krauss "Dreaming My Dreams With You" 1999

Mac Davis "Everyone But Me and You" 1994

Emmylou Harris "Gold" (with Dolly Parton and Vince Gill) 2008

Mary Kay Place "Good Ole Country Baptizin'" (with Dolly Parton and Herb Pedersen) 1976

Emmylou Harris "Green Pastures" 1980

Sonya Isaacs "Healing Hands" 2000

Paula Cole "Heart Door" 2001

Rhonda Vincent "Hearthreaker's Alibi" 2006

Aaron Crisler "High and Mighty*" (duet with Dolly Parton) 2003

Martina McBride "I Still Miss Someone" 2005

Jerry D "I Will Always Love You*" 2005

Stephanie J. Block "I Will Always Love You*" 2009

Herb Pederson "If I Lose" (with, Dolly Parton Linda Ronstadt) 1977

The Bellamy Brothers "If I Said You Had A Beautiful Body (Would You Hold It Against Me)" 2005

Stevens Sisters "I'll Never Say Goodbye*" 2002

Randy Kohrs "It Looked Good On Paper" 2004

Ray Benson "Leave That Cowboy Alone*" 2003

Deana Carter "Love Is Like a Butterfly*" 2007

Ralph Stanley "Loving You Too Well" 2001

Johnny Russell "Making Plans" 2000

Holly Dunn "Most of All Why*" 1989

Bill Anderson "My Perfect Reason" 2007

Janis Ian "My Tennessee Hills 2004

Selah "Once Upon a Christmas*" 2002

Kathie Lee Gifford "Only My Pillow Knows" 2000

Steve Martin "Pretty Flowers" (With Dolly Parton and Vince Gill) 2009

Altan "Pretty Young Girl, The" 2002

Ronnie Milsap "Rollin' My Sweet Baby's Arms" 1975 (RCA *In Concert* LP)

Vestal Goodman "Satisfied" 1999

Hank Locklin "Send Me the Pillow that You Dream On" 2001

Billy Dean "Silent Night" 2005

Stella Parton "Sisters" 1989

Floyd Tillman Slippin' Around 2004

Paul Brewster "Slowly I'm Falling To Pieces" 2001

Bryan Sutton "Smoky Mountain Memories*" 2000

The Larkins "Steady as The Rain*" 2003

Brian Waldschlager "Sweet Touch Of A Dove" 2000

Brenda Lee "This Old House" 2007

Tom Astor "To Daddy*" 2008

Solomon Burke "Tomorrow is Forever*" 2006

Eric Lee Beddingfield "Train, Train" 2005

Hal Ketchum "Two of the Lucky Ones" 2001

Kenny Rogers "Undercover*" 2003

Ricky Scaggs "A Vision of Mother" 1983

Pam Tillis "Violet And A Rose" 2002

The Grascals "Viva Las Vegas" 2004

Patty Loveless "Waiting for the Phone to Ring" 1991

Emmylou Harris "When I Stop Dreaming" 1977

Emmy Rossum "When Love Is New*" 2001

George Jones "Where The Grass Won't Grow" (with Dolly Parton, Trisha Yearwood and Emmylou Harris) 1994

Margo O'Donnell "Wrong Direction Home*" (with Dolly Parton and Maura O'Connell) 1999

Margo O'Donnell "God's Coloring Book*" 1999

Leslie Jordan "Where The Soul Never Dies" April 2021

Other Records:

1.) Dolly Parton / 2.) Frank Zappa –What's It All About?
An interview record with clips of their then current albums
TRAV– MA 1755 / August 1979 / 7" 33⅓ RPM

Le Streghe – Ballerino / Dolly Parton – Baby I'm Burnin'
Spaghetti Records – JPB 6308, RCA – JPB 6308
Vinyl, 7", 45 RPM, Jukebox Italy 1979

The air dates presented here are from the original broadcasts in Nashville, TN

Episode 1 (9th taped) September 13, 1976
Guest: Robert Keeshan as Captain Kangaroo

Songs: "Joy to the World" (Dolly); "How Much Is That Doggie" (Dolly); "Three Little Fishes" (Dolly and Captain Kangaroo); "Thank Heaven for Little Girls" (Captain Kangaroo); "My Tennessee Mountain Home" (Dolly); "Coat of Many Colors" (Dolly); "Abadaba Honeymoon" (Dolly); "Sleepyhead" (Captain Kangaroo); "I Will Always Love You" (Dolly)

Episode 2 (5th taped) September 20, 1976
Guests: Anne Murray and Randy Parton

Songs: "Let Me Be There" (Dolly); "The Battle of New Orleans" (Dolly); "Blue Finger Lou" (Anne Murray); "Tennessee Born" (Randy Parton); "All I Can Do" (Dolly with Anne Murray and Randy Parton); "Drift Away" (Dolly with Anne Murray and Randy Parton); "Golden Oldie" (Anne Murray); "I Will Always Love You" (Dolly)

Episode 3 (7th taped) September 27, 1976
Guest: Kenny Rogers

Songs: "Knock Three Times" (Dolly); "Bad, Bad Leroy Brown" (Dolly); "Love Lifted Me" (Kenny Rogers); "He's Got the Whole World in His Hands" (Dolly and Kenny Rogers); "Joshua" (Dolly); "The World Needs a Melody" (Kenny Rogers); Medley: "Spanish Eyes" / "Brown Eyed Handsome Man" / "Blue Eyes Crying in the Rain" (Dolly and Kenny Rogers); "I Will Always Love You" (Dolly)

Episode 4 (1st taped) October 4, 1976
Guest: Ronnie Milsap

Songs: "Bad, Bad Leroy Brown" (Dolly); "Me and Little Andy" (Dolly); "Pure Love" (Ronnie Milsap); "The Night Life" (Dolly); "Rollin' in My Sweet Baby's Arms" (Dolly and Ronnie Milsap); "A Legend in My Time" (Ronnie Milsap); "I Believe in Music" (Dolly and Ronnie Milsap); "I Will Always Love You" (Dolly)

Episode 5 (3rd taped) October 11, 1976
Guest: The Hues Corporation

Songs: "Thank God I'm a Country Girl" (Dolly); "I'll Take a Melody" (The Hues Corporation); "Today I Started Loving You Again" (Dolly and the Hues Corporation); "Down on Music Row" (Dolly); "Rock the Boat" (The Hues Corporation); Medley: "Blues Stay Away from My Door" / "Song Sung Blue" / "My Blue Tears" (Dolly); "I Will Always Love You" (Dolly)

Episode 6 (4th taped) October 18, 1976
Guests: Emmylou Harris and Linda Ronstadt

Songs: "Silver Threads and Golden Needles" (Dolly with Emmylou Harris and Linda Ronstadt); "My Blue Ridge Mountain Boy" (Emmylou Harris); "I Can't Help It (If I'm Still in Love with You)" (Linda Ronstadt); "Applejack" (Dolly, Emmylou Harris and Linda Ronstadt); Do I Ever Cross Your Mind (Dolly); "The Sweetest Gift" (Dolly, Emmylou Harris and Linda Ronstadt); Bury Me Beneath the Willow Tree (Dolly, Emmylou Harris and Linda Ronstadt); "I Will Always Love You" (Dolly)

Episode 7 (6th taped) October 25, 1976
Guest: Tennessee Ernie Ford

Songs: "Jolene" (Dolly); Medley: "Sunshine on My Shoulder" / "Walking in the Sunshine" (Dolly); "I've Been to Georgia on a Fast Train" (Tennessee Ernie Ford); "I Believe" (Dolly and Tennessee Ernie Ford); "Tiptoe Through the Tulips" (Dolly); "Sixteen Tons" (Tennessee Ernie Ford); "The Twelfth of Never" (Dolly); "I Will Always Love You" (Dolly)

Episode 8 (10th taped) November 1, 1976
Guests: Billy Davis Jr. and Marilyn McCoo
Songs: "Proud Mary" (Dolly); "Rhinestone Cowgirl" (Dolly); "I Hope We Get to Love in Time" (Billy Davis Jr. and Marilyn McCoo); "Love Is Like a Butterfly" (Dolly); "You Can Change My Heart" (Billy Davis Jr. and Marilyn McCoo); "Take These Chains from My Heart" (Dolly, Billy Davis Jr. and Marilyn McCoo); "You" (Dolly); "I Will Always Love You" (Dolly)

Episode 9 (2nd taped) November 8, 1976
Guest: Jim Stafford
Songs: "Hey, Lucky Lady" (Dolly); "Jasper Dan" (Jim Stafford); "Queen of the Silver Dollar" (Dolly); Medley: "Yesterday" / "For the Good Times" / "Help Me Make It Through the Night" / "Bridge Over Troubled Water" (Dolly); The Nickel Pickin' Song" (Jim Stafford); "Spiders and Snakes" (Dolly and Jim Stafford); "I Will Always Love You" (Dolly)

Episode 10 (11th taped) / November 15, 1976
Guest: Anson Williams
Songs: "Love Will Keep Us Together" (Dolly); "Early Morning Breeze" (Dolly); "Everybody Needs a Rainbow" (Anson Williams); "Everything Old Is New Again" (Dolly); "In the Middle of the Night" (Anson Williams); "Mack the Knife" (Dolly and Anson Williams); "The Bargain Store" (Dolly); "I Will Always Love You" (Dolly)

Episode 11 (12th taped) / November 22, 1976
Guest: Lynn Anderson
Songs: "That'll Be the Day" (Dolly and Lynn Anderson); "Sweet Talkin' Man" (Lynn Anderson); "Swanee" (Dolly); "Cry" (Lynn Anderson); "Gettin' Happy" (Dolly); "Taking Care of Business" (Dolly and Lynn Anderson); "We Used To" (Dolly); "Dumb Blonde" (Dolly and Lynn Anderson); "I Will Always Love You" (Dolly)

Episode 12 (16th taped) / November 29, 1976
Guest: Rod McKuen
Songs: "China Grove" (Dolly with Rod McKuen), "A Boy Named Charlie Brown" (Rod McKuen), "Feelings" (Dolly and Rod McKuen), "The World I Used to Know" (Rod McKuen); "My Funny Valentine" (Dolly), "All I Can Do" (Dolly and Rod McKuen), "Every Loner Has to Go Alone" (Dolly and Rod McKuen); "I Will Always Love You" (Dolly)

Episode 13 (13th taped) / December 6, 1976
Guests: KC and the Sunshine Band
Songs: "Flowers on the Wall" (Dolly); "Get Down Tonight" (KC and the Sunshine Band); "That's the Way I Like It" (KC and the Sunshine Band with Dolly); "He Would Know" (Dolly); "In the Ghetto" (Dolly); "Shake Your Booty" (KC and the Sunshine Band); "Cryin' Time" (Dolly and KC and the Sunshine Band); "I Will Always Love You" (Dolly)

Episode 14 (17th taped) / December 13, 1976
Guest: Bobby Goldsboro
Songs: "The Door Is Always Open (Dolly with Bobby Goldsboro); "Watching Scotty Grow" (Bobby Goldsboro); "A Little at a Time" (Dolly); "Butterflies" (Bobby Goldsboro); "The Carroll County Accident" (Dolly); "Proud Mary" (Dolly and Bobby Goldsboro); "Let It Be Me" (Dolly and Bobby Goldsboro); "I Will Always Love You" (Dolly)

Episode 15 (14th taped) / December 20, 1976
Guest: Chuck Woolery
Songs: "Burning Love" (Dolly); "Sittin' on the Dock of the Bay" (Dolly); "Growing Up the Country Way" (Chuck Woolery); "Hello, Dolly!" (Dolly and cast); "Little Green Apples" (Chuck Woolery); "Help Me

Make It Through the Night" (Dolly and Chuck Woolery); "Thank God I'm a Country Girl/Boy" (Dolly and Chuck Woolery); "I Will Always Love You" (Dolly)

Episode 16 (18th taped) / December 27, 1976
Guest: The Staple Singers
Songs: "Gypsy Fever" (Dolly); "Let's Do It Again" (The Staple Singers); "The House of the Rising Sun" (Dolly); "Love Me, Love Me, Love Me" (The Staple Singers); "Love with Me" (Dolly); "Highway Headin' South" (Dolly); "The Seeker" (Dolly and the Staple Singers); "I Will Always Love You" (Dolly)

Episode 17 (15th taped) / January 3, 1977
Guest: Pure Prairie League
Songs: "Slippin' Away" (Dolly); "Two Lane Highway" (Pure Prairie League); "Down from Dover" (Dolly); "Gypsie Fever" (Dolly); "Afternoon Delight" (Dolly with Debbi Jo and Richard Dennison); "Dance" (Pure Prairie League); "Bye Bye Love" (Dolly and Pure Prairie League); "I Will Always Love You" (Dolly)

Episode 18 (21st taped) / January 10, 1977
Guests: John Hartford and La Costa
Songs: "When Will I Be Loved" (Dolly with John Hartford and La Costa); "Circle Game" (Dolly); "Skippin' in the Mississippi Dew" (John Hartford); "Shenandoah" (La Costa on harmonica); Medley: "Old Man River" / "Dixie Land" / "Battle Hymn of the Republic" (La Costa); "Gentle on My Mind" (Dolly, John Hartford and La Costa); "How Great Thou Art" (Dolly); "I Will Always Love You" (Dolly)

Episode 19 (20th taped) / January 17, 1977
Guest: Tom T. Hall
Songs: "Sneaky Snake" (Dolly with Tom T. Hall); "Coat of Many Colors" (Dolly); "Old Dogs, Children and Watermelon Wine" (Tom T. Hall); "Cracker Jack" (Dolly); "I Love" (Dolly and Tom T. Hall); "I Care" (Tom T. Hall); "I Will Always Love You" (Dolly)

Episode 20 (19th taped) / January 24, 1977
Guest: Ray Stevens
Songs: "Great Balls of Fire" (Dolly); "Get Crazy with Me" (Ray Stevens); "Lying Eyes" (Dolly); "Happy, Happy Birthday Baby" (Dolly and Ray Stevens); "Sir Thanks-a-Lot" (Ray Stevens); "City of New Orleans" (Dolly); "Searchin'" (Dolly and Ray Stevens); "I Will Always Love You" (Dolly)

Episode 21 (24th taped) / January 31, 1977
Guests: The Parton Family (Dolly's parents, Robert Lee and Avie Lee; and siblings, Willadeene, Stella, Cassie, Randy, Floyd, Freida, and Rachel)
Songs: "Old Black Kettle" (Dolly and the Parton Family); "I'm Not That Good with Goodbye" (Stella Parton); "Down" (Randy Parton); "I Got a Brand New Pair of Roller Skates" (Dolly and Stella Parton); "Morning" (Willadeene Parton); "In the Pines" (Dolly and the Parton Family); "In the Sweet By-and-By" (Dolly and the Parton Family); "I Will Always Love You" (Dolly)

Episode 22 (ninth taped) / February 7, 1977
Guests: Karen Black
Songs: "Gettin' Happy" (Dolly); "The First Time Ever I Saw Your Face" (Dolly); "Satin Sheets" (Karen Black); "What Ain't to Be Just Might Happen" (Dolly); "Did You Ever Wonder" (Karen Black); "Me and Bobby McGee" (Dolly and Karen Black); "I Will Always Love You" (Dolly)

Episode 23 (23rd taped) / February 14, 1977
Guests: Mel Tillis
Songs: "The Entertainer" (Dolly with Mel Tillis); "The Last Time I Saw Him" (Dolly); "Good Woman Blues" (Mel Tillis); "Brother Love's Traveling Salvation Show" (Dolly); "I Order One for Me" (Mel Tillis); "Don't Let Go" (Dolly and Mel Tillis); "I Will Always Love You" (Dolly)

Episode 24 (22nd taped) / February 21, 1977
Guests: The 5th Dimension
Songs: "Promised Land" (Dolly); "We'll Sing in the Sunshine" (Dolly); "Working on a Groovy Thing" (The 5th Dimension); "Does Your Chewing Gum Lose Its Flavor on the Bedpost Overnight" (Dolly and the 5th Dimension); "With Pen in Hand" (Dolly); "If That's the Way You Want It" (The 5th Dimension); "I Will Always Love You" (Dolly)

Episode 25 (26th taped) / February 28, 1977
Guest: Freddy Fender
Songs: "(Your Love Has Lifted Me) Higher and Higher" (Dolly); "Wasted Days and Wasted Nights" (Freddy Fender); "Mr. Bojangles" (Dolly); "Lovin' Cajun Style" (Dolly); Medley: "Dixie Land" / "Battle Hymn of the Republic" (Dolly); "Before the Next Teardrop Falls" (Dolly and Freddy Fender); "I Will Always Love You" (Dolly)

Episode 26 (25th taped) / March 7, 1977
Guests: Jim Ed Brown and Helen Cornelius
Songs: "Loves Me Like a Rock" (Dolly); "I Don't Want to Have to Marry You" (Jim Ed Brown and Helen Cornelius); "The Way We Were" (Dolly); "Saying Hello, Saying I Love You, Saying Goodbye" (Jim Ed Brown and Helen Cornelius); "Midnight Train to Georgia" (Dolly); "Looking Back to See" (Dolly, Jim Ed Brown and Helen Cornelius); "Bubbling Over" (Dolly); "I Will Always Love You" (Dolly)

Notes / Trivia:

- On February 27, 2007 six episodes of the series were released on DVD under the title *Dolly Parton & Friends*. The episodes are: Disc one: Emmylou Harris and Linda Ronstadt / Anne Murray and Randy Parton / Ronnie Milsap Disc two: Rod McKuen / Kenny Rogers / Billy Davis Jr. and Marilyn McCoo. Also included were two episodes of The Porter Wagoner Show from 1969 and 1971.
- In September 2020 Time–Life released a 19–disc boxed set titled: *Dolly: The Ultimate Collection – Deluxe Edition.* On one disc (Vol. 1 / Disc 4) it features a selection of six episodes of the series, two of which had previously been released on the *Dolly Parton & Friends* DVD in 2007. However, five of the six episodes in the box set have been heavily edited due to copyright issues. To date only 10 of the series' 26 episodes have been released. Also on disc 4 is the bonus: *Dolly in Her Own Words.*
- The show was also the first time Dolly worked with Kenny Rogers. Seven years later the two would hit the top of the country and pop charts with their 1983 mega hit "Islands in the Stream."
- Sadly, despite the hard work that went into the show and the diversity of guests, Dolly was said to have been less than happy with the end result, as she found herself singing standards like "My Funny Valentine," which she felt didn't suit her voice or musical style, and interacting with guests with whom she had little in common. She told Alanna Nash in 1977: *"I liked all of the people that were on...but I would have had a totally different lineup of guests myself. It was really bad for me, that TV show. It was worse for me than good, because the people who didn't know me who liked the show thought that's how I was...I mean, I still come through as myself, even with all the other stuff, but not really like I should. Not my real, natural way. And the people who did know me thought I was crazy. They knew that wasn't me. Including me. I didn't know that woman on TV!"*
- The show boasted a budget of up to $100,000 per episode, an impressive sum for a syndicated series, making it the most expensive show to be produced out of Nashville at that time.

→

Episode 1 / September 27, 1987

Guests: Dudley Moore / Hulk Hogan / Paul Reubens as Pee-wee Herman / Oprah Winfrey / Ed Koch
Songs: "Baby I'm Burning" (Theme); "Bubbling Over" (Dolly); Dudley Moore takes Dolly on a date for the Dolly's Date section; Dolly wrote an original song about a rag mag story called "Headlock on My Heart" and Hulk Hogan appears in the video segment with her. "Do I Ever Cross Your Mind" (Dolly) "Hey Good Lookin'" (Dolly and Pee Wee Herman); "Someone to Watch Over Me" (Dolly); Dolly chats with Oprah Winfrey which leads to a skit with Dolly playing a dingy actress trying out for the play *Porgy and Bess*. Dolly sneaks up on NYC Mayor Ed Koch during the "Out and About" segment. "Coat of Many Colors" (Dolly); "Look on the Bright Side" (Dolly and Acapella); Dolly does a Q&A chat with the audience. "This Little Light of Mine" (Dolly and Oprah with choir) The show wraps up with Dolly singing "I Will Always Love You."

Episode 2 / October 4, 1987

Guests: Burt Reynolds / Whoopi Goldberg / Alabama

Dolly opens the show from her bath. The show's theme song "Baby I'm Burning" plays over the opening segment. Dolly starts the the show off with "Savin' It for You" from her new album *Rainbow*. Burt Reynolds is Dolly's guest for the "Dolly's Date" section. Dolly and Acapella sing the song "Holdin' on to You." During the shows "Out and About" segment Dolly goes to a fire station and takes a ride on a firetruck. Alabama perform the song "Chosen Few." During the "Solo Spotlight" Dolly performs "Don't Get Around Much Anymore." In the following section Dolly tries to talk a fourteen and a half year old valley girl, Whoopi Goldberg, out of getting into a van with a guy, but only manages in talking her out of a haircut. Dolly starts off the "Tennessee Mountain Home" section by singing the title song. Afterwards Dolly is joined by Alabama and they sing "I Saw the Light" and "(Play Me Some) Mountain Music" together, followed by Dolly singing "Tiptoe, Tiptoe Little Dolly Parton." Dolly and Acapella sing "Look on the Bright Side,", and then Dolly does a Q & A session with the audience. Dolly performs the Biblical song "My Name Is Jonah" with a group of young children. The show ends with Dolly singing "I Will Always Love You."

Episode 3 / October 1, 1987

Guests: Bruce Willis / Emmylou Harris / Linda Ronstadt / Daniel Rosen

Dolly gives an introduction from her bubble bath. The shows theme "Baby I'm Burning" is heard over the opening credits. The episode starts with Dolly singing "The Fire That Keeps You Warm." Bruce Willis is Dolly's guest for the "Dolly's Date" section and they sing a bit of "Under the Boardwalk" together. Dolly begins the "Tennessee Mountain Home" portion by singing the title song, she then introduces Emmylou Harris and Linda Ronstadt. The Trio sing "My Dear Companion," "Hobo's Meditation" and "Those Memories of You." A new section of the show called "Dixie's Place" features Dolly ("Dixie") working in a diner where she sings "Hollywood Potters." Acapella performs "Jukebox Saturday Night." The shows "Out and About" section takes place at Yankee Stadium and Dolly visits with the New York Yankees. Another new section of the show titled, "The Novelty Club" featuring Daniel Rosen. Dolly does a Q & A session with the audience. The show ends with singing "I Will Always Love You."

Episode 4 / October 18, 1987

Guests: Patti LaBelle / Patrick Duffy / Christine Ebersole / The Flying Karamazov Brothers

Dolly talks to the viewers from her bubble bath. The song "Baby I'm Burning" is heard over the opening credits. Dolly opens the show by singing "A Better Place to Live." Patrick Duffy is Dolly's guest for the "Dolly's Date" section. Dolly and Acapella sing "Shattered Image." Patti LaBelle performs "I've Been Loving You Too Long." After the song Patti and Dolly have a conversation. The "Dixie's Place" sectionof the show follows, featuring Christine Ebersole and she sings "Sittin' on the Front Porch Swing" with Dolly. Dolly starts the "Tennessee Mountain Home" portion by singing the title song, before singing "Traveling Man." Dolly introduces the Flying Karamazov Brothers and then sings a short version of "Great Balls of Fire" towards the end of their spectacular act. Dolly and Acapella sing "Look on the Bright Side" and then Dolly does a Q & A session with the viewers. Patti LaBelle then sings "Up Above My Head" with Dolly. The show ends with Dolly singing "I Will Always Love You."

Episode 5 / October 25, 1987
Guests: Jim Henson as Kermit the Frog / Delta Burke / Terence Trent D'Arby / The Oak Ridge Boys

Dolly talks to the viewers from her bubble bath. The shows theme song, "Baby I'm Burning" plays over the opening. The show starts with Dolly singing "How Does It Feel." Kermit the Frog is Dolly's guest for the "Dolly's Date" section of the show and they sing "Everyday People." Up next is Oak Ridge Boys who sing "This Crazy Love." Delta Burke is the guest with Dolly during the "Vanity Fair" segment. Terence Trent D'Arby sings "If You Let Me Stay." During the "Dixie's Place" segment Dolly performs "A Cowboy's Ways." Dolly starts the "Tennessee Mountain Home" section off by singing the title song, before singing "Elvira" / "Swing Down Sweet Chariot" and "Have a Little Talk with Jesus" with the Oak Ridge Boys. Dolly and Acapella sing "Look on the Bright Side" and then Dolly does a Q & A session with the audience. Dolly performs "Oh, No!" with a gathering of young children. The show ends with Dolly singing "I Will Always Love You."

Episode 6 / November 1, 1987
Guests: Ned Beatty / Jackée Harry / Jon Lovitz / Mat Plendl / Tom Petty and the Heartbreakers

The show opens with Dolly performing "Don't Stop Dreaming." Jackée Harry joins Dolly for the "Vanity Fair" section where they sing "Here You Come Again." Tom Petty and the Heartbreakers sing "Think About Me." For the Solo Spotlight" Dolly sings "Night Life." Nd Beatty in the guest in the "Dixie's Place" section and Dolly performs "I'm a Drifter." Jon Lovitz is Dolly's guest for the "Dolly's Date" portion. Dolly begins the "Tennessee Mountain Home" segment with the title song, she then sings "Appalachian Memories." Mat Plendl performs for the second installment of "The Novelty Club." Dolly and Acapella sing "Look on the Bright Side" and then Dolly has a Q & A meeting with the audience. Dolly performs "The Seeker" and then show closes with Dolly singing "I Will Always Love You."

Episode 7 / November 8, 1987
"A Tennessee Mountain Thanksgiving"
Guests: Family Show

Dolly speaks to the viewers from her bubble bath. The show opens with Dolly singing "My Tennessee Mountain Home" on the front porch of the Tennessee Mountain Home where she grew up, interspliced with footage from the Great Smoky Mountains. Dolly goes to "Dolly Day" in downtown Sevierville, Tennessee. The Gatlinburg-Pittman-Seymour High School and Sevierville High School bands perform "9 to 5" at the event. Dolly speaks to some of her former classmates before singing "Mountain Magic." Dolly then gives a quick tour of Dollywood, showcasing the rides, stores, and entertainment. Then she sings "Rocky Top," followed by the traditional American folk song "In the Pines" with her brothers, Randy and Floyd. Dolly strolls the fields near the Tennessee Mountain Home and talks about growing up there in the mountains. She then brings her parents, Lee and Avie Lee Parton, onto the front porch and they think back through their memories of living there. Dolly performs "In the Good Old Days" (When Times Were Bad)." Dolly highlights Craftsman's Valley at Dollywood and sings "Poor Folks Town." Then Dolly introduces her uncle, John Henry Owens III and her aunt Dorothy Jo Owens who sings "Daddy Was an Old Time Preacher Man" with Dolly providing backing vocals and various other family members also performing. Dolly sings "On Top of Old Smoky" with her sisters, Stella and Frieda, in front of the Dr. Robert F. Thomas Chapel. Inside the chapel, Dolly along with her family perform "In the Sweet By-and-By" then Dolly's grandfather, Jake Owens, leads the group in a verse of "Amazing Grace" and "At the Cross." Dolly then performs "The Better Part of Life" with her siblings. Dolly ends the show with "I Will Always Love You."

Episode 8 / November 15, 1987
Guests: Juice Newton / Jerry Reed / Frank Oz as Miss Piggy

Miss Piggy talks to the viewers from Dolly's bubble bath. The shows theme song "Baby I'm Burning" plays over the opening segment. The show begins with Dolly singing "Could I Have Your Autograph." Dolly then goes to a Hollywood party. Miss Piggy takes control over Dolly's dressing room and schemes to get Dolly off the show before Dolly arrives and they perform "Friendship." Juice Newton sings "Tell Me True" and then Dolly joins her for "Ride 'Em Cowboy." Jerry Reed is the guest in the "Dixie's Place" portion and Dolly performs "Down." Miss Piggy sings "Someone to Watch Over Me" for the "Solo Spotlight" section, before a producer interrupts her. Dolly sings "Hoedown Showdown" and then has a short Q & A session with the viewers. Jerry and Dolly perform "She Got the Goldmine (I Got the Shaft.)" Juice Newton then joins them for "Oh, Lonesome Me." Dolly ends the show singing "I Will Always Love You."

Episode 9 / November 22, 1987
Guests: The Smothers Brothers / Allyce Beasley / Louis Nye / Willie Nelson

The show begins with Dolly singing "Hoedown Showdown" followed by "Two Doors Down." Then Dolly holds a Q & A session with the viewers. Dolly and Acapalla sing "This Old House." The Smothers Brothers perform a short a capella song for Dolly. Dolly shows Allyce Beasley around the set while the Smothers Brothers do a comedy sketch. Willie Nelson sings "Stardust" and then joined by Dolly and together they sing a medley of "Crazy," "Funny How Time Slips Away," "On the Road Again," "Blue Eyes Crying in the Rain," and "Family Bible." Dolly and Allyce Beasley go on a double date with the Smothers Brothers for the "Dolly's Date" section. Willie Nelson sings "Still Is Still Moving" before being joined on stage by Dolly, Allyce Beasley and the Smothers Brothers for "To All the Girls I've Loved Before." The show ends with Dolly singing "I Will Always Love You."

Episode 10 / November 29, 1987
"A Down Home Christmas Christmas"
Guests: Mac Davis / Burl Ives / Joanna Barnes / Robert Mandan / The Peppercorn Players

Dolly, dressed as Santa, introduces the show from the roof of the ABC Prospect Studio and then disappears down a chimney. She then appears inside and performs "With Bells On" and then her guests join in with her. Dolly remembers back about Christmases in Tennessee and sings "A Down Home Country Christmas" with Burl Ives, Mac Davis and The Peppercorn Players. The Peppercorn Players then sing "Grandma Got Run Over by a Reindeer," "All I Want for Christmas Is My Two Front Teeth" and "Jingle Bells" then Dolly leads them in the song "Santa Claus Is Going on a Diet." Dolly and Mac think back about Christmas when they were younger and Dolly performs "I Remember" which leads into a transition section of young Dolly at Christmas. Dolly shows a corn cob doll like one she had a child and sings "Little Tiny Tasseltop" which was one of the first songs she ever wrote. Dolly reads "The Letter" which blurs into a flashback segment of her first Christmas after moving to Nashville. Mac joins her and sings "Fall in Love with Your Wife" and "Drinkin' Christmas Dinner All Alone" before they sing "White Christmas" together. Joanna Barnes, Robert Mandan, and Burl Ives are the guests in the "Dixie's Place" segment. Dolly is then joined by Mac and Burl for a medley of "We Need a Little Christmas," "Jingle Bells," "O Little Town of Bethlehem," "Caroling, Caroling," "Silent Night," "O Come, All Ye Faithful" and "Joy to the World." Dolly ends the show with "Once Upon a Christmas."

Episode 11 / January 3, 1988
Guests: Joe Piscopo / Ricky Skaggs / Tammy Wynette

The show starts with Dolly singing "Hoedown Showdown," followed by "9 to 5." Dolly then hosts a Q & A session with the viewers. Dolly and Joe Piscopo, as Frank Sinatra, perform a medley of "Hello, Dolly!," "My Tennessee Mountain Home," and "I Get a Kick Out of You." Tammy Wynette sings "Talkin' to Myself Again" before Dolly joins her for a medley of "Stand by Your Man," "Apartment No. 9," "D-I-V-O-R-C-E," "I Don't Wanna Play House," and "Your Good Girl's Gonna Go Bad." Dolly performs "Heartbreak Express" during the "Dixie's Place" section. Dolly and Joe then chat and sing "I'm on Fire" with Joe as Bruce Springsteen. Ricky Skaggs performs "I'm Tired" and then duets with Dolly on "The Pain of Loving You." Tammy Wynette joins them on "Hallelujah, I'm Ready to Go." The show ends with Dolly singing "I Will Always Love You."

Episode 12 / Jan 10, 1988
Guests: Mary Hart / Holly Dunn / Brett Butler / Merle Haggard

The show begins with Dolly singing "Hoedown Showdown" followed by "Jolene." Dolly then holds a Q & A with the audience. Mary Hart joins Dolly for a comedy sketch. Merle Haggard performs "Twinkle, Twinkle Lucky Star" before Dolly joins him to perform a medley of "Workin' Man Blues," "Swinging Doors," "Today I Started Loving You Again," "Mama Tried," and "Okie from Muskogee." Mary returns to sing "Footloose" before Brett Butler performs a comedy skit. Holly Dunn sings "Strangers Again" and then Dolly joins her for "Daddy's Hands." All of the guests return to the stage with Dolly to sing "Rollin' in My Sweet Baby's Arms." Dolly ends the show by singing "I Will Always Love You."

Episode 13 / January 16, 1988
"Dolly's Birthday"
Guests: Kenny Rogers / James Gregory / Charles Durning

The show begins with Dolly singing "Hoedown Showdown," followed by "Islands in the Stream" with Kenny Rogers. Dolly and Kenny then do a Q & A with the audience. Kenny presents Dolly with a birthday cake and leads the audience in singing "Happy Birthday to You." James Gregory performs a comedy routine. Dolly and Kenny perform a medley of "We've Got Tonight," "Anyone Who Isn't Me Tonight," "Don't Fall in Love with a Dreamer," and "Real Love." Charles Durning is the guest in the "Dixie's Place" section and Dolly performs "The Stranger." Charles Durning performs "The Sidestep" from their 1982 film *The Best Little Whorehouse in Texas*. Dolly, Kenny Rogers and Charles During perform "Blaze of Glory." The show wraps up with Dolly performing "I Will Always Love You."

Episode 14 / January 23, 1988
Guests: Tom Jones / Lee Majors / Paul Rodriguez / The McCarters

The show begins with Dolly singing "Hoedown Showdown," followed by "Here You Come Again." Dolly then holds a Q & A with the audience. Tom Jones performs a medley of his hits: "She's a Lady," "Delilah," "What's New Pussycat?," "Without Love," and "It's Not Unusual." Dolly joins him for "Green, Green Grass of Home." Paul Rodriguez performs a comedy vignette. The clip of "Headlock on My Heart" music video with Hulk Hogan from the first episode is shown again. The McCarters perform "Timeless and True Love" and then clog dance to "Foggy Mountain Breakdown." Lee Majors gust stars in the "Dixie's Place" section of the show and Dolly performs "Kentucky Gambler." Acapella performs "Stand by Me." Dolly, Tom Jones and The McCarters join Acapella to perform "My Soul Is a Witness." Dolly ends the show by performing "I Will Always Love You."

Episode 15 / January 30, 1988
Guests: Glen Campbell / Brenda Lee / Lee Horsley / Exile / Ann Madison / The California Raisins

Dolly opens the show with "Hoedown Showdown," followed by "Baby I'm Burnin'." Dolly tells a humorous story and then has a Q & A with the audience. Next Glen Campbell performs "I Remember You." Dolly and Acapella sing "Amazing Grace" while Glen Campbell plays the bagpipes. The California Raisins sing "I Heard It Through the Grapevine." Ann Madison performs a musical comedy sketch. Exile sings their hit "Feel Like Foolin' Around." Lee Horsley is the guest in the "Dixie's Place" section and performs "Let It Be Me" with Dolly. Brenda Lee performs "I Can't Help It (If I'm Still in Love with You)." Dolly and Glen join Brenda and Lee for a medley of "Southern Nights," "Break It to Me Gently," "The Hand That Rocks the Cradle," "Sweet Nothin's," "Rhinestone Cowboy," "Wichita Lineman," "Galveston," "I'm Sorry," "By the Time I Get to Phoenix," "Dum Dum" and "Jambalaya (On the Bayou)." Dolly ends the show by performing "I Will Always Love You."

Episode 16 / February 6, 1988
"My Hawaii"
Guests: Malveen Lead / Danny Kaus / Al Harrington / Norm Compton / Danny Kallekeni

My Hawaii (Dolly); I Want To Be A Cowboys Sweetheart (Dolly); Paniolo Country (Dolly and Malveen Lead); Madame Pele (Goddess of Fire) (Dolly); Hoedown Showdown (Hawaiian Style) 9Dolly); At Home in the Islands (Danny Kaus); Unchained Melody (Dolly); Honolulu Nightlife (Dolly and Norm

Compton); Across the Sea (Dolly); Hawaiian Wedding Song (Dolly and Danny Kallekeni); Blue Hawaii (Dolly and Al Harrinfton); Little Grass Shack (Dolly, Al Harrington and Danny Kallekeni); How Great Thou Art (Dolly with the Honolulu Boy's Choir).

Episode 17 / February 13, 1988
Guests: Barbara Mandrell / Smokey Robinson / The Temptations / Tom Selleck

The show begins with Dolly singing "Hoedown Showdown," followed by "All I Can Do." Dolly tells a joke and then has a Q & A with the viewers before she is joined by Tom Selleck. Barbara Mandrell performs "Angels Love Bad Men." Smokey Robinson performs "Love Don't Give No Reason" before Dolly joins him to premiere the music video for their duet; "I Know You by Heart." Barbara Mandrell guest stars in the "Dixie's Place" portion and performs "Just the Way You Are" with Dolly. The Temptations perform "I Wonder Who She's Seeing Now" and then Dolly, Smokey Robinson, and Barbara Mandrell join them for a medley of "My Girl," "Baby, Baby I Need You," "Get Ready," "I Second That Emotion," "Two Lovers," "Shop Around," "Papa Was a Rollin' Stone," "The Tears of a Clown," and "I'm Gonna Make You Love Me." Dolly ends the show with "I Will Always Love You."

Episode 18 / April 9, 1988
Guests: Tyne Daly / Randy Travis / Rich Little / Nell Carter

Dolly opens the show with Dolly singing "Hoedown Showdown," followed by "(Your Love Has Lifted Me) Higher and Higher." Dolly tells a cute joke and then has a Q & A with the audience. Rich Little performs a comedy skit. Randy Travis performs "I Told You So" before Dolly joins him on "Blue Blue Day." Tyne Daly is the guest at "Dixie's Place" and performs "If I Could Be There (Too Hard To Be Soft)" with Dolly. Dolly and Rich Little do an old-time movie sketch together. Dolly sings "Wildflowers" during the "Tennessee Mountain Home" section. Nell Carter sings "Back in the High Life Again" before Dolly joins her for a medley of "Operator (Give Me Jesus on the Line)" and "I'll Fly Away." The show ends with Dolly singing "I Will Always Love You."

Episode 19 / April 16, 1988
"Nashville Memories"

Guests: Porter Wagoner / Fred Foster / Buck Trent / Faron Young / Ralph Emery / Bill Owens / Curly Putman / Bill Phillips / Jimmy C. Newman / Bill Carlisle / Johnny Russell / Chet Atkins / Minnie Pearl / Jan Howard / Skeeter Davis / Jeanne Pruett / Jean Shepard / Del Wood / Norma Jean / Kitty Wells / Stella Parton / Roy Acuff / Bill Monroe / Ben Smathers and his Stoney Mountain Cloggers / Melvin Sloan and the Melvin Sloan dancers.

This show was taped on location in Nashville, Tennessee at the Grand Ole Opry, Ryman Auditorium, Tootsie's Orchid Lounge, and RCA Studio B. It opens with Dolly singing "Down on Music Row" at the Grand Ole Opry. Then Ben Smathers and his Stoney Mountain Cloggers and Melvin Sloan and his Dancers perform. Dolly and Porter Wagoner sing "Black Draught Theme" at Ryman Auditorium. They view some vintage clips from *The Porter Wagoner Show* and then sing a medley of "The Last Thing on My Mind," "Fight and Scratch," "Holding on to Nothin'," "Daddy Was an Old Time Preacher Man." Dolly thinks back at Tootsie's Orchid Lounge with Fred Foster, Buck Trent, Faron Young, Ralph Emery, Bill Owens, Curly Putman, Bill Phillips, Jimmy C. Newman, Porter Wagoner, Bill Carlisle, and Johnny Russell. Dolly and Bill Phillips perform "Put It Off Until Tomorrow." Dolly is joined by Chet Atkins at RCA Studios to remember back and perform "Black Smoke's a-Risin'" and "Foggy Mountain Top." Dolly is then inducted into the Star Walk in Nashville. At Ryman Auditoriurm, Dolly joins Minnie Pearl, Jan Howard, Skeeter Davis, Jeanne Pruett, Jean Shepard, Del Wood, Norma Jean, and Kitty Wells. They all sing the Kitty Wells hit "It Wasn't God Who Made Honky Tonk Angels." Back at the Grand Ole Opry, Dolly introduces her sister Stella who performs "The Reason I'm Living." Roy Acuff performs Wabash Cannonball," Jimmie C. Newman sings "Cajun Way," Jean Shepard sings "Second Fiddle to an Old Guitar," Bill Monroe performs "Mule Skinner Blues (Blue Yodel No. 8)," Jeanne Pruett performs "Satin Sheets," Del Wood performs a piano solo, Skeeter Davis sings "The End of the World" and Porter Wagoner performs "Ole Slew Foot" and is joined by Dolly and all the other performers. Dolly brings all present members of the Opry on stage and together they sing "I Saw the Light." The show ends with Dolly singing "I Will Always Love You."

Episode 20 / April 23, 1988
Guests: Bob Hope / Frank Oz as Miss Piggy / Loretta Swit / Jerry Lee Lewis

The show begins with Dolly singing "Hoedown Showdown," followed by "Star of the Show" and then she introduces her band members. Dolly gets a laugh with a joke and then asks if anyone in the audience have any jokes to tell or questions for her, then Miss Piggy comes on stage. Bob Hope and Dolly perform a comedy skit and sing "Buttons and Bows." Dolly and Miss Piggy have a conversation before The Desert Rose Band perform "He's Back and I'm Blue." Jerry Lee Lewis performs "Meat Man" and "Great Balls of Fire" before Dolly joins him and they sing "Why You Been Gone So Long." Dolly joins Miss Piggy on her tour bus. Loretta Swift is the guest in the "Dixie's Place" portion and she performs "Stop! In the Name of Love" and "If We Never Meet Again." Dolly and Miss Piggy perform "I'm a Hog for You Baby." The show ends with Dolly singing "I Will Always Love You."

Episode 21 / April 30, 1988
"Down in New Orleans"

Guests: Doug Kershaw / George Kirby as Louis Armstrong / Pete Fountain / Irma Thomas / Allen Toussaint / The Dixie Cups / Neville Brothers / Dr. John / Good Rockin' Dopsie and the Twisters / Paul Prudhomme

This show was taped on location in New Orleans, Louisiana. It opens with Dolly marching down the street in a funeral parade. She then gets on a steamboat and performs "Down by the Riverside" with Pete Fountain. Dolly talks about the steam calliope and the Mississippi River with Captain Doc Holley. Dolly sings "New Orleans" on the deck of the steamboat, once again with Pete Fountain. Dolly then takes a tour of the city in a mule-drawn carriage. The Dixie Cups sing "Iko Iko" in the streets of New Orleans and then are joined by the Neville Brothers who sing "When You Go to New Orleans." Dolly talks about riding on a float at the Mardi Gras parade and video is shown of the parade and her singing "When the Saints Go Marching In" at the Super Dome. George Kirby sings "What a Wonderful World" as Louis Armstrong at Storyville in the French Quarter. Dolly then sings "The House of the Rising Sun." Dr. John sings "Right Place, Wrong Time." Next, Allen Toussaint sings "Southern Nights" followed by Irma Thomas singing "Breakaway." Dolly brings Dr. John, Allen and Irma on stage and together they perform "Working in the Coal Mine." Dolly and Doug Kershaw talk about Cajun food with cook Paul Prudhomme. Dolly then sings "Rock-a-Bye Baby" before attending a party where Good Rockin' Dopsie and the Twisters sing "Fais Do-Do." Doug Kershaw then performs "Jambalaya (On the Bayou)" and "Louisiana Man." He and Dolly then perform "Louisiana Saturday Night." Dolly sings "Shall We Gather at the River" and "Gather on the Other Side" with a choir on a riverbank. Dolly ends the show by singing "Blue Bayou."

Episode 22 / May 7, 1988
Guests: Loretta Lynn / Dabney Coleman / Mike Snider / Jackie Mason

The show starts with Dolly performing "Hoedown Showdown," followed by "When Will I Be Loved." Dolly then tells a joke and asks if anyone in the audience has any jokes to share or any questions for her. Loretta Lynn performs "Who Was That Stranger" from her new album of the same name before Dolly joins her for a medley of "Coal Miner's Daughter," "You Ain't Woman Enough," "Don't Come Home a Drinkin' (With Lovin' on Your Mind)," "Blue Kentucky Girl," "One's on the Way," "The Pill," and a reprise of "Coal Miner's Daughter." Jackie Mason performs a comedy bit. Dolly sings "Applejack" during the "Tennessee Mountain Home" portion. Dabney Coleman is the gust star in the "Dixie's Place" section and Dolly performs "Waterloo." Mike Snider performs "Satellite "T.V." Blues." Dolly and Loretta Lynn join him for "I Shall Not Be Moved." Dolly wraps up the series with "I Will Always Love You."

Notes / Trivia:

- Some of the writers of this series were Fannie Flagg and Bruce Vilanch.
- The author has master copies of these shows and thoroughly enjoyed the research!

<ins>This is not every TV appearance by Dolly. Just some highlights.</ins>

Cas Walker Farm and Home Hour (1956-1964) (First television appearances)
The Early Morning Show (June 2, 1964)
The Ralph Emery Early Morning Show (1967)
Music City USA (1967)
The Wilburn Brothers Show (1967 and 1973)
The Porter Wagoner Show (1967 -1974 / 218 episodes)
The Kraft Music Hall (1968, 1969, 1970)
An Old-Time Country Christmas (1969) (TV Special)
Hee Haw (1970, 1972, 1975)
The Nashville Sound (1970) (Documentary)
The Mike Douglas Show (1970, 1974, 1977)
The David Frost Show (1971)
That Good Ole Nashville Music (1971)
The Rowan and Martin Special (1973) (TV Special)
RCA's Opening Night (1973) (TV Special)
Burt Reynolds' Late Show (1973) (TV Special)
Dinah's Place (1974)
8th Annual Country Music Association Awards (1974) (TV Special)
In Concert (this episode was released on LP by RCA Records) *(1975)*
Sing Country 1975 (1975) (TV Special)
The Ronnie Prophet Show (1975)
Candid Camera (1975)
Dinah! (1976)
Dolly! (1976-1977 / 26 episodes)
Festival of Entertainment (1976) (TV Special)
Sing Country 1976 (1976) (TV Special)
The Mac Davis Show (1976)
The Hollywood Squares (1976 / Five episodes)
10th Annual Country Music Association Awards (1976)
The 4th Annual American Music Awards (1977)
The 19th Annual Grammy Awards (1977)
Captain Kangaroo (1977)
Musikladen (1977)
Cher... Special (1978) Dolly was nominated for an Emmy in the category

of "Best Supporting Actress in a Variety or Musical Special." (TV Special)
The Hollywood Squares (1978 / One episode)
50 Years of Country Music (1978) (TV Special)
Dolly and Carol in Nashville (1979) (TV Special)
The Seventies: An Explosion of Country Music (1979) TV Special
The Barbara Mandrell Show (1980)
Lily: Sold Out (1981) (TV Special)
Kenny & Dolly: A Christmas to Remember (1984) (TV Special)
Kenny Rogers and Dolly Parton Together (1985) (TV Special) later released on home media as: Kenny and Dolly: Real Love.
The Winning Hand (1985) (TV Special)
A Smoky Mountain Christmas (1986) (TV Movie)
Dolly (1987-1988 / 22 episodes)
Bob Hope's Christmas Special (1988) (TV Special)
Kenny, Dolly and Willie: Something Inside So Strong (1989) (TV Special)
Designing Women (1990)
Babes (1991) (Dolly was an executive producer)
Wild Texas Wind (1991) (TV Movie)
Unlikely Angel (1996) TV Movie
Get to the Heart: The Barbara Mandrell Story (TV Movie / Cameo) (1997)
The Simpsons (1999)
Blue Valley Songbird (1999) (TV Movie)
Bette (2000)
Reba (2005)
Dolly Celebrates 25 Years of Dollywood (2010)
Kenny & Dolly: An Intimate Conversation (2013)
Dolly Parton's Coat of Many Colors (2015) (TV Movie)
Dolly Parton's Christmas of Many Colors: Circle of Love (2016)
Dolly & Friends: The Making of a Soundtrack (2018) (The making of the Dumplin' soundtrack)
Dolly Parton's Heartstrings (2019) (Eight episodes produced)
Christmas at Dollywood 2019 (TV Movie)
Dolly Parton's Comin' Home for Christmas (2020) (TV Special)
Christmas on the Square 2020 (TV Movie / Musical)

9 to 5
(Released: December 19, 1980)
Dolly's introduction to the big screen came in this funny and heartwarming comedy. Three friends who are all working women (Dolly, Lily Tomlin, and Jane Fonda) are tired of their "sexist, egotistical, lying, hypocritical bigot" of a boss (Dabney Coleman) and his demeaning demands. The film's title song was written and recorded by Dolly. There is a possible sequel in the works.

The Best Little Whorehouse in Texas
(Released: July 23, 1982)
Texas brothel madame Mona (Dolly) has developed a good, working relationship with the small town where she resides, mostly thanks in part to her romantic past with the local sheriff (Burt Reynolds). But when a big city nosey reporter (Dom DeLuise) reveals this arrangement, Mona's life is turned upside down. Dolly was nominated for her second Golden Globe Award for this screen adaptation of the 1978 Broadway musical of the same name. (Her first nomination was for *9 to 5*). She re-recorded her 1974 chart-topping single "I Will Always Love You" for this film.

Rhinestone
(Released: June 22, 1984)
Jake Farris (Dolly) makes a bet with her boss, a sleazy club manager (Ron Leibman), to get out of her long-term contract at a New York City urban cowboy nightclub. The bet is that she can turn the next person who walk s through the front door into a country star. He accepts. Then New York cabbie Nick Martinelli (Sylvester Stallone) who thinks country music is "worse than liver" happens to walk in. Jake has a big challenge ahead of her. The film didn't do well at the box office, but it did produce two top 10 country hits for Dolly: "Tennessee Homesick Blues" and "God Won't Get You."

Smoky Mountain Christmas
(Aired: December 14, 1986)
Way before Hallmark started making yearly Christmas movies there was ABC-TV. In this Dolly Parton made-for-TV holiday movie she plays Lorna Davis, a discouraged and played-out country music star. For the Christmas season Lorna decides to take a break and head for the cabin a friend said she could use to unwind and get away from everyone pulling at her. But soon after she arrives, she discovers seven orphans who ran away from the local orphanage in town hiding out there. What Lorna doesn't realize is that he has been followed to the cabin by a reporter who is determined to to let everyone know where she is. Other characters come into the picture making things difficult. You'll have to watch for yourself. John Ritter stars as the judge who fixes everything.

Steel Magnolias
(Released: November 22, 1989)
This is the true life story of a Louisiana born mother-and-daughter (and Julia) who bring a whole group of long-time friends (and some new friends) together through a tragedy. Truvy (Dolly Parton) has a salon in Chinquapin, Louisiana and it is the place to go for a beauty treatment served with a hearty side of gossip. Along with her overeager assistant Annelle (Daryl Hannah), Truvy spoils her small-town clients with hairdos, manicures and all kinds of unsolicited advice. Anybody who's anybody is a regular: There's the doting M'Lynn (Sally Field) and her soon-to-be-married daughter Shelby (Roberts), the moody Ouiser (Shirley MacLaine) and the well-to-do widow Clairee (Olympia Dukakis). Through witty banter and wisecracks, this hodgepodge group of long-time friends form an even stronger friendship... one as strong as steel, which they are forced to lean on when a sudden tragedy strikes.

Wild Texas Wind
(Aired: September 23, 1991)

The story of this Made-for-TV movie revolves around country singer Thiola Rayfield (Dolly Parton) and her band *Big T & The Texas Wheelers*. The story follows the band's quick rise to success as well as Thiola's troubled relationship with their violently abusive and alcoholic manager Justice Parker (Gary Busey). In the middle of everything, a murder takes place, leaving the officials with a trio of suspects and a murder to solve.

Straight Talk (1992)
(Released: April 3, 1992)

Arkansas based dance teacher Shirlee Kenyon (Dolly) decides to leave her loser boyfriend Steve who does nothing but stomp on her dreams and belittle her and head to the big city—Chicago—for a fresh start. But along the way Shirlee runs into some trouble and bad luck. After a series of bad job interviews she is hired to run the switchboard at a local radio station even though she has no experience with the equipment. During a coffee break she accidentally wonders into the studio and is mistaken for the new call in therapist, is put on the air, and begins hesitantly talking with the show's callers. Upon completion of the show, the program director arrives, sees this is not the new therapist (who never showed up) and fires Shirlee, along with the producer and engineer, who had made the mistake of putting Shirlee on the air. However the listening audience really liked Dr. Shirlee and wants her back. She is brought back with a nice contract (but no credentials). Noisy local television reporter Jack (James Woods) hears of this new popular radio show and of the doctor, and he begins to look into her past, which shows she is not who she claims she is. But luckily for Kenyon, Jack seems to fancy her as much as he fancies excavating her past.

The Beverly Hillbillies
(Released: October 15, 1993)

Dolly plays herself is this early 1990's comedy film. She is brought in to sing at Jed Clampett's birthday party. Dolly did write and record the song "If You Ain't Got Love" for the film soundtrack which was released on CD and cassette tape by Fox Records and marketed by RCA. Film also stars: Jim Varney, Cloris Leechman, Dabney Coleman, Lily Tomlin, Lea Thompson, Buddy Ebsen. Filming took place February 22, 1993 to May 4, 1993.

Unlikely Angel (1996)
(Aired: December 17, 1996)

Country star Ruby Diamond (Dolly Parton) dies unexpectedly in a car accident after a gig. Arriving at heaven's gate she learns that but before she can cross into heaven, she has to do some good deeds back on Earth first. Saint Peter (Roddy McDowall) sends her back to help a workaholic father (Brian Kerwin) to reunite with his children for the holidays. Ruby can sing like an angel, but can she act like one? *Unlikely Angel* features two original Dolly Parton songs and a lot of holiday cheer. No known soundtrack was released from the film, but Dolly wrote "Unlikely Angel" and "Whatcha Tryin' To Do To Me."

The Blue Valley Songbird (1999)
(Aired: November 1, 1999)

A popular country singer named Leanna Taylor (Dolly Parton) longs for more recognition but finds her ambitions restricted by her controlling boyfriend Hank (John Terry). Turning to her guitarist Bobby (fellow country singer Billy Dean), she not only manages to face up to her boyfriend, but also confronts old troubles, namely her estranged mother and dead father. No soundtrack was released, but Dolly wrote all the material except for "Amazing Grace" and "Angel Band." Dolly and Billy Dean team up for several songs including; "I Hope You're Never Happy," "We Might Be In Love" and "Runaway Feeling."

Frank McKlusky, C.I.
(Limited Release: June 27, 2002)

In this film Dolly plays Edith McKlusky, the overprotective mother of Frank who decides to go undercover to find the reason behind his best friends premature death. The story revolves around an insurance claims investigator who takes his job very seriously. In 1979 as a child Frank (Dave Sheridan) watched his daredevil father wipe out in a motorcycle jumping stunt, and since then, Frank's developed an unhealthy aversion to any kind of risk: he lives with his parents, wears a helmet and knee pads everywhere he goes, and lives his life strictly by the rules. When his partner is killed in the line of duty, Frank's forced to come out of his shell to crack the case.

Miss Congeniality 2: Armed and Fabulous
(Released: March 24, 2005)

Dolly plays herself in this film. Sandra Bullock's character is investigating some shady dealings at a pageant and thinking that Dolly looks like a suspicious Dolly impersonator chases her and tackles her to the ground.

Gnomeo & Juliet
(Released: January 23, 2011)

This is an animated feature released by Walt Disney Studios Motion Pictures under the Touchstone Pictures banner in which Dolly plays "Dolly Gnome," the lawnmower race announcer, and Mankini Gnome's (Julio Bonet) love interest. Based loosely on *Romeo & Juliet*. The main characters are played by James McAvoy, Emily Blunt, Michael Caine, Maggie Smith, Patrick Stewart.

The Year Dolly Parton Was My Mom
(March 4, 2011 / Canada)

Dolly provides only a voice cameo in this Canadian coming-of-age film. Set in Manitoba in 1976. The main character, Elizabeth wants to be older. She is only 11, but *nearly* 12 she points out. Her mother Marion, points out that being nearly 12 "makes you still 11." Elizabeth and her best friend, Annabelle, are looking forward to their bodies maturing, including the possibility that they might get "big boobs" like Dolly Parton. Her father, Phil, answers her questions about the family's blood types for a school project. When the project is reviewed in her science class, it reveals that her blood type means that she is not her parents' natural child. Elizabeth is angry and hurt, and soon dreams of the possibility of Dolly being her real mother. Annabelle's mother, Stella, who is active in the woman's movement, admires Dolly as a strong independent business woman, which adds to Elizabeth's fantasy. Elizabeth tries to ride her bike to a Dolly concert in Minneapolis, but is stopped hours later at the Emerson border crossing. Marion drives to get her, and the two form a stronger connection over the next two days, as Marion takes her to Minneapolis to meet Dolly.

Joyful Noise
(Released January 13, 2012)

Hard times in Pacashau, Ga. result in an unlikely partnership- a choir director's widow, G.G. Sparrow (Dolly Parton) and a single mom of two teenagers Vi Rose (Queen Latifah) come together to try to save a small Georgia town's gospel choir at Divinity Church Choir. But it doesn't go as planned, as the two fuss and fight regularly and publicly. Vi Rose (Queen Latifah) believes that a traditional style is the key to victory, but G.G. (Dolly Parton) thinks tried-and-true means tired-and-old. As the hopes of keeping their choir alive fade, the two learn to put aside their differences aside and find a harmonious chord or risk losing everything.

Hollywood to Dollywood
(August 31, 2012)

Twin brothers Gary and Larry Lane, originally from Goldsboro, North Carolina, have written a screenplay for their idol Dolly Parton called *Full Circle*. After several unsuccessful attempts at trying to get their work to Dolly, the brother decided to drive from Los Angeles where they currently live to the Dollywood theme park in Pigeon Forge, Tennessee to hand the script directly to Dolly. They had met Dolly once before at the 25th Anniversary celebration of Dollywood. They make their way east in their RV named "Jolene" after Dolly's hit 1974 song. On board with them is driver Michael Bowen who is also Gary's partner. Michael hopes to give Dolly a birdhouse he made which is a replica of her Tennessee Mountain Home. During the 2000+ mile trip down Interstate 40, Gary and Larry revise their script, encounter a tornado, meet many people along the way and discuss growing up gay in North Carolina. The floods in Nashville in 2010 nearly cause them to miss getting to Dollywood in time. This documentary reveals the twins concerns with how their hometown will react to the film (and to the brothers' homosexuality) and their desire for acceptance from their Southern Baptist mother.
Hollywood to Dollywood includes appearances from several of the Lane twins' friends, including actors Leslie Jordan, Chad Allen, Beth Grant and Ann Walker and Oscar–winning screenwriter Dustin Lance Black.

Dolly Parton's Christmas on the Square
(Aired November 22, 2020)

A wealthy woman named Regina Fuller (Christine Baranski), plans to return to the small town she was raised in, evict the residents and sell the land to a mall developer without regard for their feelings, receives a visit from an angel (Dolly Parton).

- Dolly wrote all of the songs featured in the film. A soundtrack album was not released, although Parton did record versions of "Christmas Is" and "Christmas on the Square" for her 2020 album *A Holly Dolly Christmas*. "Main Title" – Orchestra / Medley: "Christmas Is - Christmas on the Square - Gotta Get Out - Maybe, Just Maybe - So Sorry" (Dolly Parton, Christine Baranski, Josh Segarra, Mary Lane Haskell, Jeanine Mason, and Ensemble) / "You" – Josh Segarra and Mary Lane Haskell / "Queen of Mean" – Jenifer Lewis / "Keeper of Memories" – Treat Williams / "Everybody Needs an Angel" – Dolly Parton / "Light Your Lamp" – Dolly Parton / "Wickedest Witch of the Middle" – Josh Segarra and Ensemble / "Try" – Josh Segarra, Mary Lane Haskell, and Ensemble / "Fairytale" – Selah Kimbro Jones & Christine Baranski / "Maybe, Just Maybe" (Reprise 1) – Christine Baranski / "A Father's Prayer" – Douglas Sills / "Everybody Needs an Angel" (Reprise) – Dolly Parton and Jeanine Mason / "Rearview Mirror / Happy Town / Just Dance" – Dolly Parton, Christine Baranski, and Ensemble / "Maybe, Just Maybe" (Reprise 2) – Christine Baranski / "A Father's Prayer" (Reprise) – Matthew Johnson / "Christmas Is" (Reprise) – Jeanine Mason / "Try" (Reprise) – Mary Lane Haskell / "Angels Know" – Dolly Parton / "Maybe, Just Maybe" (Reprise 3) – Christine Baranski / "Try" (Gospel Reprise) – Jenifer Lewis and Ensemble / "An Angel's Prayer" – Dolly Parton / "Forgive Me" – Christine Baranski / "Christmas Is / Christmas on the Square" (Finale) – Cast / "Try" (End Credits) – Dolly Parton
- Directed and choreographed by Debbie Allen

If you would like to learn more about this amazing person I suggest a few books. There are bound to be many more available by doing a search such as on Amazon or Google. These were the books I was able to really enjoy the most of all the books about Dolly Parton that I have read.

Dolly by Alanna Nash (1978)
Just the Way I Am: Poetic Selections on Reasons to Live, Reasons to Love and Reasons to Smile from the Songs of Dolly Parton (1979)
Dolly Parton: My Life and Other Unfinished Business (1994)
Coat of Many Colors (1996)
Dolly's Dixie Fixin's: Love, Laughter and Lots of Good Food (2006)
I Am a Rainbow (2009)
Dream More: Celebrate the Dreamer in You (2012)
Dolly on Dolly by Randy Schmidt (2017)
Songteller: My Life in Lyrics (2020)
Female Force: Dolly Parton comic book (March 31, 2021)
My Little Golden Book About Dolly Parton (September 21, 2021)

A Decade of Recording Information 1968 – 1978

Just Because I'm a Woman (Release Date: April 15, 1968)
Side 1

No.	Title	Writer(s)	Recording date	Length
1.	"You're Gonna Be Sorry"	Dolly Parton	December 11, 1967	2:16
2.	"I Wish I Felt This Way at Home"	Harlan Howard	December 11, 1967	2:29
3.	"False Eyelashes"	Demetrius Tapp, Bob Tubert	December 20, 1967	2:30
4.	"I'll Oilwells Love You"	Dolly Parton, Bill Owens	December 20, 1967	2:16
5.	"The Only Way Out (Is to Walk Over Me)"	Neal Merritt	December 11, 1967	2:55
6.	"Little Bit Slow to Catch On"	Curly Putman	December 18, 1967	2:19

Side 2

No.	Title	Writer(s)	Recording date	Length
1.	"The Bridge"	Dolly Parton	December 20, 1967	2:34
2.	"Love and Learn"	Bill Owens	December 20, 1967	2:33
3.	"I'm Running Out of Love"	Bill Owens	December 18, 1967	2:06
4.	"Just Because I'm a Woman"	Dolly Parton	December 18, 1967	3:04
5.	"Baby Sister"	Shirl Milete	December 18, 1967	2:39
6.	"Try Being Lonely"	Charles Trent, George McCormick	December 20, 1967	2:42

In The Good Old Days (When Times Were Bad) (Release Date: February 3, 1969)
Side 1

No.	Title	Writer(s)	Recording date	Length
1.	"Don't Let It Trouble Your Mind"	Dolly Parton	October 9, 1968	2:12
2.	"He's a Go–Getter"	Dolly Parton	October 9, 1968	2:03
3.	"In the Good Old Days (When Times Were Bad)"	Dolly Parton	September 9, 1968	2:45
4.	"It's My Time"	John D. Loudermilk	September 10, 1968	2:37
5.	"Harper Valley PTA"	Tom T. Hall	September 9, 1968	3:10
6.	"Little Bird"	Dolly Parton	September 10, 1968	1:44

Side 2

No.	Title	Writer(s)	Recording date	Length
1.	"Mine"	Dolly Parton	October 9, 1968	2:03
2.	"The Carroll County Accident"	Bob Ferguson	October 9, 1968	2:56
3.	"Fresh Out of Forgiveness"	Bill Owens, Gene Gill	October 9, 1968	2:01
4.	"Mama, Say a Prayer"	Dolly Parton	October 9, 1968	2:45
5.	"Always the First Time"	Joyce McCord	September 9, 1968	2:01
6.	"D–I–V–O–R–C–E"	Bobby Braddock, Curly Putman	September 10, 1968	2:43

My Blue Ridge Mountain Boy (Release Date: September 8, 1969)
Side 1

No.	Title	Writer(s)	Recording date	Length
1.	"In the Ghetto"	Mac Davis	June 2, 1969	2:50
2.	"Games People Play"	Joe South	June 2, 1969	2:26
3.	"'Til Death Do Us Part"	Dolly Parton	May 14, 1969	3:09
4.	"Big Wind"	Wayne P. Walker / Alex Zanetis / George McCormick	June 2, 1969	2:18
5.	"Evening Shade"	Dolly Parton	May 21, 1969	3:22
6.	"I'm Fed Up with You"	Bill Owens	June 2, 1969	2:00

Side 2

No.	Title	Writer(s)	Recording date	Length
1.	"My Blue Ridge Mountain Boy"	Dolly Parton	May 20, 1969	
2.	"Daddy"	Dolly Parton	September 9, 1968	2:50
3.	"We Had All the Good Things Going"	Merv Shiner / Jerry Monday	May 14, 1969	2:45
4.	"The Monkey's Tale"	Leona Ross	May 14, 1969	1:51
5.	"Gypsy, Joe and Me"	Dolly Parton	May 21, 1969	3:13
6.	"Home for Pete's Sake"	Rudy Preston	May 14, 1969	1:59

The Fairest of Them All (Release Date: February 2, 1970)
Side 1

No.	Title	Writer(s)	Recording date	Length
1.	"Daddy Come and Get Me"	Dolly Parton / Dorothy Jo Hope	October 31, 1969	3:01
2.	"Chas"	Dolly Parton	October 30, 1969	2:24
3.	"When Possession Gets Too Strong"	Dolly Parton / Louis Owens	October 31, 1969	2:04
4.	"Before You Make Up Your Mind"	Bill Owens	October 31, 1969	2:10
5.	"I'm Doing This for Your Sake"	Dolly Parton	September 10, 1968	2:11
6.	"But You Loved Me Then"	Dolly Parton	May 21, 1969	1:52

Side 2

No.	Title	Writer(s)	Recording date	Length
1.	"Just the Way I Am"	Dolly Parton	October 31, 1969	2:28
2.	"More Than Their Share"	Dolly Parton	October 31, 1969	2:20
3.	"Mammie"	Dolly Parton	May 13, 1969	3:11
4.	"Down from Dover"	Dolly Parton	September 4, 1969	3:46
5.	"Robert"	Dolly Parton	September 4, 1969	2:39

The Golden Streets of Glory (Release Date: February 15, 1971)
Side 1

No.	Title	Writer(s)	Recording date	Length
1.	"I Believe"	Ervin Drake / Jimmy Shirl / Irvin Graham / Al Stillman	May 13, 1970	2:17
2.	"Yes, I See God"	Dorothy Jo Hope	May 13, 1970	2:15

No.	Title	Writer(s)	Recording date	Length
3.	"The Master's Hand"	Dolly Parton	May 12, 1970	2:41
4.	"Heaven's Just a Prayer Away"	Tommy Tomlinson	May 12, 1970	2:45
5.	"The Golden Streets of Glory"	Dolly Parton	May 11, 1970	2:54

Side 2

No.	Title	Writer(s)	Recording date	Length
1	"How Great Thou Art"	Stuart K. Hine	May 12, 1970	3:34
2	"I'll Keep Climbing"	Dorothy Jo Hope	May 12, 1970	2:41
3	"Book of Life"	Jake Robert Owens	May 13, 1970	1:44
4	"Wings of a Dove"	Bob Ferguson	May 11, 1970	2:35
5	"Lord, Hold My Hand"	Dolly Parton, Ginny Dean	May 13, 1970	2:03

Joshua (Release Date: April 12, 1971)

Side 1

No.	Title	Writer(s)	Recording date	Length
1.	"Joshua"	Dolly Parton	October 21, 1970	3:02
2.	"The Last One to Touch Me"	Dolly Parton	February 11, 1971	3:04
3.	"Walls of My Mind"	Dolly Parton	October 31, 1969	2:32
4.	"It Ain't Fair That It Ain't Right"	Bob Eggers, Janice Eggers	April 20, 1970	2:18
5.	"J.J. Sneed"	Dolly Parton, Dorothy Jo Hope	January 26, 1971	2:53

Side 2

No.	Title	Writer(s)	Recording date	Length
1.	"You Can't Reach Me Anymore"	Dolly Parton, Dorothy Jo Hope	October 31, 1969	2:38
2.	"Daddy's Moonshine Still"	Dolly Parton	January 26, 1971	3:29
3.	"Chicken Every Sunday"	Charlie Craig, Betty Craig	October 21, 1970	2:35
4.	"The Fire's Still Burning"	Dolly Parton, Dorothy Jo Hope	October 31, 1969	2:49
5.	"Letter to Heaven"	Dolly Parton	January 26, 1971	2:29

Coat of Many Colors (Release Date: October 4, 1971)

Side 1

No.	Title	Writer(s)	Recording date	Length
1.	"Coat of Many Colors"	Dolly Parton	April 27, 1971	3:05
2.	"Traveling Man"	Dolly Parton	April 16, 1971	2:40
3.	"My Blue Tears"	Dolly Parton	April 16, 1971	2:16
4.	"If I Lose My Mind"	Porter Wagoner	April 27, 1971	2:29
5.	"The Mystery of the Mystery"	Porter Wagoner	April 27, 1971	2:28

Side 2

No.	Title	Writer(s)	Recording date	Length
1.	"She Never Met a Man (She Didn't Like)"	Dolly Parton	October 30, 1969	2:41
2.	"Early Morning Breeze"	Dolly Parton	January 26, 1971	2:54

No.	Title	Writer(s)	Recording date	Length
3.	"The Way I See You"	Wagoner	April 27, 1971	2:46
4.	"Here I Am"	Dolly Parton	April 27, 1971	3:19
5.	"A Better Place to Live"	Dolly Parton	October 30, 1969	2:39

Touch Your Woman (Release Date: March 6, 1972)
Side 1

No.	Title	Writer(s)	Recording date	Length
1.	"Will He Be Waiting?"	Dolly Parton	December 14, 1971	2:31
2.	"The Greatest Days of All"	Dolly Parton	December 14, 1971	2:41
3.	"Touch Your Woman"	Dolly Parton	December 14, 1971	2:43
4.	"A Lot of You Left in Me"	Dolly Parton	January 1, 1972	2:31
5.	"Second Best"	Dolly Parton	January 12, 1972	2:57

Side 2

No.	Title	Writer(s)	Recording date	Length
1.	"A Little at a Time"	Dolly Parton	January 1, 1972	2:14
2.	"Love Is Only as Strong (As Your Weakest Moment)"	Bill Owens	January 12, 1972	2:05
3.	"Love Isn't Free"	Dolly Parton	October 30, 1969	2:34
4.	"Mission Chapel Memories"	Dolly Parton, Porter Wagoner	January 1, 1972	3:09
5.	"Loneliness Found Me"	Porter Wagoner	Unknown	

My Favorite Songwriter, Porter Wagoner (Release Date: October 2, 1972)
Side 1

No.	Title	Recording date	Length
1.	"Lonely Comin' Down"	May 3, 1972	3:10
2.	"Do You Hear the Robins Sing"	May 4, 1972	2:27
3.	"What Ain't to Be, Just Might Happen"	June 19, 1972	2:22
4.	"The Bird That Never Flew"	May 4, 1972	3:13
5.	"Comes and Goes"	May 2, 1972	3:15

Side two

No.	Title	Recording date	Length
1.	"Washday Blues"	May 3, 1972	2:04
2.	"When I Sing for Him"	May 4, 1972	2:58
3.	"He Left Me Love"	May 2, 1972	2:57
4.	"Oh, He's Everywhere"	May 3, 1972	3:01
5.	"Still on Your Mind"	January 12, 1972	2:41

My Tennessee Mountain Home (Release Date: April 2, 1973)
Side 1

No.	Title	Recording date	Length
1.	"The Letter"	September 5, 1972	2:03
2.	"I Remember"	October 3, 1972	3:42
3.	"Old Black Kettle"	September 5, 1972	2:32
4.	"Daddy's Working Boots"	September 1, 1972	2:52
5.	"Dr. Robert F. Thomas"	October 2, 1972	2:36
6.	"In the Good Old Days (When Times were Bad)"	October 2, 1972	3:26

Side 2

No. Title	Recording date	Length
1. "My Tennessee Mountain Home"	September 1, 1972	3:05
2. "Wrong Direction Home"	September 1, 1972	2:28
3. "Back Home"	October 3, 1972	2:44
4. "The Better Part of Life"	October 3, 1972	3:13
5. "Down on Music Row"	September 5, 1972	2:58

Bubbling Over (Release Date: September 10, 1973)
Side 1

No. Title	Writer(s)	Recording date	Length
1. "Bubbling Over"	Dolly Parton	May 22, 1973	2:20
2. "Traveling Man"	Dolly Parton	April 9, 1973	2:12
3. "Alabama Sundown"	Dave Kirby, Danny Morrison	December 14, 1971	2:31
4. "Afraid to Live and Afraid of Dying"	Porter Wagoner	May 19, 1972	2:04
5. "Love with Me"	Dolly Parton	February 1, 1973	2:15

Side 2

No. Title	Writer(s)	Recording date	Length
1. "My Kind of Man"	Dolly Parton	December 12, 1972	2:25
2. "Sometimes an Old Memory Gets in My Eye"	Bill Owens	February 1, 1973	2:20
3. "Pleasant as May"	Dolly Parton	January 26, 1971	2:34
4. "The Beginning"	Dolly Parton	January 11, 1972	2:35
5. "Love, You're So Beautiful Tonight"	Porter Wagoner	May 19, 1972	3:09

Jolene (Release Date: February 4, 1974)
Side 1

No. Title	Writer(s)	Recording date	Length
1. "Jolene"	Dolly Parton	May 22, 1973	2:43
2. "When Someone Wants to Leave"	Dolly Parton	December 26, 1973	2:06
3. "River of Happiness"	Dolly Parton	December 26, 1973	2:19
4. "Early Morning Breeze"	Dolly Parton	December 26, 1973	2:45
5. "Highlight of My Life"	Dolly Parton	December 3, 1973	2:18

Side 2

No. Title	Writer(s)	Recording date	Length
1 "I Will Always Love You"	Dolly Parton	June 12, 1973	2:56
2 "Randy"	Dolly Parton	December 26, 1973	1:53
3 "Living on Memories of You"	Dolly Parton	December 26, 1973	2:47
4 "Lonely Comin' Down"	Porter Wagoner	May 3, 1972	3:13
5 "It Must Be You"	Blaise Tosti		

Love Is Like A Butterfly (Release Date: September 16, 1974)
Side 1

No. Title	Writer(s)	Recording date	Length
1. "Love Is Like a Butterfly"	Dolly Parton	July 16, 1974	2:22
2. "If I Cross Your Mind"	Porter Wagoner	July 18, 1974	2:40
3. "My Eyes Can Only See You"	Dolly Parton	July 16, 1974	2:48
4. "Take Me Back"	Dolly Parton	July 16, 1974	2:37

No.	Title	Writer(s)	Recording date	Length
5.	"Blackie, Kentucky"	Dolly Parton	July 16, 1974	3:30

Side 2

No.	Title	Writer(s)	Recording date	Length
1	"Gettin' Happy"	Dolly Parton	July 16, 1974	2:38
2	"You're the One That Taught Me How to Swing"	Dolly Parton	July 18, 1974	2:07
3	"Highway Headin' South"	Wagoner	July 18, 1974	2:05
4	"Once Upon a Memory"	Dolly Parton	July 16, 1974	3:11
5	"Sacred Memories"	Dolly Parton	September 1, 1972	2:42

The Bargain Store (Release Date: February 17, 1975)

Side 1

No.	Title	Writer(s)	Recording date	Length
1.	"The Bargain Store"	Dolly Parton	December 4, 1974	2:44
2.	"Kentucky Gambler"	Dolly Parton	May 23, 1973	2:40
3.	"When I'm Gone"	Dolly Parton	December 11, 1974	2:16
4.	"The Only Hand You'll Need to Hold"	Dolly Parton	December 4, 1974	2:12
5.	"On My Mind Again"	Dolly Parton	December 11, 1974	2:51

Side 2

No.	Title	Writer(s)	Recording date	Length
1	"I Want to Be What You Need"	Dolly Parton	December 9, 1974	2:42
2	"Love to Remember"	Porter Wagoner	December 11, 1974	2:33
3	"You'll Always Be Special to Me"	Merle Haggard	December 11, 1974	2:23
4	"He Would Know"	Dolly Parton	December 9, 1974	2:34
5	"I'll Never Forget"	Dolly Parton	December 11, 1974	2:47

Dolly (Release Date: September 15, 1975

Side 1

No.	Title		Recording date	Length
1.	"We Used To"	Dolly Parton	December 9, 1974	3:14
2.	"The Love I Used to Call Me"	Dolly Parton	December 26, 1973	2:50
3.	"My Heart Started Breaking"	Dolly Parton	April 16, 1971	3:23
4.	"Most of All, Why?"	Dolly Parton	May 24, 1974	3:03
5.	"Bobby's Arms"	Dolly Parton	December 1, 1973	2.40

Side 2

No.	Title		Recording date	Length
1.	"The Seeker"	Dolly Parton	December 9, 1974	3:02
2.	"Hold Me"	Dolly Parton	February 1, 1973	2:36
3.	"Because I Love You"	Dolly Parton	unknown	2:16
4.	"Only the Memory Remains"	Dolly Parton	unknown	2:49
5.	"I'll Remember You as Mine"	Dolly Parton	August 22, 1972	2:48

All I Can Do (Release Date: August 16, 1976)

Side 1

No.	Title		Recording date	Length
1.	"All I Can Do"	Dolly Parton	February 18, 1976	2:23
2.	"The Fire That Keeps You Warm"	Dolly Parton	February 19, 1976	2:49

No.	Title	Writer(s)	Recording date	Length
3.	"When the Sun Goes Down Tomorrow"	Dolly Parton	unknown	2:05
4.	"I'm a Drifter"	Dolly Parton	February 17, 1976	2:53
5.	"Falling Out of Love with Me"	Dolly Parton	February 18, 1976	2:47

Side 2

No.	Title	Writer(s)	Recording date	Length
1.	"Shattered Image"	Dolly Parton	February 17, 1976	2:23
2.	"Boulder to Birmingham"	Emmylou Harris, Bill Danoff	February 19, 1976	4:13
3.	"Preacher Tom"	Dolly Parton	February 17, 1976	3:40
4.	"Life's Like Poetry"	Merle Haggard	unknown	1:48
5.	"Hey, Lucky Lady"	Dolly Parton	December 9, 1974	2:20

New Harvest...First Gathering (Release Date: February 14, 1977)

Side 1

No.	Title	Writer(s)	Recording date	Length
1.	"Light of a Clear Blue Morning"	Dolly Parton	August 19, 1976	4:53
2.	"Applejack"	Dolly Parton	December 10, 1976	3:20
3.	"My Girl (My Love)"	William Robinson, Ronald White	December 3, 1976	3:44
4.	"Holdin' on to You"	Dolly Parton	August 22, 1976	2:46
5.	"You Are"	Dolly Parton	August 20, 1976	5:14

Side 2

No.	Title	Writer(s)	Recording date	Length
1.	"How Does It Feel"	Dolly Parton	November 21, 1976	3:13
2.	"Where Beauty Lives in Memory"	Dolly Parton	December 10, 1976	3:50
3.	"(Your Love Has Lifted Me) Higher and Higher"	Gary Jackson, Carl Smith	December 16, 1976	2:52
4.	"Getting in My Way"	Dolly Parton	August 21, 1976	2:40
5.	"There"	Dolly Parton		

Here You Come Again (Release Date: October 3, 1977)

Side 1

No.	Title	Writer(s)	Recording date	Length
1.	"Here You Come Again"	Barry Mann, Cynthia Weil	June 15, 1977	2:58
2.	"Baby, Come Out Tonight"	Kath McCord	June 15, 1977	3:28
3.	"It's All Wrong, But It's All Right"	Dolly Parton	July 22, 1977	3:17
4.	"Me and Little Andy"	Dolly Parton	August 2, 1977	2:40
5.	"Lovin' You"	John Sebastian	June 16, 1977	2:24

Side 2

No.	Title	Writer(s)	Recording date	Length
1.	"Cowgirl & the Dandy"	Bobby Goldsboro	August 5, 1977	3:46
2.	"Two Doors Down"	Dolly Parton	August 1, 1977	3:07
3.	"God's Coloring Book"	Dolly Parton	August 1, 1977	3:13
4.	"As Soon as I Touched Him"	Norma Helms, Ken Hirsch	August 1, 1977	3:09
5.	"Sweet Music Man"	Kenny Rogers	June 15, 1977	3:08

Heartbreaker (Release Date: July 17, 1978)

Side 1

No.	Title	Writer(s)	Recording date	Length
1.	"I Really Got the Feeling"	Billy Vera	March 7, 1978	3:09
2.	"It's Too Late to Love Me Now"	Rory Bourke Gene Dobbins Johnny Wilson	March 9, 1978	3:02
3.	"We're Through Forever ('Til Tomorrow)"	Blaise Tosti	March 8, 1978	3:51
4.	"Sure Thing"	Dolly Parton	March 9, 1978	3:33
5.	"With You Gone"	Dolly Parton	March 10, 1978	3:07

Side 2

No.	Title	Writer(s)	Recording date	Length
1.	"Baby I'm Burnin'"	Dolly Parton	March 8, 1978	2:37
2.	"Nickels and Dimes"	Dolly Parton Floyd Parton	March 7, 1978	3:24
3.	"The Man"	Dolly Parton	March 10, 1978	3:16
4.	"Heartbreaker"	Carole Bayer Sager David Wolfert	March 7, 1978	3:35
5.	"I Wanna Fall in Love"	Dolly Parton	March 8, 1978	2:26

On this tape box legend, filled out by engineer Tom Pick, it shows that *Jolene* and *Bubbling Over* were recorded the same day (June 12, 1973) at RCA Studio A, located at 30 Music Square West. A majority of the legends I was able to see on Dolly are *all* marked "Studio A." A few were Studio "B." "RS" is for assistant engineer Roy Shockley. Dolly and Porter also usually used Studio A, *not* Studio B a majority of the time. Studio A opened on March 29, 1965. 16 track 2" tape at 15 IPS.
CWA4–1126 ("Jolene" master number) CWA4–1127 ("Bubbling Over" master number)

**List of Dolly Parton albums including compilation (US and foreign) and some bootlegs.
Not all these releases appear in this book.**

1967 – Hello, I'm Dolly
1968 – Just Because I'm A Woman
1969 – In The Good Old Days (When Times Were Bad)
1969 – My Blue Ridge Mountain Boy
1970 – A Real Live Dolly
1970 – As Long As I Love
1970 – The Best Of Dolly Parton
1970 – The Fairest Of Them All
1971 – Coat Of Many Colors
1971 – Golden Streets Of Glory
1971 – Joshua
1972 – Just The Way I Am
1972 – My Favorite Songwriter, Porter Wagoner
1972 – The World Of Dolly Parton (2 LP's)
1972 – Touch Your Woman
1973 – Bubbling Over
1973 – Mine
1973 – My Tennessee Mountain Home
1974 – I Believe
1974 – Jolene
1974 – Love Is Like A Butterfly
1975 – The Bargain Store
1975 – The Best Of Dolly Parton Vol. 2
1975 – The Seeker / We Used To
1976 – All I Can Do
1977 – A Personal Music & Dialogue With Dolly Parton (New Harvest Radio Show)
1977 – Here You Come Again
1977 – New Harvest...First Gathering
1978 – Heartbreaker
1978 – In The Beginning (1st LP re–issued)
1979 – Dance With Dolly Parton (Special Disco Mix)
1979 – Great Balls Of Fire
1980 – 9 To 5 And Odd Jobs
1980 – Dolly, Dolly, Dolly
1981 – Heartbreak Express
1982 – Greatest Hits
1982 – The Best Little Whorehouse In Texas (OST)
1982 – The World Of Dolly Parton Vol. 1
1982 – Willie, Kris, Brenda & Dolly – The Winning Hand (Live)
1983 – Burlap And Satin
1983 – The Love Album
1984 – Favourites
1984 – The Great Pretender
1984 – Dolly Parton & Kenny Rogers – Once Upon A Christmas
1984 – Dolly Parton & Sylvester Stallone – Rhinestone Cowboy (OST)
1985 – Collectors Series
1985 – Real Love
1985 – The Love Album Vol. 2
1986 – 16 Top Tracks
1986 – Think About Love

1987 – Rainbow
1987 – The Best Of Dolly Parton Vol. 3
1987 – The Best There Is
1987 – Dolly Parton, Emmylou Harris & Linda Ronstadt – Trio
1988 – The World Of Dolly Parton Vol. 1
1988 – The World Of Dolly Parton Vol. 2
1988 – Dolly Parton & Donna Fargo – The Queens Of Country (The Collection)
1989 – Country Heroes
1989 – White Limozeen
1990 – Home For Christmas
1990 – Dolly Parton & Kenny Rogers – Gold
1990 – Dolly Parton, Donna Fargo & Lynn Anderson – 16 Great Songs
1991 – Best Love Songs
1991 – Country Girl
1991 – Eagle When She Files
1991 – Simply The Best (Her Greatest Hits)
1992 – As Long As I Love (Sony Music Special Product)
1992 – Jolene
1992 – Straight Talk (OST)
1993 – Dolly Parton And Friends – Gold
1993 – Slow Dancing With The Moon
1993 – The Collection
1993 – The Little Things (18 Great Country Songs)
1993 – The RCA Years 1967–1986 (2CD Set)
1993 – Dolly, Loretta & Tammy – Honky Tonk Angels
1994 – Golden Hits
1994 – Best Selections
1994 – Heartsongs Live From Home
1995 – Something Special
1995 – The Essential One (I Will Always Love You)
1996 – Honky Tonk Angel
1996 – I Will Always Love You And Other Greatest Hits
1996 – Legendary Country Singers
1996 – Super Hits
1996 – Treasures
1997 – A Life In Music (The Ultimate Collection)
1997 – I Believe (The Encore Collection)
1997 – Peace Train (Remixes)
1997 – The Best Of Dolly Parton
1997 – The Encore Collection
1997 – The Essential Dolly Parton Vol. 2
1998 – Hungry Again
1998 – Dolly Parton, Kris Kristofferson, Willie Nelson & Brenda Lee – The Winning Hand
1998 – Dolly Parton, Emmylou Harris & Linda Ronstadt – Trio 2
1999 – Love Songs
1999 – Precious Memories
1999 – Super Hits
1999 – Super Hits 2
1999 – The Grass Is Blue
1999 – The Great Dolly Parton
1999 – Walking On Sunshine (Remixes)
2000 – A Discography – All The Charted Hits (4CD Set)
2000 – Honky Tonk Angel

- 2000 – Legendary Dolly Parton (3 CD Set – Australia)
- 2001 – Everything's Beautiful
- 2001 – Gold (Greatest Hits)
- 2001 – Here You Come Again – The Best of
- 2001 – Legends (3CD Set)
- 2001 – Midnight Country: Dolly Parton
- 2001 – Little Sparrow
- 2001 – Joshua & Coat of Many Colors
- 2001 – Mission Chapel Memories 1971–1975
- 2001– Jolene & My Tennessee Mountain Home
- 2001 – Queen Of Country (2CD Set)
- 2002 – Greatest Hits
- 2002 – Halos & Horns
- 2002 – Coat of Many Colors: Best of the Best
- 2002 – RCA Country Legends
- 2002 – Songs Of Love And Heartache
- 2002 – Dolly Parton & Sandy Posey – The Company You Keep
- 2003 – All American Country
- 2003 – For God And Country
- 2003 – From Nine to Five (Australia) (2 CD box set)
- 2003 – Just Because I'm A Woman
- 2003 – The Bluegrass Collection
- 2003 – Ultimate Dolly Parton
- 2003 – Dolly Parton & Kenny Rogers – Kenny & Dolly
- 2004 – Live And Well (2CD Set)
- 2004 – The Only Dolly Parton Album You'll Ever Need
- 2004 – The Great Dolly Parton (Australia) (three–disc box set)
- 2004 – Platinum & Gold Collection
- 2004 – The Acoustic Collection 1999–2002 (3 CD Set)
- 2004 – The Early Years
- 2005 – Live From Molson Amphitheater, Toronto, Ont. CA (Bootleg)
- 2005 – The Monument Sessions
- 2005 – Those Were The Days
- 2005 – Dolly Parton & Friends – Retro Gold
- 2006 – Dolly 'N' Friends
- 2006 – Love Songs
- 2006 – Puppy Love
- 2006 – The Collection
- 2007 – 16 Biggest Hits
- 2007 – All American Country Vol. 2
- 2007 – Jolene (Re–Issue With Bonus Tracks)
- 2007 – Singer, Songwriter & Legendary Performer (Mail On Sunday release U.K.)
- 2007 – The Very Best Of
- 2007 – The Very Best Of Vol.2
- 2008 – Backwoods Barbie
- 2008 – Covered By Dolly Parton
- 2008 – Dolly Parton And Country Friends
- 2008 – Playlist: The Very Best of Dolly Parton
- 2008 – Live In Berkeley, CA 08–05–08
- 2008 – Live In Stockholm, Sweden 06–13–08 (2CD Set)
- 2008 – The Tour Collection (4CD Set)
- 2009 – 9 To 5 And Odd Jobs (Re–Issue)
- 2009 – Dolly (4CD Set)

2009 – Live From London (02 Arena 2008)
2009 – Sha–Kon–O–Hey! Land Of Blue Smoke (EP – 8 tracks)
2010 – A Real Live Dolly (1970 – Limited Edition Reissue)
2010 – Letter To Heaven (Songs Of Faith And Inspiration)
2010 – The Fairest Of Them All & My Favorite Songwriter, Porter Wagoner
2010 – The Gospel Collection
2010 – Wanted
2011 – Better Day
2012 – An Evening With Dolly
2013 – 9 To 5 The Musical (Dolly's Demos)
2013 – Message To Booksellers
2013 – Dolly Parton's My People – The Original Cast Album
2014 – Blue Smoke
2014 – Blue Smoke (EP)
2014 – Dolly Parton: The Box Set Series (four–CD box set)
2014 – Dolly Parton & Linda Ronstadt – Live At The Boarding House, San Francisco
2015 – Country Girl In The Big Apple (Live 1977)
2015 – Dolly Parton: Nashville Stories
2016 – Pure & Simple
2016 – Live At Glastonbury (2014 recording)
2017 – I Believe in You
2020 – Holly Dolly Christmas

Though Dolly does not appear on this album I wanted to include it for it rareness

The Parton Family Sings In The Garden
LPS–1083

Track Listing:
In The Garden / Sweet By and By / How Great Is Jesus / Great Speckled Bird / He Will Make the Flowers Bloom / Great Judgment Morning / Someone to Care / How Great Thou Art / Don't Cry and Weep / Little Lost Lamb / Twelve Roses / Just As I Am

Production Information:
Produced by: Louis Owens and Marion R. Mangrum
Recorded at: Hilltop Studios, Nashville, TN
Engineers: Jack Linneman
Musical Arrangements / Production: Bill Owens
Cover Photography: Lee Wilkinson
Cover Layout & Design: Duke Pierce Jr.

Notes / Trivia:

- This album was released in 1968
- Extremely rare Parton family gospel LP with Avie Lee Parton (mother) sisters: Stella, Cassie & Willadeen. Back jacket below.

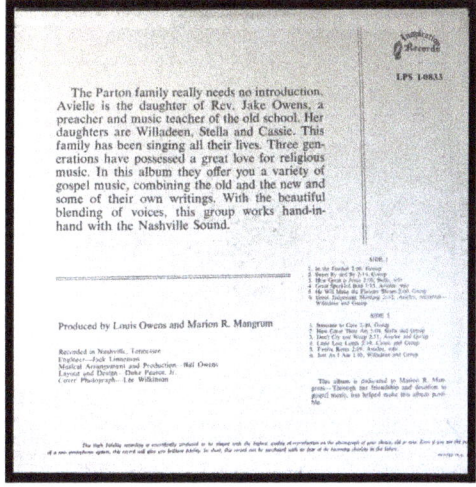

Also available from Daniel Selby / BearManor Media
310 pages / Full color

www.ingramcontent.com/pod-product-compliance
Lightning Source LLC
Chambersburg PA
CBHW061126010526
44116CB00022B/2983